CRÉCY

OSPREY
PUBLISHING

MICHAEL LIVINGSTON

CRÉCY

BATTLE OF FIVE KINGS

OSPREY PUBLISHING
Bloomsbury Publishing Plc
Kemp House, Chawley Park, Cumnor Hill, Oxford OX2 9PH, UK
29 Earlsfort Terrace, Dublin 2, Ireland
1385 Broadway, 5th Floor, New York, NY 10018, USA
E-mail: info@ospreypublishing.com
www.ospreypublishing.com

OSPREY is a trademark of Osprey Publishing Ltd

First published in Great Britain in 2022

A catalogue record for this book is available from the British Library.

ISBN: HB 978 1 4728 4705 8; PB 978 1 4728 4706 5; eBook 978 1 4728 4704 1; ePDF 978 1 4728 4702 7; XML 978 1 4728 4703 4

22 23 24 25 26   10 9 8 7 6 5 4 3 2 1

Plate section image credits are given in full in the List of Illustrations (pp. 17–20).
Maps by www.bounford.com
Index by Zoe Ross

Typeset by Deanta Global Publishing Services, Chennai, India
Printed and bound in Great Britain by CPI (Group) UK Ltd, Croydon, CR0 4YY

To find out more about our authors and books visit www.ospreypublishing.com. Here you will find extracts, author interviews, details of forthcoming events and the option to sign up for our newsletter.

Contents

Foreword

By Bernard Cornwell

Historical novelists are heavily dependent on historians for their research and I can only wish that Michael Livingston had written this book before the year 2000 when I wrote *Harlequin*, which ends with a long description of the battle of Crécy.

It is, of course, one of the most famous battles in English history, given spice by the exploits of the Black Prince in a victory which had pitted a small desperate army of Englishmen against a much larger and confident French force. Before writing the novel I made a pilgrimage to northern France and visited the site of the battle, gazing down from the ridge where King Edward III watched as his archers and men-at-arms destroyed the enemy.

And, though the battle's site was well signposted and marked, it seems I was in entirely the wrong place. That is just one of the revelations contained in this book, and it is a remarkable piece of detective work. As for the story of the battle itself I was relieved to discover that my fictional account was not entirely fictional, though had I known what Michael Livingston would uncover I would certainly have changed my tale.

It is a splendid story: how a small English army is trapped during its attempt to escape from France, and how they fight back against a much larger and better supplied army. It features the English war bow against the professional crossbowmen from Genoa, and the horrific clash of armoured men-at-arms colliding in hand-to-hand combat. Crécy is a forerunner of Agincourt, an equally famous battle which Sir John Keegan described in his great book *The Face of Battle*. Of Agincourt he wrote, 'It is a victory of the weak over the strong, of the common soldier over the mounted knight … it is a set-piece demonstration of English moral superiority … It is also a story of slaughter yard behaviour and of outright atrocity.' The same could be written of Crécy, and in this book Michael Livingston brings immediacy to the battle. It is a well-known, oft-told story, but no future historian, let alone novelist, will be able to ignore this book which enhances and corrects over six centuries of misconception.

Like Crécy itself, this book is a triumph and the tale it tells gives an old story new life.

Preface

On 27 July 1361, King Jean II of France wrote of the toll suffered on both sides of the war with England that had begun 24 years earlier:

> in these wars many deadly battles have been fought, people slaughtered, churches pillaged, bodies and souls destroyed, young girls and virgins deflowered, respectable wives and widows dishonored, towns, manors, and buildings burned, and robberies, cruelties, and ambushes committed on the paths and roads.[1]

It is a picture of absolute devastation, a reality in which, he goes on to say, 'justice has failed'. Indeed, the country's war with England left so deep a wound across the countryside – on its people, on its prosperity, and even on its physical landscape – that he confesses how his mind quakes to see its totality: 'so many other evils and horrible things have followed from these wars that they cannot be spoken, numbered, or written down.' When he had signed the Treaty of Brétigny with England the previous year, Jean the Good, as the French king would become known, surely thought peace was at hand. For all the blood, for all the battle, for all the burning of the past 23 years, peace had come at last.

The king didn't live to see how very wrong he was.

Jean died in English hands in 1364. The conflict continued, hot and cold, until 1453. None who saw its beginning saw its end: the Hundred Years War, as these 116 years of conflict are called today, was a generational war.

Those long years of struggle brought pageantry and tragedy, incredible honour and absolute terror together on what can seem like a series of grand stages of geopolitical theatre. It should hardly surprise us that writers as different as Shakespeare and Mark Twain – and songwriters, filmmakers, and artists beyond count – have been drawn again and again to the powerful setting of the Hundred Years War.

Among these many grand stages, few have stood more firmly in history's memory than one of its first great engagements: the battle of Crécy, fought on 26 August 1346. One of the most famous and widely studied military engagements of all time, it was an unmitigated disaster for the French, and an astonishing victory for the English. Crécy had enormous impact even beyond the tens of thousands of men who fought and died there: this was a battle of wide international scope, where massive armies collided in bloody tumult under the command of five men who were or would later become kings. For good reason, Winston Churchill once wrote that the astounding English victory at Crécy ranked alongside 'Blenheim, Waterloo, and the final advance in the last summer of the Great War as one of the four supreme achievements' of the English military.[2]

Today, the fields around the Forest of Crécy seem an unlikely place for a battle. No massive fortifications loom over the scene. No vast store of natural resources sits nearby waiting to be conquered and plundered. Yet in 1346 these now-quiet fields stood witness to unimaginable horror. Here tens of thousands of men and horses scrambled through a bloody and brutal melee amid hurtling arrows. Here thousands of people bled their last.

And here multiple national myths were born. The English army yearning to fight. The hooves of the French knights deliberately pounding through the terrorized lines of their own Genoese crossbowmen. The English longbows pulsing wave after wave of arrows up into the heavens and down into a hell on earth. John, the blind and aged king of Bohemia, being led into the bloody melee so that he might die with his sword in his hand. The English king, Edward III, watching the carnage from a windmill atop a hill, insisting that his son, the 16-year-old Black Prince, 'earn his spurs' as a knight in leading the first line of battle. And that same heroic lad, after the battle, finding the body of the king of Bohemia and honouring him by taking his crest to be that of the prince of Wales.

The battle has left its mark in the landscape, too, with the very 'battlefield' that tourists are pointed towards today. The trouble is, archaeologists have found no physical evidence that a struggle of any kind whatsoever occurred at the battle's supposed site. New investigations using archived manuscripts, satellite technologies, and old-fashioned field research have unlocked a stunning explanation: the battle wasn't fought there. And this just scratches the surface of the secrets now being exposed. In ways both large and small, every one of the famous stories I just mentioned is misleading. Most of what we think we know about Crécy is simply untrue.

The Battle of Five Kings is the battle of Crécy as we know it now. My primary aim in this book is to create an accessible and accurate story of this astonishing conflict – telling not just *what* happened but *why* it happened. My secondary aim is to tell a story about the present – *how* we have learned that so many of those famous myths about Crécy aren't true.

HISTORY AND TRUTH

As we step into these twin stories, it's of vital importance that we understand what history is and is not.

I've used various analogies to define history to my students. We can, for instance, think about history as an investigation into a car crash: the constraints of the evidence, including the constrained views of whatever eyewitnesses we have, inevitably limit our ability to reconstruct what happened. We don't ever really have the 'full truth' of anything, so the best we can do is create a story that makes the most sense of what we have.

Another analogy is mathematics. (Don't worry, the maths in this book will more or less end with this example!) Think about a simple maths problem where we divide 1 by some other number: $1 \div x$, in mathematical terms. If x is 2, the solution is 0.5. If x is 4, the solution is 0.25. If x is 1,000, the solution is 0.001. Plugging in bigger and bigger numbers gets us smaller and smaller solutions, closer and closer to zero. But, and this is the important bit, our answer will never *be* zero. Dividing 1 by an infinitely large number may give us an infinitely small number, but it will still be a number. Zero is the mathematical limit in this example (mathematicians call it the asymptote). For the historian, truth is precisely such a limit: something forever approached but never reached. We arrive at our story by cutting away what we know not to be true, again and again and again. With each cut we shape our story closer and closer to the truth of the past – but we will never, ever have it exactly as it was.

This book won't give you the 'truth' of Crécy. No book can. What it will give you instead is a *story* of Crécy that *approaches* the truth as closely as we can manage with the facts as we currently know them.

KEY REFERENCES

Though you'll see that I've tried to ensure that credit is given where due in both the endnotes and acknowledgement sections of the book, I've kept academic historiography to a minimum in the course of the narrative. That said, I need to explain the heavy use of one particular work of scholarship that will be frequently cited in this book (and echoed in the opening you just read): *The Battle of Crécy: A Casebook*, co-edited with my colleague Kelly DeVries, which was published by Liverpool University Press in 2015. The *Crécy Casebook*, as I'll refer to it in the run of the text, contains over 80 14th-century primary sources about the battle, presented both in their original language and in translation. We've discovered a few more accounts of Crécy since the book came out, but not many. Rather than sending the reader across hill and dale looking for 80 different books to find the primary sources I'll be using, I think it will be a lot easier to direct you to this one-stop shop.

NAMES IN THIS BOOK

There are exceptions, but many of the names in this book will not be Anglicized. In English histories the French king at Crécy is often recorded as Philip, but here he will be Philippe. Many a John will be Jean. I suspect most of you reading this book will be English speakers, and I realize that these non-English names will make the text a little more difficult to read. For that, I apologize.

It's important, though, to recognize that I'm not here to tell the *English* history of Crécy. The battle doesn't belong to the English or to the French, to you or to me. It belongs to the men who fought and died there. Though it might be a small gesture in light of what they saw and did that day, giving them their names as they knew them is the least we can do.

MILITARY TERMINOLOGY

If medieval names are problematic, medieval military terminology is a nightmare: even for something as simple as what constitutes a 'knight', our sources aren't consistent with each other (or, at times, even with themselves). It can be maddening.

It's also not historically unusual or even slightly surprising.

When I was a kid, my older brother and I used some buckets to categorize our toy army men. You know the ones: perhaps an inch or two high, forever frozen in one fighting position or another, in various colours to represent armies. There was an initial division of green and beige men, of course, but further divisions were made of the types of soldiers in each army. The organization we came up with wasn't at all consistent with the actual roles or ranks of the Armed Forces of the United States of America. Our buckets were instead determined by the appearance of the men and how we used them.

Most people in the Middle Ages saw medieval armies in much the same way. For Crécy, the buckets they usually put soldiers into are common infantry, archers, men-at-arms, knights, and nobles. It's important to understand why our sources divide soldiers up this way – and what they usually meant when they did so.

The first thing to know is that these medieval military divisions generally correspond to medieval social divisions. The key distinction between a knight and a similarly outfitted man-at-arms would be that the knight had status, whereas the man-at-arms could be anything from a mercenary to a nobleman. In combat, all knights and men-at-arms might be fairly interchangeable, but in society they most definitely were not. Given this, it's no surprise that our sources will often emphasize the number of knights in a given battle, because doing so emphasizes how important the engagement was for the rich and powerful men who generally ran things.

The second thing to know is that these categories have a direct effect on the tactics and actions on the field of battle. An army dominated by common infantry and archers would be very different from an army dominated by knights and men-at-arms. At a basic level, common infantry and archers are likely fighting on foot, wearing little to no armour. The archers would be using ranged weapons like bows or crossbows unless forced into sudden melee combat (at which point daggers or whatever else was handy could be used). The common infantry would have a motley mix of arms and armaments. Pressed into service or called out as a local militia, they used whatever they could get their hands on: from rudimentary clubs and axes to pillaged pikes and hand-me-down swords. But there were professional infantry, too, who were more highly trained and far better armoured. Quite different even from these were the knights and men-at-arms, who often fought mounted, wearing expensive heavy armour, using a variety of hand-held weapons – like lances and swords – that were built and maintained for war.

I'm using a lot of 'wiggle-room' wording here – 'likely', 'generally', 'often' – because as with my childhood piles of toy soldiers, these categories don't really conform to any official standard. What constitutes a 'knight' ultimately depends on who's talking about it. These are buckets of perception and probable use, which means that when one source counts up the 'knights' in the battle it might include the men-at-arms, whereas another source on the same event might distinguish them. As military historians we tend to use sharper distinctions in these categories than our sources do, but the same is true of most specialists in a field. The general populace talks about 'the flu', but for good reason the doctors and researchers fighting it use far more detailed language of distinction. All that to say that for this book I've tried not to get into the weeds of terminology and detail unless it's necessary to understand the military actions on the field.

ON TRADITIONS AND THE *VULGATO*

Traditions are hard things to shake. Repeated year by year, voice by voice, they take on a momentum of their own – a quality of ancient wisdom – that lends them greater and greater authority. If all these knowledgeable people repeated it, surely it must be true?

Not always. The earth isn't the centre of the universe. A fever isn't caused by excess humour in the blood. There are no dragons in the world. Yet all these things were believed and repeated by very knowledgeable people over the ages.

When Kelly DeVries and I were working on *The Battle of Crécy: A Casebook*, our Florentine friend Count Niccolò Capponi was working through the relevant Italian materials. He referred to the thing commonly said about the battle, the thing repeated so often it was assumed to be true, as the *vulgato* (meaning, in Italian, the widespread belief).

Dismantling such traditions wasn't the aim of writing the *Crécy Casebook*, but it's undeniable that much of the Crécy *vulgato* was torn apart by our work. And a number of people were exceedingly angry as a result.

This isn't surprising. Saying that 'the way it's always been' is wrong inevitably disturbs those people who have built their authority upon their repetition of the received tradition.

But upsetting people was never the point. And it isn't the point of *this* book, either, which builds upon and refines those earlier discoveries. I'm not setting out to attack the *vulgato*, but I'm also more than willing to set it aside. It doesn't matter how many generations of great luminaries have said something ... if it simply isn't true.

What that means is that you're about to read a new story of Crécy. Comparing it to the old Crécy *vulgato*,

King Edward wasn't doing what we thought he was.

The battle wasn't fought where we thought it was.

It wasn't fought for the reasons we thought it was.

The Genoese disaster wasn't what we thought it was.

The Black Prince wasn't the hero we thought he was.

The battle wasn't even the same number of days as we thought it was.

Even some of my own thoughts, formulated just a few years ago, now stand corrected.

Repeated enough, this new story of the battle might become a new *vulgato*, but it will always be a story of the truth, not the truth itself. I've put the puzzle of this event together as well as I can. I've tried to show how I've done so – no tricks, as transparent and as objectively as possible – and I stand ready to revise my thoughts if new evidence comes to light. This is, after all, how history is supposed to work.

It's not about being right.

It's about getting it right.

List of Illustrations

Fig. 8:   In 1340, Edward III quartered the arms of England with those
           of France – a visual declaration of his political claims. This
           new coat of arms appears here in a stained glass piece made a
           decade or two later. (Philadelphia Museum of Art: Gift of
           Fitz Eugene Dixon, Jr., 2010, 2010-2-2)
Fig. 9:   A crusader kneels to be knighted in this image from the
           Westminster Psalter. (Photo by Photo12/UIG/Getty Images)
Fig. 10:   The battle of Sluys, 24 June 1340, brought England one of its
           first victories in the Hundred Years War. (Photo by: Universal
           History Archive/ Universal Images Group via Getty Images)
Fig. 11:   A page of William Retford's *Kitchen Journal*, which was
           maintained during the Crécy campaign in 1346. The day of
           the battle begins eight lines up from the bottom of the main
           block of text. (Michael Livingston)
Fig. 12:   The English attack on Caen was far more chaotic, and far
           bloodier, than illustrations could ever show. (Photo by Fine
           Art Images/Heritage Images via Getty Images)
Fig. 13:   The English make their way across the Seine at Poissy in this
           imaginative scene from a 14th-century manuscript in the
           British Library. (© British Library Board. All Rights
           Reserved / Bridgeman Images)
Fig. 14:   Cassini's 1757 map of the region, overlaid with major roads
           and information discussed in the text. The red dashed line
           traces the likely route of the English to the battle site. The
           dashed blue line does the same for the two approaches of the
           French: the vanguard following the route to the north along
           the Chaussée Brunehaut. (Michael Livingston)
Fig. 15:   Edward and the English fight their way across the Somme at
           Blanchetaque in this imaginative 19th-century illustration.
           (Photo by The Print Collector via Getty Images)
Fig. 16:   A close-up of Guillaume de l'Isle's 1704 map of Artois: the
           earliest map to mark the battle of Crécy in its traditional
           location. (Carte d'Artois et des environs où l'on voit le ressort
           du Conseil provincial d'Artois / par Guillaume de l'Isle by
           Delisle, Guillaume (1675–1726). Cartographe – 1704 –
           National Library of France, France – No Copyright – Other
           Known Legal Restrictions.
           https://www.europeana.eu/en/item/9200517/ark__12148_
           btv1b8592522q)

the taller trees at right centre: the wagenburg stood on the high ground of the Mount of Crécy behind it. (Michael Livingston)

Fig. 26: The initial moments of the battle of Crécy, as pictured in the late 14th century. Note that the illustration is missing the English wagenburg completely. (Photo by Photo12/UIG/ Getty Images)

Fig. 27: Though the man firing it is out of proportion – he should be perhaps twice as tall – this image of a hand-cannon from 1405 is otherwise a good approximation of the artillery fired at Crécy. (fol. 104v, 2° Cod. Ms. philos. 63 Cim, Niedersächsische Staats- und Universitätsbibliothek Göttingen)

Fig. 28: The remains of John of Bohemia's body within his tomb in Luxembourg, published by anthropologist Emanuel Vlček in 1993. (Vlček)

Fig. 29: The remains of John of Bohemia as they appeared when his tomb was opened in 1980. (© National museum of history and art – Luxembourg)

Fig. 30: Nearly everything about Julian Russell Story's The Black Prince at Crécy (1888) – an imaginative depiction of the finding of the king of Bohemia – is inaccurate, but it is nevertheless a magnificent testament to the lasting memory of Crécy. (Telfair Museum of Art, Savannah, Georgia, Bequest of Carl L. Brandt, 1905.2, Photo: Peter Harholdt)

Fig. 31: This casting of Auguste Rodin's The Burghers of Calais (modelled 1884–95, cast 1985) is housed in The Metropolitan Museum of Art New York. (The Metropolitan Museum of Art, New York, Gift of Iris and B. Gerald Cantor, 1989, CC0, www.metmuseum.org)

Fig. 32: Edward III is depicted as a Channel-spanning king in this coin issued after his conquest of Calais. (powerofforever/ Getty Images)

Fig. 33: Edward III's effigy atop his tomb in Westminster Abbey. (Photo by Angelo Hornak/Corbis via Getty Images)

List of Maps

Introduction

The Crécy Dead, 28 August 1346

The crows won.

King Edward III and the English had the victory. But the bloody reality of battle was that no one had really won but the scavengers that followed war. And as the summer sun rose ever higher on 28 August 1346, it was clear that the black wings circling over the scene could never eat their fill.

Colins de Beaumont was in shock. Only two days earlier, when the English army had at last given up its flight north and decided to make its final, desperate stand upon this rolling bit of high ground, this field would have been the deep greens and ripening golds of an ample harvest. A brief summer storm had passed over the opposing armies as they had formed up, and it left a strange beauty in its wake. The rain had tamped down the dust of marching feet, and the passing wet would have brought the colours of the scene into vibrant life: bold men and their shining arms, with bright swatches of heraldry upon their tunics and gently flapping banners. In those moments between the storm of nature and the storm of men, the field would have been alive with vivid colour.

It was nothing like that now.

The bells of mourning were not yet tolling over the streets of Paris, and it would be days before news of the victory would raise cheers through the halls of London. The recriminations that follow disastrous defeat and the celebrations that follow unexpected victory had hardly begun. What Colins saw now would not have been a glorious fanfare but the far more practical tasks that occupied the survivors of battle: tending wounds, dragging the living from the piles of corpses, and the horrible, bitter chore of burying the mangled dead.

We don't know how old Colins was this day. We don't know where he was born or where he died. What little we have of him comes from a single piece of writing he left behind, a nearly forgotten poem that he apparently composed upon this field. In it, he tells us that he had come to Crécy as a herald for Jean, lord of Beaumont, a barony in the southern Netherlands near Hainaut. This role, which would have required him to introduce Jean at court and in other official duties, hints at a man prized for both his wit and his eloquence. His poem certainly underscores these traits. His lord, Jean, was born in 1288, and by the time of the battle his career had traversed several countries. Ironically, in 1326 he was one of the leaders of the forces that had helped Queen Isabella and the exiled Roger Mortimer reach England to depose King Edward II and put his 14-year-old son on the throne as Edward III. Now, just two decades later, that same Edward III had invaded France, and Jean de Beaumont had rallied to the flag of King Philippe VI. Jean would survive the battle of Crécy, but his son-in-law, Louis II, count of Blois, would not.

Even if they'd never met, the herald, Colins, would have known the count, Louis II, by his coat of arms: the arms of the house of Blois was a blue shield with a thick diagonal stripe of silver flanked by thinner lines of gold. It was a herald's duty to know such things. That knowledge was what had brought him back to the field.

The scene that stretched before him was one of horrific devastation. Where the battle had begun on the previous afternoon, the bodies had fallen in a patchwork of carnage across the gentle sweep of a sloping hillside. Other gatherings of the slain surrounded that bloodied killing ground: places where flights from the battle had fallen short, where many heroic but quickly forgotten last stands were made.

However old Colins was when he had come to Crécy, he surely felt far older now, as he made his lonely way through these despairing fields of the dead and dying. He had but one mission: to uncover the names of those who had fallen. So that the victor could know the totality of his victory. So that the defeated could know the totality of his loss. So that the loved ones that the dead left behind could grieve. So that the dead themselves could have prayers to carry their souls to an eternal rest.

There were thousands of mangled corpses in this feast for the crows. Colins would name more of them than anyone else.

He identified 33.

DEALING WITH THE DEAD

In the aftermath of medieval battle, it was often the case that local churchmen – typically monks – would help gather the bodies and transport them back to holy ground for burial and the attempted salvation of their souls. Friend or foe, ally or enemy, they deserved that grace at least. Whatever the count on this day, there were far too many to transport. As that late August sun was rising with the birds above the field, the bishop of Durham came forth from the ranks of the victors. Using his travelling kit for Mass, the Englishman consecrated the ground and made it safe for an eternal rest.

It seems apparent that the total numbers of the dead mattered relatively little to the victorious King Edward III. On 3 September 1346, a week after the battle, the English king wrote in a letter that 'in a small area where the first onslaught occurred more than 1,500 knights and squires died, even aside from the others who died afterwards on all parts of the battlefield'. What goes unspoken speaks volumes: it was the 'knights and squires' who mattered to him, the men of title that he had destroyed. Unlike the 'others' who had given their lives, *they* mattered very much indeed.

And so, as the wounded tended to their injuries as best they could with the help of anyone with medical knowledge on the campaign – and maybe a few conscripted from the nearby towns – the king ordered many of the remaining men to begin digging pits. Meanwhile, he designated one detachment, led by Reginald de Cobham, to begin sorting through the remains.

Cobham was in his early fifties, and for several years he had served as a knight in the personal service of his king. He would prove an able diplomat through much of his career, but he was a fighter, too. Cobham's tomb at Lichfield Church was certainly intended to convey the impression of him as a martial man: his carved stone effigy depicts him as a physically fit, long-necked man in armour, his sword and helm at his side. It was this man who likely met Colins when he came to the terrible field. Cobham had fought Frenchmen in the battle, had treated them as the mortal enemies they were in the heat of the melee. But now was not the time for fighting. However well he'd fought in the battle, Cobham's task in its aftermath was far from glorious. He needed to know which men of status had died, and for that he needed the help of men like Colins.

One of their first discoveries would have been that the French king was not among the dead. King Philippe VI of France had fled in the night to Labroye after the first day of slaughter. At dawn of the next day, as a second French force arrived and stumbled upon the English position only to be destroyed in turn, the king was on his horse again, riding first east and then south. Philippe gave the English position a wide berth as he retreated towards the strong fortifications of Amiens. By the time the English were sorting the fallen, by the time Colins was making his lonely walk through the battlefield devastation, Philippe was safe behind thick walls, perhaps still wondering what had happened. Did he feel guilt? Did he pray in the magnificent cathedral of John the Baptist in Amiens?

What seems clear is that the French king was, at the very least, seeking to assign blame. In the initial stages of the battle, a large contingent of Genoese crossbowmen in his employ had gone forward, presumably intended to soften up the English defences for the charge of his knights. Such was the haste and confidence of the French that the Genoese were sent up without their armour or even their *pavises*, the large shields meant to protect them from missile attacks while they made ready their slow-loading weapons.

The Genoese never had a chance. The longbowmen along Edward's front loosed upon them, and the Genoese were forced to flee back towards the lines in fear of their lives. Yet the first line of the French knights were already coming forward, eager to follow the Genoese bolts and ride through and over the hated enemy. Where the lines of crossbowmen and knights ran into and over each other, chaos erupted. It would take more hours of deadly fighting for the battle to be done, but it seems no stretch of the imagination to say that in that fateful moment the French had already lost.

We will discuss how we know all this later in the book. For now, it's enough to know that Philippe, back safe in Amiens after it was all done, initially blamed the Genoese for what had happened. Rumours were flying that they might not even have loosed their bolts against the English before they fled and sent the battle plan into confusion. Worse, some people were saying that the Genoese were traitors, paid off by the English to bungle their attack. Word of this had reached the English, too: in a letter, King Edward reported back to England that he'd heard that 'a great number of the Genoese' had been executed in Amiens on just such a charge.[1] Corroborating this rumour is the independent chronicle of Gilles li Muisit, which records that Philippe ordered 'a great massacre' of the Genoese survivors until he 'realized the cause of the flight ... and caused the slaughter to cease'.[2]

If there *was* an attack on the Genoese, it cannot have been as massive as these statements imply. The same Genoese mercenary captains, we now know, would continue to serve in Philippe's employ for years to come, which makes the number of these supposed executions likely to be small – and their participation in some kind of English conspiracy very unlikely indeed. Still, the accusation of Genoese treachery would linger for centuries through the course of the Crécy story.

COUNTING THE DEAD

The dead became legend, too.

On 12 September 1346, less than two weeks after the battle, a German knight named Johann von Schönfeld wrote a letter from Bruges to the bishop of Passau. In it, he informed the bishop that he'd fought on the side of the English, and that he'd been wounded: he had an inch-deep wound from an arrow on the right side of his face. He gave a rough approximation of the battle's location, but he recounted none of its tactics. Instead, he simply provided a list of those who died on the French side, which included 'the old king of Bohemia, the king of Majorca, the count of Alençon, the legitimate brother to the king of France through both his father and his mother, the count of Flanders and two bishops, as well as 13 counts, as well as 1,500 among the barons, knights, and nobles, and 16,000 men.'[3] We'll see that there were an estimated 13,000 men in Edward's army, and facing him had been a French force that would have totalled roughly 26,000 fighting men, so it might be easy to imagine von Schönfeld's report of the number of dead to be at least plausible. But whether or not we put full trust in the accuracy of his early report, we can surely trace the rapid movement of the battle into myth through the increasing exaggeration of the dead. Even before the end of 1346 the numbers were rising as news of the battle swiftly spread across Europe. Written in Ferrara later that year, *The Chronicle of the Este Family* shows that rumours had reached Italy that around 21,600 had died.[4] Around the same time, *The Annals of Zwettl*, written in a Cistercian monastery in modern-day Austria, records that an astounding 50,000 men had been killed.[5]

The numbers would range even more wildly as time went on. The chronicler Jean Froissart was clearly unable to keep himself from moving towards larger and larger numbers. In his first account of the battle, he gives an account of the dead that is close to that of von Schönfeld, but in a second account he claims that some 24,000 French died.[6] Still later, revising and expanding his tale again, Froissart further increases the numbers: 'eleven princes had fallen there, together with eighty bannerettes, 1,200 knights bachelor and about 30,000 other men'.[7] And Froissart's contemporary Thomas Burton went further by implausibly claiming that the battle's losses included 20 great lords, 'along with other lords, barons, baronets, and 80 viscounts, more than 20,000 knights and squires, and over 100,000 infantry and militia'.[8] Within the span of 60 years, the dead had very much become a myth of their own.

Part of what made the battle of Crécy such a receptive centre for this myth-making was its international nature (see Map 1). Like

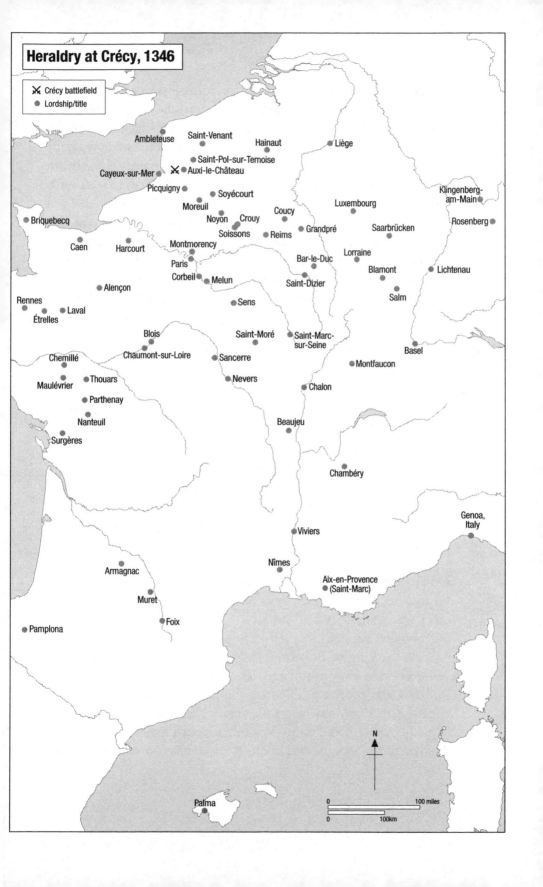

Heraldry at Crécy, 1346

✕ Crécy battlefield
● Lordship/title

Ambleteuse
Saint-Venant
Hainaut
Liège
Saint-Pol-sur-Ternoise
Cayeux-sur-Mer
✕ Auxi-le-Château
Picquigny
Soyécourt
Klingenberg-am-Main
Moreuil
Luxembourg
Rosenberg
Briquebecq
Noyon
Crouy
Coucy
Saarbrücken
Soissons
Reims
Grandpré
Caen
Harcourt
Montmorency
Lorraine
Lichtenau
Paris
Bar-le-Duc
Blamont
Corbeil
Melun
Saint-Dizier
Alençon
Salm
Rennes
Sens
Étrelles
Laval
Blois
Saint-Moré
Saint-Marc-sur-Seine
Basel
Chaumont-sur-Loire
Sancerre
Chemillé
Montfaucon
Maulévrier
Thouars
Nevers
Chalon
Parthenay
Nanteuil
Beaujeu
Surgères
Chambéry
Viviers
Genoa, Italy
Nîmes
Armagnac
Aix-en-Provence (Saint-Marc)
Muret
Foix
Pamplona

N

0   100 miles
0   100km

Palma

a great drama, the field at Crécy hosted an extraordinary cast of characters, and it was this assemblage of persons – in particular, the losses among the cast – that dominated the spreading news of the event: the vast majority of our sources incorporate what typically amounts to a catalogue of the dead, a listing of names that almost invariably forms a separate, distinct section of the narrative, usually at the conclusion of the account of the battle. Interestingly, this was true even from some of the earliest remembrances. In Edward III's aforementioned letter written on 3 September, the king reports essentially nothing about the tactics of the battle – or hardly anything specific about the location, the difficulty, or the course of the engagement. Yet reporting the results of the noble dead is very clearly worth his time:

> There were killed the king of Bohemia, the king of Majorca, the duke of Lorraine, the archbishop of [Sens], the bishop of Noyon, the Grand Prior of the Order of the Hospital of France, the abbot of Corbeil, the count of Alençon, the count of Flanders, the count of Blois, the count of Harcourt and his son, the count of Salm, the count of Auxerre, the count of Montbéliard, the count of Grandpré, the viscount of Melun, the viscount of Coucy, the lord of Rosenberg, the lord of Moreuil, the lord of Cayeu, the lord of Saint-Venant, and many other counts and barons and other great lords, men whose names are not yet known.[9]

Similar, though not usually identical, catalogues occur throughout our sources. In some cases, a list of the fallen is all that is preserved: Crécy was defined by its dead.

Only, as it happens, not *all* these men had died.

True, the king of Bohemia was dead, but the king of Majorca would not pass away until 1349. The duke of Lorraine was certainly dead (he was probably killed in the morning of the second day of battle), and so, too, were Alençon, Flanders, Blois, Harcourt, Salm, Rosenberg, and Saint-Venant. Cayeu might also have been killed. But, for certain, roughly half of the men on Edward III's list assuredly did *not* die on the field at Crécy. The archbishop of Sens would live until 1376. The bishop of Noyon would live until 1349. The lord of Coucy died in 1347, Moreuil and Melun in 1350, Grandpré in 1356, Auxerre in 1361, and Montbéliard in 1367 – more than 20 years after the battle.

This is not to say that the king of England was purposely intending to mislead. To the contrary, it seems likely that he was reporting what he thought was true – or at least what had been reported to him as true. After all, the king's own confessor, Richard Wynkeley, writing home to England on the previous day, was already expressing uncertainty regarding the death of the king of Majorca, which he said was rumoured but could not be confirmed. And Edward III was certainly not alone in propagating errors about the death count from the battle of Crécy. A recent study of the compiled list of the catalogues of the dead in all of the surviving 14th-century accounts of the battle shows that less than a third of the 50 whose death dates are known actually died at Crécy. Nor are these errors a simple problem of the initial fog of war: writing a half-century later, Froissart continues to insist on the death of the aforementioned count of Auxerre, alongside the death of the count of Aumale (died 1355).

As historians we have grown to expect numerical errors when it comes to the thousands of men who were engaged upon a given field. We have already seen the great disparity between von Schönfeld's contemporary estimation of just over 17,000 men slain and Burton's end-of-the-century report of 120,000 men dead: these numbers that our manuscripts preserve can be influenced by anything from exaggerations – intended to impress or fit some biblical precedent of battle size – to unintentional scribal errors recorded in a distant abbey. Such gross inaccuracies may frustrate us, but they're no surprise at all.

The basic factual errors among the lists of the dead, however, appear to be something apart. These are reports that specific, well-known men had died on the field at Crécy, when in fact they had not.

How our sources could have got such simple facts so very wrong returns us to the battlefield and its circling birds. As Cobham and his men turned over the bodies, many of them pillaging the corpses even as they prepared them for burial, they knew to look for the insignia of titled men. These were, in their time, the equivalent of the modern 'dog tag' for military personnel: an identification that might save the combatant's life if he were deemed useful to the other side … or ensure prayers for his soul if he were struck down.

Sigils could be on almost anything: on coats of arms and banners, but also on shields, sword pommels, saddle fittings, or jewellery. These they pulled from the piles, and at Cobham's direction they gathered them together in a great pavilion raised upon the field, where the initial accounting and attempts at identification were made.

The men responsible for much of this identification process were the heralds. In particular, because so many of their number had died, French heralds were sought out by the English and given the important task of combing through the collected detritus of war. One of these was our Colins, who recounted his experience in the 566-line poem *On the Crécy Dead*. It's an absolutely incredible eyewitness account of the battle – one that historians ignored for centuries.

HOW HISTORY IS MADE

Because we all experience the world through our unique upbringings and experiences, seeing it through our own individual lenses, each participant in an event – in our case, a battle – has a unique story to tell. So let's imagine a box filled with each and every one of these individual stories, each one of them a fragment of the complete book of the event itself. They're all in the box at first, but we won't get to know them all. So before we turn to what Colins wrote about what he saw that day, it's important to pause for a moment to understand how his voice survived at all, and what this tells us about how many past voices didn't make it to the present … and all the problems that come with this.

The first eraser of the stories in our imaginary box of stories is death on the field: as the old pirate saying goes, dead men tell no tales. And not everyone who experiences war survives it. Our reports about what happened are already biased by virtue of being the reports of the survivors. This doesn't make them wrong, by any means. It simply makes them intrinsically incomplete and biased by the measure of their individuality.

The second eraser of stories is death off the field. It comes for everyone in the end, and, sadly, most people leave this world with their tales unheard.

The third eraser is interest: not everyone who has a story can tell a story, and not everyone who has a story has a story that others consider worth telling. For a story to survive, it must be of interest, and it must catch and hold that interest.

The fourth eraser is opportunity: a story, to survive long term, needs the opportunity to be preserved in a way that it can outlast the storyteller's mortal life. Given the literacy rates of much of the pre-modern world, this isn't common.

The fifth eraser is chance: a great story can be amazing and written down and *still* not survive due to simple bad luck. The library with the one copy of it might be struck by lightning and burned to the ground. Or the ink with which it was written might be improperly mixed: if it's too acidic, the writing will burn holes straight through the pages meant to preserve it. Or maybe worms ate the pages. Or they simply rotted. There is an endless list of calamities that can befall stories.

The poem that Colins de Beaumont wrote on the battlefield of Crécy survived each and every one of these great erasures. Of the thousands of men who fought there – the thousands of stories in the box – his is one of only a dozen or so whose accounts made it unscathed to the 21st century.

Everything we know of Colins comes from the text of his Old French poem and the Latin headnote that accompanies it in the one place it survives: a chronicle written by Gilles li Muisit. The chronicler, who was at the time of the battle around 74 years old and losing his eyesight, lived all his life in the city of Tournai, which is today in Belgium, some 80 miles from the field of Crécy. He'd survived Edward's siege of Tournai in 1340, no doubt learning much about the tragedies of warfare. By 1346, he was abbot for the abbey of Saint-Martin, and he had likely just begun composing the chronicle for which he is now known best: a history of the world as he knew it, from Creation to his present day. When it came to present events, it appears he relied on the accounts of others. For Crécy, his informant was likely Jean de Beaumont – whose herald was Colins. We probably only have the account of Colins because he worked for a man who gave the poem to the abbot when he told him about what happened at the battle ... and that li Muisit's chronicle, in turn, survived the erasures of history (see Figure 2).

Which brings us to the sixth, final, and perhaps most tragic eraser of the stories of the past. Us.

None of us can comprehend the fullness of our present moment, much less recollect the fullness of our past. This means that our memories of ourselves are largely a kind of highlight reel of who we have been. More accurately, they're a reel of who we believe we have been. I may remember an embarrassing childhood incident as being positively definitional in the way that everyone, including myself, perceives me – when the truth is that a week after the fact everyone had forgotten it but me. Which recollection is 'true' – mine or theirs – depends entirely on which of us is telling the story: in their telling, my single greatest event would fail to be preserved at all. If we're going to approach the past, we inevitably face choices about which story we'll favour.

This means, at a most basic level, that history is something we make from our choices. It doesn't exist until we actively create it for ourselves through every decision we make about which stories we'll listen to, which tales we'll preserve, and which tales – even if it's through our benign neglect – we erase.

Colins de Beaumont's story survived. Through all those hurdles of chance, it made it to the present day. Yet without anyone to choose to listen to him, his voice was silent until very recently.

There are probably a couple of reasons that Colins' breathtaking work wasn't in our histories. The first is that it's written in a difficult French dialect. There exists today only a small number of specialists who can read it. That said, the battle of Crécy is a rather big deal in history, something lots of historians write about. So surely someone would on that basis alone have long ago translated it and made it more widely available. The fact that this didn't happen might be the second reason the work had been erased: it's a poem.

Poetry doesn't have the widest readership today, which is one reason why this book is in prose rather than in poetic lines. Even among its fans, poetry has a reputation for often being difficult to parse, dense with meanings, and rarely direct in its intent. Poetry, as some of my students complain, is just *hard*.

Perhaps so. But an enormous part of the written record of our past is poetic. Homer. Chaucer. Dante. Shakespeare. And so many of the voices who have given us their stories of Crécy.

People like Colins de Beaumont.

His account, written in 1346, was printed first in the original French in 1826 and then again in 1841. Yet for one reason or another – for nearly *two centuries* – it was ignored by historians of the battle.

And what a loss this was!

Judging only from his sole surviving work, we can see that Colins was a poet of no meagre quality. *On the Crécy Dead* is a mortuary roll: it is an attempt to publicize the names of the dead to churchmen who would pray for their souls. Such rolls were more typically a list of names, but powerful individuals were often accorded more elaborate, poetic rolls. It is a testament to the immediate impact of Crécy that its dead warranted this grand treatment by Colins. His poem is a powerful record of battle and the far too real costs of war: a tour de force of energy and imagery. Most remarkable of all, it appears to have been composed by Colins within a few days of the battle, very likely on the field itself, making it one of the earliest responses to a battle that reverberated across Europe and left an enduring mark on history.

Colins opens his poem with beautiful language, both evocative of time and space while infused with a foreboding despair of the death that would come:

When the summer is in decline,
And the sun abandons its lofty course,
And the weather gets cold,
And the chill withers the foliage
And renders the green trees yellow,
One sees come to death
All the fruit that issued from the blossom.[10]

In the poem, Colins describes falling asleep at this end of summer and experiencing a fantastical dream-vision in which he meets the personifications of medieval virtues: the ladies Fame, Prowess, Loyalty, Largesse, Courtesy, and Joy. The sequence begins as the poet-dreamer is led into the empty hall of 'a ruined castle'. He wanders down a corridor to 'a closed room' from which emanates 'a strong scent of incense, / Softly fragrant and full of sweet balm'. The poem is built around the death that those scents are meant to overpower. It's not a surprise that from within the room he hears 'a lady / Lamenting, weeping, and despairing greatly', and a sound of terrible lamentation that is beyond his ability to describe.[11]

He hears words through the sorrows, as the personified virtues speak of the deaths of great men on the field of battle, beginning with King John of Bohemia. When all hope for victory was lost, Lady Largesse reports, he was led on horseback into the melee so that he could die with his sword in his hand. Too old to see the way, he was harnessed by the chains of his armour to two knights who pulled him forward to his death like a cart behind running horses.

The poet describes chaos as being everywhere upon the field of Crécy as standards fell and the noblemen beneath them were broken and crushed. The death of the count of Blois gives an insight into the remarkable fact, to which we will return, that the Black Prince was captured in the battle:

> I saw him fighting on foot.
> Loyalty saw it, she was there.
> Indeed, Prowess, so were you.
> How did you dare start such an enterprise?
> You made him descend from his horse
> With a meager retinue of men.
> There was his sword bathed in blood;
> There I saw him bleeding and wounded,
> Going on, fighting on foot,
> Always ahead without turning back,
> Until he had brought the standard
> Of the Prince of Wales all the way to the ground
> And held it in his arms
> As he died. Lord, what valor![12]

Colins continues, accounting the deaths of these great lords through the fiction of these personified virtues, but already the veil between the poet and this dream-vision is beginning to slip, as it does when Fame declares her horror at what has happened:

> Ah, Lord! So many fine men died there,
> Whom I observe remembered here,
> That never in the realm of France
> Has such a loss occurred as I see here.[13]

And see it Colins had. The 'castle' to which the poet has come is the pavilion that the English had raised upon the field to house the various sigils that the searching parties had found:

> There I saw cast in the middle of the floor
> Many a ragged standard
> And many a befouled coat-of-arms,

And many a shield so shattered and so scratched
That no color nor hue appeared upon them,
And all of this greatly saddened my heart.
I clearly recognized the eight standards
Of a king, a duke and six counts,
In memory of whom this account has been produced.
And I saw anew a whole mountain of others.[14]

That Colins presents what are apparently eyewitness images within the framework of a dream-vision – that is, a fantasy – should hardly surprise us. Like J.R.R. Tolkien fictionalizing the horrors he had witnessed at the battle of the Somme in 1916, Colins utilizes a fantasy structure to work through a trauma that must have been too mentally crippling to address directly.[15] Not only had the poet witnessed death on a scale that we can only imagine in the worst of nightmares, but he had been given the daunting and gruesome task of using his knowledge of heraldry to identify the dead.

The pressure that these heralds were under is clear. Colins says that his heart aches because he knows that an inability to identify a coat of arms could mean that prayers would not be adequately said for the soul of the departed, adding a spiritual trauma to the emotional and physical trauma of what he had just witnessed. As he again relates:

Ah, Lord! I was so anguished
That I was seeing so many insignia there
And none that I could recognize,
Whether it were a little pennant or a standard,
A shield, a surcoat, or a pommel ornament:
All were dismantled and all were broken.[16]

He did what he could, and Colins' poem holds our most complete record of the Crécy dead: 33 named men. Ten more than any other source.

Yet 33 is far less than the thousands of mangled dead that day. When the poet asks Fame for a means to identify the items of heraldry that he does not know, she observes that there is no means for him to be taught: the royal standard bearer and many of the other greater heralds are dead. Colins is told that the herald Guillaume of Surgières would be an excellent source of further information, as would a man named Huet Cholet.[17] Not at all to be listened to, Fame insists, are two other heralds – Colins names them – for they were captured by the English and led away from the battle while it was ongoing: in addition to not being present for the whole engagement, Fame notes that their honour is in question for allowing themselves to be taken. Far more reliable and honourable, we are told, are the aforementioned Guillaume and Huet, but the horrors of their experiences have left them muted by their shock:

> Guillaume, however, was discovered
> Among the dead, wounded in the face and body,
> The night after the battle,
> And then indeed Huet Cholet, without doubt,
> Was found on the third day after the battle,
> Which was certainly directly confirmed.
> Let Honor have them, I insist,
> Ranged with the dead in her records,
> For they had been left for dead.[18]

The otherwise unknown Colins de Beaumont left us a remarkable, first-hand account of one of the most important battles in the Middle Ages. He left us an account of its impact, its horror, and the ways in which the living tried to assuage their guilt amid the fallen. He told us first-hand how the dead were identified. He left us, too, with a striking look at the ways in which one man dealt with the trauma of it all – and indirectly he revealed how other men were crippled by that same trauma, as Guillaume and Huet remain as voiceless as the dead under which they had fallen.[19]

It is perhaps best for our own psyches that we do not often think of such scenes as we study history, but at the same time there is great importance in looking such horror in the face here at the start of our journey to Crécy. Though we can never achieve it completely, history remains the pursuit of truth. In that pursuit, we must confront the reality of war in any age. This is particularly true for an age in which so much depended – both in this life and in the next – on knowing who had fallen in any given conflict.

This reality also helps us to understand the errors in the lists of the dead. After all, under such conditions it is to be expected that mistakes would be made. A herald – even one as earnest as Colins – might misidentify a coat of arms. It is also inevitable that in the chaos of both the melee and the subsequent retreat heraldic items were left behind by those who survived – a fact that is assuredly behind many of our 'false positives', like the early declarations that the king of Majorca had died on the field. Viewed against the full scope of what we now know, it seems likely instead that his banner or some other key heraldic symbol of his station had been left behind, leading to the erroneous conclusion that he had perished. As sources copied sources, these errors promulgated. Tracing the lists of the dead is one of several ways we can track where sources were probably getting their information.

More than this, though, the errors among the lists of the dead at Crécy serve to remind us of the brutality of conflict. Amid the detritus of the slain, there was little to distinguish the king from the commoner.

Few of us ponder these scenes. We speak of the battle strategy perhaps – distilling the lines of the men into coloured blocks, their final actions melded into arrows that push this way or that across a sanitized topographic map, each movement marking death. Or we speak of the political interests of the kings who ordered the lines forward – setting aside the lingering affective trauma upon both the winners and losers in order to ponder the simpler goals of power relationships amid the men – sadly, most often men – who made up the top echelon of society.

There is utility to such discussions, and we will turn to them in due course. The operative battle strategies, like an orchestral arrangement, help us to grasp the grand sweep and flow of actions that can be so difficult to understand in individual isolation. The effects of the battle on political fates is of obvious importance given the high degree to which medieval societies were driven from the crown down – the head that led the body politic, as the common medieval metaphor presented it. While we will look at this impact in later chapters, we don't want to ignore the pressing reality of those days as they were experienced.

* * *

This, then, was the field after the battle of Crécy. How it came to be, and what it came to mean – for those who survived and for those who came generations afterwards – is a gripping tale in and of itself. But let's first step back from the crows and Colins' bitter walk to understand why this battle happened at all.

Let's turn to the roots of the Hundred Years War, to the seeds that were sown in bloodied soil across the English Channel with the death of another king in 1066.

PART ONE

Before the Campaign, to 1346

*Sundered nations, tormented peoples, forsaken provinces, the
wholeness of the western church – consumed by laments, souls
contrite and humbled – beg you, whom God appointed over
peoples and kingdoms in all fullness of power: please, let the
wails of the afflicted enter your ears, for our calamities are
multiplied beyond counting.*

Eleanor of Aquitaine, in a letter
to Pope Celestine III, 1193[1]

I

Roots of War, 1066–1308

In the early days of 1066, Edward the Confessor, the childless king of England, lay dead. By the time that tumultuous year was out, two more men had worn his crown, a third king had died trying to get it, and the seeds had been sown for the Hundred Years War some two and a half centuries later.

This isn't the place for a popular account of 1066 and all that, but a basic understanding of that pivotal year is nevertheless vital to understanding Crécy.

When Edward the Confessor died, multiple people could have theoretically laid claim to the crown. The modern monarchy of England has worked hard to establish clear and unquestionable lines of succession, but its early medieval counterpart had no such thing. A bloodline could make a man eligible for the office, but actually *being* king required the support of the ruling class of the country: its rich landowners and its often richer churchmen who would pledge loyalty to the crown and be supported by it in turn. This exchange, established through formal oaths of fealty, undergirded much of the medieval period.

Those who were in the immediate family of an existing king – his children, his brothers – were certainly in a more privileged position to achieve the necessary support to rule, but by no means was this likelihood a guarantee. A claim, no matter how strong it might seem, was nothing without a willingness of those in power to defend it. No support, no throne.

Edward the Confessor, it was reported, had on his deathbed designated the richest and most powerful of those landowners – and the brother of his queen – to take the crown. The man's name was Harold Godwinson, and he agreed to do it.

The problem, as most English schoolchildren learn, was that William, the duke of Normandy, claimed that Harold had a couple of years earlier promised to support *his* claim to the same throne. What exactly Harold's earlier promise was – for that matter, *if* it was – is an interesting question. But what matters here is that William complained he'd been wronged, and enough allies on the Continent supported his complaint for him to be able to raise a massive army and navy to prepare to cross the English Channel and attack Harold.

Meanwhile, Harold's estranged and exiled brother, Tostig Godwinson, was riling up other potential claimants to make a play for the same crown – with the promise that they would, in return, restore him to his previous position of privilege and power. He was turned away by several leaders before he found a taker. Harald Hardrada, king of Norway, agreed that the English crown should be his and promptly began building an army and navy of his own.

Harold expected the Norman invasion, but it seems he had no hint of the Norwegian one, which struck first. The English king was on the south shore of England, waiting to fend off William, when news arrived that Harald and Tostig had come ashore far to the north. Harold immediately set off to meet them. Behind him – by dumb luck or fate – the shifting of the prevailing winds enabled William to make his own passage over the sea.

On 25 September, Harold defeated Harald and Tostig at the battle of Stamford Bridge, just outside York. Both enemy leaders were killed. So thorough was the English army's victory that it was said that the Norwegian army which had come to England in over 300 ships returned home in just 24.

Harold raised cups to his victory, only to hear – just three days later – that William had landed on his abandoned southern shore.

Once more the English king and his army high-tailed the length of England to defend his claim against a claimant for the crown.

On 14 October the two armies fought in what has become known as the battle of Hastings. Harold was struck down by swords and killed (Figure 3). In the weeks and months that followed, William's forces took more and more control over the country, and it became more and more clear that no one could muster a suitable defence in favour of a different claimant. Edward the Confessor's great-nephew Edgar Atheling was apparently suggested, but it seems that no one was willing to die for the foreign-born teenager. And so, on Christmas Day, the duke became the Conqueror: William was crowned king at Westminster Abbey.

A NON-ENGLISH VIEW OF ENGLAND

It's a human trait to gravitate towards those whom we perceive to be 'like' us – whether that common ground is where we live, how we look, or what football team we root for (and, for that matter, what sport 'football' is!). This gravitational pull of the familiar may be instinctive, but it's nevertheless short-sighted. We learn far more about ourselves by moving outside the familiar than we do by staying within it.

There are life lessons in this, but there are also history lessons.

Many English speakers tend to be drawn to (or even limited to) a history written by English writers. Those writers, in turn, are likely to have been drawn to (or even limited to) previous English writers. As this goes on, it can create what we might call a 'bubble' of history that focuses more exclusively on what the English did, what it meant for England, and so forth. Perhaps inevitably, some of these English speakers will view this Anglocentric history as the only history that there is because it's the only one they ever hear.

I tend to push back against this – not because I think there's anything inherently wrong with that English viewpoint, but because I think it's ultimately limiting not to have the whole picture. Think about it as a football match: it's rather hard to understand the actions on the field if all the camera ever shows us is what one team is doing.

Take, for instance, William and the Norman Conquest of England.

1066 is one of the most well-known dates in English history, and rightly so. It changed England's political structures, class structures, legal structures, even the English language itself. Seemingly nothing went untouched. One cannot overstate its importance for England, which for most English speakers puts it in a central place in history – full stop.

Confirmation seems readily apparent even in the event itself. After all, William went to a lot of trouble to conquer England. He built, bought, or borrowed the ships to create an enormous fleet to transport an equally enormous army across the English Channel. His victory at Hastings came relatively quickly – and his coronation, too – but he would spend *years* as king working hard to quash pockets of rebellious Englishmen. Clearly, for William, England held high value. It must have been enormously important.

Only it wasn't.

The island was of course vitally important to the English who lived there, but Europeans in general thought of it as little more than a backwater – if they thought of it at all. The place held no geographical centrality to them, the way Rome did. It had no weight of cultural memory, the way Charlemagne's Holy Roman Empire did. It didn't even have a large population or any great wealth to speak of: the natural resources that in earlier centuries had made the island so important to the Roman Empire had long been in decline. William's conquest may have overturned the life of nearly every Englishman, but the rest of Europe hardly noticed.

This was even true of the French, just across the English Channel (or, from their perspective, *la Manche*). Up until 1066, the two countries, as one historian put it, 'traveled in completely different orbits'.[1] And even after 1066, though they'd spend the better part of the next millennium in on-and-off conflict with the English, the French only rarely showed any interest in English lands in England.

Instead, their goal was to seize English lands *in France* – which was a crucial but complicated result of the Norman Conquest: by right of his victory, William had become the king of England, but back home he was still the duke of Normandy and count of Maine. When it came to *those* lands, he still owed fealty to the king of France. He was subject to a continental king – but a subject who could also pull upon the weight of an island kingdom behind him. In modern terms, the king of France had become both the rival and the boss of the king of England.

It's easy to see how this could be a problem.

To his credit, William seems to have recognized the immediate problem and deftly navigated it by dividing his Norman and English lands between his heirs. The fact that his eldest, Robert, became the duke of Normandy, while his second son, William II Rufus, became king of England, probably says a great deal about how even the Conqueror valued his conquest relative to his lands on the Continent. So, too, does the fact that William was buried in Caen, the capital of Normandy, rather than in England. Whatever importance England had to him personally as a crown, it was apparently second place in the political reality of where prestige could be found.

William II died in a hunting accident in 1100. It's convenient to suspect – but no means possible to prove – that he was assassinated at the instigation of the Conqueror's *third* son, who in any case quickly claimed the throne of England as King Henry I. His surviving brother, Robert of Normandy, fought the claim, but Henry shrewdly won the early support of a number of powerful barons and churchmen. In 1101, Robert agreed to what's called the Treaty of Alton: he recognized Henry as king of England in exchange for a significant yearly stipend and agreements from Henry that would support his own continued power in Normandy. Just five years later, though, Henry reneged on the agreement. He invaded Robert's lands on the Continent, and he won. Robert was captured and died in prison.

Despite his long reign, Henry died in 1135 without a clear heir. As it was in 1066, blood filled the vacuum.

This time it was a civil war, which erupted between the supporters of Henry's daughter, Matilda, and the supporters of his nephew, Stephen of Blois. Stephen was nominally king throughout this crisis – a period from 1135 to 1153 quite aptly called the Anarchy – but in the end his 'victory' was an agreement that while he would be allowed to keep the crown until his death, it would be Matilda's son – not his own – who would succeed him. Because of who that man was – more accurately, who his *wife* was – the already complex relationship between England and France was about to grow far more dangerously complicated.

ELEANOR AND HER CHILDREN

Her name was Eleanor, and she was born in Poitiers to the duke of Aquitaine. On her father's death in April 1137, she had taken over control of the vast holdings of this powerful duchy – roughly speaking, Aquitaine is the south-western quarter of France – and become one of the most powerful people in Western Europe. She was astonishingly wealthy, exceedingly powerful ... and just 15 years old. That July, only months into her rule as duchess, she married the heir to the French throne. Within a week, *his* father was dead, and preparations had begun for her husband to take the throne as King Louis VII. That Christmas Day, the teenaged Eleanor became the queen consort of France.

For the next 15 years, Eleanor helped her husband rule France, engaging in multiple acts of diplomacy at home and abroad. But her relationship with her husband grew increasingly strained: she'd accomplished a great many things, but the one thing she hadn't done was the one thing the king most needed. She hadn't borne him a son and heir. This wasn't at all her fault, but her husband didn't see it that way. In 1152, their marriage was annulled. No longer a queen, Eleanor was once more 'only' the very powerful duchess of Aquitaine.

Almost at once, though, Eleanor was wedded again. This time, it was to one of the few nobles of France who might be her equal in status: none other than the son of Matilda, who'd been made the duke of Normandy in 1150 and the count of Anjou and Maine in 1151, and now would be, with their marriage in 1152, the duke of Aquitaine. When King Stephen died less than two years later, Eleanor's husband was crowned as King Henry II. Eleanor, for the second time in her life, was a queen.

Eleanor and Henry's relationship is somewhat famous for its tumultuousness, but she nevertheless bore him five sons, three of whom would wear the crown of England. One daughter would become queen of Castile, while another would become queen of Sicily. Her other children were dukes and duchesses, counts and countesses. Few figures in history managed to stand so firmly in the centre of their age as Eleanor was in hers.

Beyond all this, Eleanor also inadvertently provided the tinder that would ignite the Hundred Years War. Because while Henry already problematically held substantial lands in submission to the king of France, Eleanor brought even more lands into the peculiar situation: the English crown could now claim *her* homelands, too.

For the first years of Henry II's reign, we can be sure that the French king Louis VII – Eleanor's previous husband – was anything but pleased to see that the English king stood in such a strong position within France. At least initially, he made few moves to combat Henry directly. Instead, the relationship between the two men took on something of a 'Cold War' feeling. Tensions were high and constant, and each man jockeyed third parties to take favour over the other. Peace talks were regular and inconclusive. Here and there local disputes brought arms to the field only to have cooler heads prevail. Things grew more heated when Louis' son, Philippe II Augustus, succeeded to the throne of France after his father's death in 1180. Yet neither side, it seemed, had much interest in outright war, even though neither side had any interest in giving up its territories or ceasing attempts to expand them.

This book isn't the place to go through all the twists and turns of these years, fascinating though that would be.[2] It's enough to know that Henry devoted the entirety of his reign to the solidification of English holdings in France: Normandy, Gascony, and much else, too. He was building an empire on the Continent, and he was doing it at the expense of the kings of France. By the time he died in 1189, more than half of France – its western half and much more besides – was in his hands: the Angevin Empire.

As early as 1172, Henry had tried to divide these vast holdings among his many sons. His eldest, Henry the Young King, would take England, Anjou, and Normandy; Richard would receive Aquitaine. Geoffrey would get Brittany. And the youngest, John, would receive nothing at all. John 'Lack-land', he was called – though perhaps not to his face. Two of these four sons – Henry and Geoffrey – died before the king, so it was Richard who was given the crown of England.

Richard the Lionheart, as he came to be known, packed a fair bit of adventure into his ten years on the throne. Little of it was in England: perhaps only six months or so. His first order of business was to join the effort to wrest control of Jerusalem from Saladin. He, his father, and Philippe had all promised to do this in previous years, but nothing had come of it. Now, because neither king trusted the other to leave his lands alone while on crusade, Richard and Philippe made a grand show of joining forces for what would be called the Third Crusade.

The crusaders set sail in the summer of 1190, but they didn't arrive in the Holy Land until the following year after being delayed by affairs in Sicily and Cyprus. They besieged Acre and took it, but Philippe decided to return home to France. He was, it was said, ill with dysentery – hardly unusual on such a campaign – but he was also well aware that Richard's absence on campaign left him with an opportunity to press French interests back home. The property of crusaders was under Church protection while they were away, so Philippe first tried to convince the Pope to release him from his own crusader vows while also condemning Richard for what we might today call 'conduct unbecoming of an officer'. We don't have a record of exactly what Philippe said the English king had done wrong, but it's likely he brought up the fact that Richard had, after taking Acre, ordered the shocking execution of some 3,000 Muslims – including non-combatants – in an act of savagery that only served to further the cycle of animosities and reprisals between the Christians and the Muslims in the Holy Land.

Whatever the French king's exact complaints, the Pope failed to act on them. So Philippe next began spreading rumours of Richard being a traitor to his fellow crusaders while also convincing Richard's remaining brother, John, to rebel against him. 'Lack-land', no doubt long simmering with resentment towards his older brothers, was more than ready to strike out against him.

Meanwhile, back in the Holy Land, Richard and the remaining crusaders failed to take Jerusalem. On his return voyage he was shipwrecked and ultimately imprisoned by first the duke of Austria and then the Holy Roman Emperor Henry VI, who had a grudge against the English king. Since Richard was now neither on crusade nor able to make a defence himself, Philippe shrewdly began attacking his French lands. The emperor meanwhile demanded an enormous sum of money for his release. Philippe, in response, offered an enormous sum for him *not* to be released, giving him and John more time to weaken Richard's holdings.

Remarkably, we have Eleanor's viewpoint on this horrible moment. Three times in 1193 she wrote to Pope Celestine III, begging for him to intercede and have Richard freed. The last of these letters is particularly heartbreaking as the queen reflects on the losses of her two previous sons while lamenting the tragedy unfolding between the two that had survived:

Pitiful but pitied by no one, why have I – queen of two kingdoms, mother of two kings – come to this disgrace in my detestable old age? My guts are torn out. 'My generation is at an end and is rolled away from me' [Isaiah 38:12]. The young king [i.e. Henry, d. 1183] and the count of Brittany [Geoffrey II, d. 1186] sleep in dust, and their sorrowful mother is compelled to live fatally tormented by the memory of the dead. Two sons remain to comfort me – who today survive to torture me, miserable and damned. King Richard is kept in chains. John, his brother, ravages the prisoner's kingdom with the sword and lays waste to it with fire. 'In all things the Lord has become cruel to me and attacked me with the harshness of his hand' [Job 30:21]. Truly God's wrath battles against me. It makes my sons battle each other – if it can be called a fight when one is crushed by tightening chains, while the other, heaping sorrow upon sorrow, works to usurp the exile's kingdom with his cruel tyranny.[3]

The Pope did little to help, but Eleanor managed to raise sufficient funds to pay Richard's ransom and get him out of chains. Once free, Richard immediately set out against his treacherous brother. Eleanor likely had a strong hand in brokering an uneasy settlement between her two boys, after which Richard spent the better part of four years fighting to regain the territories that the French king had taken during the whole affair.

Not long after a new status quo was established – effectively the old, pre-crusade status quo – Richard attacked one of his own rebellious vassals, who was holed up in the small castle of Châlus-Chabrol. It was there, on 26 March 1199, that a crossbow bolt – loosed by a cook or a vengeful boy, depending on the story – struck the king in the shoulder or neck. Gangrene infected the wound. Richard died on 6 April.

FRANCE ASCENDING

Once more, England had a succession crisis. This time, it was between the duplicitous John, who was the youngest and last-surviving of Henry II's sons, and Arthur, who was the eldest of Henry's grandsons. Open war between the rival claimants broke out in France, and Philippe was more than happy to take advantage by supporting first one side and then the other. From the French perspective, chaos in the English leadership was a very good thing indeed. By the time Arthur died – rumour was that John had murdered him – Philippe was rolling back the English holdings with relative ease. By 1204, John had been swept out of Normandy and the rest of the English holdings in the north. John 'Lack-land' was now John 'Soft-sword' – with all that the label implied.

That same year, Eleanor died. She'd outlived all but two of her ten children.

A decade later, in 1214, John allied with the Holy Roman Emperor and a number of rebellious French lords in an attempt to overthrow Philippe and regain some semblance of what he'd lost – only to see the alliance obliterated in the disastrous battle of Bouvines. At that point John had lost every English holding in France save the south-west corner of Aquitaine called Gascony. His reign had been a train-wreck for the English monarchy: a seemingly endless crash as defeat piled onto defeat, fires rolling into bigger fires. The Angevin Empire had crumbled. In 1215 his barons forced him to sign Magna Carta, significantly curtailing the power of the English monarchy.

The French monarchy, on the other hand, was in ascendance. By the time of Philippe's death in 1223, the kingdom of France was stronger than it had ever been. The Angevin Empire had crumbled, and the next king of England, Henry III (r. 1216–72), John's son, showed little sign that he would be capable of winning any of it back. In 1224, Philippe's successor, King Louis VIII of France (r. 1223–26), seized the great port city of La Rochelle. This left Bordeaux, the capital of Gascony, as the only major port available to the English in the south of France. Henry tried to strengthen its defences, and he made a few minor attempts to push back, but it amounted to little in the end.

The feebleness of the English position is perhaps shown most clearly in the fact that the next king of France – Louis IX (r. 1226–70) – felt free to depart on the Seventh Crusade (1248–54). Whereas Richard I and Philippe II had done so in coordination so

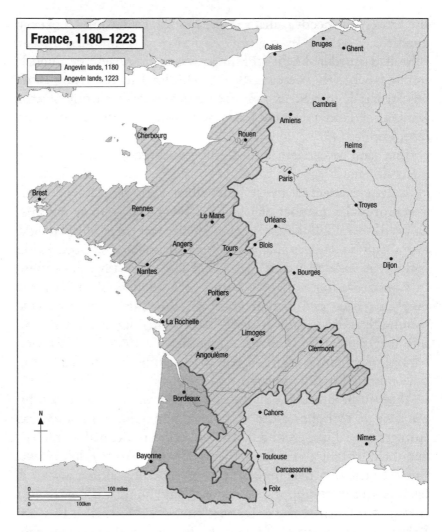

France, 1180–1223

Angevin lands, 1180
Angevin lands, 1223

Calais · Bruges · Ghent
Cambrai
Amiens
Cherbourg · Rouen · Reims
Brest
Paris
Rennes · Troyes
Le Mans
Orléans
Angers · Tours · Blois · Bourges
Nantes · Dijon
Poitiers
La Rochelle
Limoges
Angoulême · Clermont
Bordeaux
Cahors
Nîmes
Bayonne
Toulouse
Carcassonne
Foix

N

0   100 miles
0   100km

that neither could take advantage of the other's absence, Louis just upped and went.

The Seventh Crusade, as it turned out, was an enormously expensive and completely ineffectual military effort that saw his army destroyed, crusader lands lost, and the king himself in prison by 1250. But even after he was ransomed – for roughly a quarter of his kingdom's revenue – he continued to linger around the Holy Land for a further four years of largely unproductive 'crusading': no major gains despite the money and lives spent on the cause.

All this time, the English made no gains in France. In fact, Henry was so beset with worry that the English might lose Gascony to the French king that in 1259 he agreed to the Treaty of Paris. The king of England would be allowed to call himself the duke of Aquitaine, but he would be allowed lordship over *only* the Gascon portion that was still in his control – not the greater Aquitaine that had been Eleanor's. Importantly, he would have those lands in fealty to France: they were the lands of the king of France, but in return for performing the act of homage he would be allowed to 'hold' them. Furthermore, Henry relinquished English claims over any other lands in France (i.e. Normandy, Maine, Anjou, and Poitou). It may not have been the total victory that Louis would have liked – from the French monarchy's standpoint, the English shouldn't be on the Continent at all – but it was nevertheless a resounding win.

This Treaty of Paris would dominate the political exchanges between the two realms for the next century. Among its greatest problems was the fact that the exact boundaries between English and French holdings in 'Aquitaine' weren't fully defined. Nor was the division of rights between the two rulers made clear. Henry duly performed the act of homage in Paris on 4 December 1259 – but it may be that no two people present on either side would have agreed on a map of what he was doing homage for or even what the ceremony really *meant*.

In 1270, Louis took the cross yet again, showing the kind of dedication that would see him canonized as Saint Louis by the end of the century. Alas, the Eighth Crusade ended even more badly for him than the futile Seventh had: the king shat himself to death on the coast of Tunis when dysentery raged through his army – just two months into the effort. Louis' son, Philippe III (r. 1270–85), continued his father's policies as king. Back in England, Henry continued to do not much at all. After all the English losses, there was, in essence, peace.

It wouldn't last long.

THE ANGLO-FRENCH WAR, 1294–1303

Henry's son, Edward I, followed his father to the throne of England in 1272. In France, Philippe IV took over from his father in 1285. For a time, they left each other alone.

From the beginning, Edward was a man of war. Early in his reign, troubles in Wales eventually brought his armies into a full-scale campaign of conquest and control: Prince of Wales Llewelyn ap Gruffudd (r. 1258–82) was killed – his title afterwards transferred to the crown prince of England – and Edward spent massive sums of money building a ring of extraordinary castles around Wales. Not long afterwards, a succession crisis brought Edward into the heart of the political situation in Scotland, once more keeping him busy. And in between, Edward took the cross in 1287, which meant that for political reasons he could ill afford being in conflict with Philippe – though after his expenditures in Wales he could ill afford it for economic reasons, too.

With each year that the next crusade didn't materialize, however, the likelihood of war between the two realms grew. In 1293, squabbles between the sailors of English-held Bayonne and those of French-held Normandy morphed into wider skirmishes and assaults. The situation was serious enough to come to the attention of the French king, who felt the need to clarify his crown's right to protect all peoples within what he considered to be his territorial sovereignty. Accordingly, Philippe summoned the vassal in charge of Gascony – that would be King Edward I of England – to appear before him for questioning on the matter. Edward refused and sent ambassadors in his stead. Philippe rejected them, insisting that Edward himself needed to appear as his duke. If he didn't, he would face the forfeiture of his holdings in France: about the only thing the Treaty of Paris had made clear was that the English held Gascony by the hands of the French king, a fealty Edward himself had given in 1286 (Figure 4).

Philippe's threat went over like a lead balloon. Edward refused to come. But Philippe wasn't bluffing. Edward was declared to be in violation of his oaths, and Philippe declared Gascony forfeit. So in 1294, the kings were in conflict and armies were on the move.

As an opening move, Edward took advantage of growing hostilities between France and neighbouring Flanders – nominally a county of France – by sending a small army and supplies to support a rebellion by the count of Flanders. Furthermore, Edward agreed to have his son, the future Edward II, marry the count's daughter. A furious Philippe responded by imprisoning the daughter and forcing the count to publicly and embarrassingly renounce the marriage agreement. He then countered the English manoeuvre: in 1295 the French king made a pact with the Scots – it would come to be called the Auld Alliance – in which they agreed to work together: if either country was invaded by the English, the other would invade English territories in order to weaken their mutual enemy.

The English version of these events tends to cast the French in a dim light, as if Philippe was villainously back-stabbing the high-minded English. The French perspective would have Edward directly flouting the most basic standards of fealty. Both have an element of truth: each king likely welcomed the excuse to go to war.

The years that followed are a blur of battle. Edward was fighting William Wallace and his allies in Scotland. Philippe was fighting the count of Flanders and his allies. And both kings were fighting each other in Gascony.

In 1303, after a succession of inconclusive engagements in the south, Philippe recognized that his war against Edward was costing him more money than he stood to gain. More than that, a crippling defeat against the Flemings at the battle of the Golden Spurs on 11 July 1302 had left his control over Flanders on life support (Figure 5). He offered terms. Edward could retain possession of French lands under the terms of the Treaty of Paris. In return, Edward would abandon his allies in Flanders. The English accepted, and to seal the agreement Philippe promised a different engagement for Edward's son, the prince of Wales.

Instead of marrying the daughter of the count of Flanders, the future Edward II of England would marry Philippe's eldest daughter, Princess Isabella. The marriage, which took place in 1308, was never intended to produce claimants for the French throne. Philippe had three healthy and strong sons at the time, each of them fully capable of succeeding him as king and siring more sons to follow after them. Isabella was only meant to cement peace between the rival kingdoms.

Instead, the marriage would bring about the Hundred Years War.

Isabella and the Two Edwards, 1308–30

Edward II was beset by troubles seemingly from the moment his father, the ruthless but effective Edward I, died unexpectedly in 1307. Barons were furious at the high taxes that his father's wars in Wales and Scotland had required. And no one was happy with the fact that while the Welsh campaigns had been successful, those against the Scots had not gone well.

He also had to decide whether or not to get married. His engagement to Isabella of France was the fourth time that his father had arranged a marriage for him. The first three times, changes in political winds had caused his father to call off the engagements. This time, his father's death had abruptly put the decision in his own hands.

Arranged marriages were hardly unexpected among the scions of the medieval elite. Edward's status as heir to the English throne made him a particularly valuable political bargaining chip.

Isabella was in the same position. While not the heir to the French throne – she had three older brothers – she was nevertheless the daughter of a king. That had value.

In the end, Edward agreed to continue with the engagement. No doubt he hoped it would secure his hold on Gascony, giving him more time to settle matters in England and Scotland and thus cement his rule. In 1308, they were wed. Isabella was 12. Her new husband was twice her age.

There have long been questions about Edward II's sexuality. Royals often had a 'favourite' – a member of court upon whom they bestowed special attentions and awards – but Edward was so strikingly close with his favourite, Piers Gaveston, that historians have speculated that the two men were lovers.

Likely they were, and Edward was bisexual. Four years into his marriage, Isabella gave birth to his son, the future Edward III. Three other children would follow. The delay to their first child, such as it was, ought to be attributed to her young age rather than any struggles on his part. Nor was his siring of children with Isabella the result of his only 'doing his duty' – though it was indeed his duty to supply England with an heir. We know Edward had affairs with at least two other women, one of whom bore him a son. These escapades had nothing to do what was expected of him as the crown prince. They had everything to do with his sexual desires.

Edward and Gaveston's relationship caused conflict in the realm – though it should be noted that none of the grievances were centred on or even implied sexual impropriety on the part of the king. The barons were instead angered by the favour Edward showed to Gaveston. Access to his bed wasn't the issue. Access to his coffers was.

After suffering several off-and-on exiles – forced upon the crown by the angry barons – Gaveston was seized and executed without Edward's awareness in 1312. Civil war threatened in response, and discontent grew worse when the English army was badly beaten by Robert the Bruce's Scots in the battle of Bannockburn in 1314.

Edward, it had to be said, was hardly the second coming of his father.

THE BATTLE OF BOROUGHBRIDGE

Soon enough, the king had taken a new favourite: Hugh Despenser the Younger. Once again, the hostility of the other elites was high, and it only grew worse as the greed of Despenser and his father, Hugh Despenser the Elder, deepened. Gaveston had been bad. The Despensers seemed destined to be worse.

Opposition to the Despensers took deepest root in the Welsh Marches, led by the powerful Thomas, earl of Lancaster; Humphrey de Bohun, earl of Hereford; and Lord Roger Mortimer. In 1321, these 'Contrariants', as they would style themselves, attacked Despenser lands in Wales. Edward gathered forces in response, while demanding that the lords appear before him to answer charges. They refused, and the attacks grew fiercer. Edward retreated to London, and the growing forces of the Contrariants began what could be described as a low-scale siege there.

The Contrariants outside the walls weren't the only ones who hated the Despensers. Queen Isabella hated them, too.

Whatever the early state of their relationship, the years had not brought the royal couple closer together. Isabella was a woman now, and she was more and more comfortable staking a claim to her own positions whether the king liked them or not. As the barons' dissatisfaction with Edward's latest favourite had become an outright rebellion in what we now call the Despenser War, the couple had grown far apart indeed. With the situation in London deteriorating fast, the queen took the bold move of making a display of kneeling before her husband and begging him to remove the Despensers from power for the public good. Edward complied and exiled them, his fulfilment of her pleading giving him the opportunity to do what needed to be done – the numbers of the Contrariants were increasing – while seeming magnanimous in doing so.

It wasn't over. Mere months later, during a pilgrimage to Canterbury, Queen Isabella tried to stop at Leeds Castle near Maidstone, which was then under the control of Bartholomew de Badlesmere, one of the Contrariant leaders. He wasn't in the castle, but his wife was – and she refused entry to the queen. Fighting broke out. Edward's supporters rushed to the castle and besieged it. In October, it surrendered. Badlesmere was executed.

Emboldened, Edward revoked the exile of the Despensers and went to war with the Contrariants.

Hereford and Mortimer had returned to Wales to pacify their lands, and the king came after them with his army. Mortimer surrendered and was taken to the Tower of London. Hereford had meanwhile regrouped with Lancaster. They headed north, hoping to reach a friendly ally in Scotland. Edward was once more in pursuit, but it wouldn't be the king who would catch them. Instead, Hereford and Lancaster found themselves cut off at Boroughbridge by an army loyal to the king. With Edward on their heels, the rebels had no choice but to attempt to break through this force on 16 March 1322. They were vastly outnumbered – probably by four to one – and the royalists had already taken up positions across the northern bank of the River Ure. The rebels would be funnelled through the choke-point of the bridge and a nearby ford over the river.

The battle of Boroughbridge would not be a tale of improbable victory against the odds. It was, instead, an entirely predictable working out of the cold mathematics of military probability. Hereford was killed as he tried to storm the foot soldiers who held the bridge. According to a chronicle account, he died writhing on a pike thrust up through the boards of the bridge: his agonized screams signalled the retreat and rout of his men. Lancaster, meanwhile, had tried to use his cavalry to break through at the ford, but he didn't even make it out of the water before he was turned back. He retreated, tried to hole up in the town, and was eventually forced to surrender and throw himself on the mercy of the king.

Edward had none. Lancaster lost his head.

Boroughbridge was an enormous victory for the royalist cause. It was also one of the key steps in the determination of the battle-plan that the English would use at Crécy in 1346.

The fight at the ford presents the tactics in a nutshell. The royalists, as they had at the bridge, blocked the road with men-at-arms on foot, ready to receive the charging rebel cavalry with pikes and spears. This was the result of lessons learned in Scotland and paid for in blood. The English cavalry had been destroyed at Bannockburn by squares of pike-armed infantry (called *schiltrons*).[1] As shocking as it was in the moment, one chronicler wrote, perhaps it shouldn't have been: it was 'unheard of in our time for such an army to be scattered by infantry, until we remember that the flower of France fell before the Flemings' at the battle of the Golden Spurs – a battle we will hear more about shortly.[2]

Interspersed with these infantry, and probably stretching out like wings along the river's embankment, were lines of archers. As Lancaster approached, these archers loosed volley after volley into the charge, a storm of arrows that pierced his horses and men from either side. This punishment no doubt toppled many riders, who fell and were crushed by the pounding hooves around them. Those who didn't fall would have instinctively shied away from the shots, squeezing towards the centre of the road. As they packed closer together, they would tangle and lose momentum – all the while becoming easier and easier marks for the next wave of shots. The archers, in effect, were funnelling Lancaster's cavalry every bit as efficiently as the bridge had done to Hereford.

The English didn't invent this tactic, but they would come to master it. Nowhere would they better show this mastery than at Crécy.

For now, Boroughbridge marked the end of the rebellion. King Edward and the Despensers were victorious. But back in London, Mortimer managed to escape the Tower. He fled to France in 1323 and was still there when, in March of 1325, Queen Isabella sailed for Paris.

THE WAR OF SAINT-SARDOS

Writing a few decades later, the chronicler Jean le Bel – we'll hear his name often as we proceed through this book – claimed that Isabella sailed in secret. Later accounts would add further detail to her secret 'flight': she'd left London on the pretence of a pilgrimage to Canterbury, but instead surprised everyone by taking a ship from the coast bound for her French homelands.

Not true. Every indication we have is that her husband knew full well that she was headed to France. More than that, he knew why. She was going to Paris to stop a war.

The War of Saint-Sardos, as it has come to be called, is little remembered by most people today. It's overshadowed by the

Hundred Years War that would soon erupt. But understanding this short-lived conflict is essential to understanding that far more horrifying war that arose upon its ashes.

The trouble, as it had been for a while now, was Gascony. By the terms of the Treaty of Paris in 1259, the English could hold their lands in France provided they agreed to do homage for them to the king of France. Edward had performed this gesture for Philippe IV in 1308, but the French king died in 1314. Isabella's eldest brother succeeded him as Louis X, but Edward never got around to doing homage before Louis became the first tennis player in history whose name we actually know – because he died just two years later after celebrating a rousing game on the court by drinking a large measure of wine.

Louis' wife was pregnant at the time, and when she gave birth to a son a few months later the infant was crowned King Jean I. Edward didn't give homage to *him*, either, since the child-king lived a mere five days, after which his uncle – Louis' and Isabella's next surviving brother – was crowned as Philippe V in 1316. The dispute that would be called the War of Saint-Sardos began two years into his reign.

What happened was this:

On the outskirts of the otherwise obscure village of Saint-Sardos – within lands subject to the English – stood an even more obscure Benedictine priory. But within the structures of church governance, the priory was a daughter house of the abbey of Sarlat, which was within lands subject to the French. The abbot of Sarlat was keen to have the priory declared exempt from English jurisdiction – no doubt this would have simplified his life considerably – and he offered up the suggestion that if the priory was free of English control then it might be an excellent place to build a French fortification. Saint-Sardos might have been little known, but it happened to be in a key strategic location along the border between the English and French regions of control.

As Jonathan Sumption, a lawyer himself and one of the great historians of the period, once quipped, 'It was a lawyer's delight.'[3]

It was also the start of a full-blown international incident because it cut to the very root of the problem that had been plaguing the relationship between the two kingdoms since 1066: one king holding lands in fealty to another. By such terms, the kings of France were ultimately in charge of the English lands in France. The English were effectively just borrowing them. Certainly that's how the abbot viewed the matter. It's how the rest of the French did, too.

The English saw it differently. The 1259 Treaty of Paris that had put so much of this in writing was fine print, and faded at that. It had no basis in the day-to-day reality that the English were in charge of Gascony and had been for generations. This was a major reason why English kings had consistently been reluctant to pay homage to the French: to their mind, it wasn't right.

There can be no mistaking, though, that it *was* right. The terms of the treaty weren't clear on a lot of things, but the need to do homage for the lands was unquestionable. The fact that many French kings hadn't pressed the English on the matter is irrelevant.

When a legal ruling on the abbot's case finally came down in 1322, there was yet another new French king on the throne. Philippe had died of dysentery, and now his brother – the third and last of the brothers – was King Charles IV. He would be the one to deal with the mess.

And a mess it was.

The ruling was in favour of the abbot's right to be exempt from English jurisdiction. Ten months later, a royal sergeant planted a stake bearing the king's arms in the village of Saint-Sardos. From the English perspective, he'd quite literally planted a French flag on English ground.

The following night, a local English lord responded. He raided the village and massacred the French garrison. The sergeant was hanged by the very stake he'd so boldly planted in the earth.

As the situation escalated, threatening to provoke far-ranging hostilities, diplomats quickly tried to broker a solution. Edward certainly wasn't in a position to go to war across the sea. But he also wasn't in any hurry to give homage for Gascony to the latest French king, which is precisely what the French demanded. Ambassadors and letters hurried hither and yon, but they seemed ever out of tune with the fast-moving pace of events on the ground.

In the summer of 1324, Charles was entirely out of patience. The French army marched into the area. The English were shockingly ill-prepared. Towns and villages were rolled up, one after another, before a cease-fire gave space for another round of negotiations. In a mere six weeks of fighting, the French had seized nearly everything but a narrow strip of coast between Bayonne and Bordeaux and the city of Saintes.

The French made plans to continue their push – to take Bordeaux and sweep the English into the sea – but fighting a war, even one so close to home, cost substantial sums of money. Charles, still getting his feet on the ground as king, sent word to the English through the Pope: not only did he still require Edward to pay homage for the lands he had, but he also demanded that the English king cede the captured territory of the Agenais to him. Otherwise, the armies would come and he'd probably have nothing left.

Intriguingly, the Pope also passed along another piece of information. Tired of dealing with the ineffective and ill-informed English diplomats, the king of France wanted to negotiate with someone he could trust.

And it just so happened that his sister was the queen of England.

ISABELLA AND MORTIMER

Isabella arrived in Paris in the spring of 1325, ostensibly to negotiate a new peace on behalf of Edward. It is likely that neither side trusted her completely. To the French, her sympathies might have seemed to be with the enemy despite the fact that she was Charles' sister. To the English, her sympathies might have seemed to be with the enemy *because* she was Charles' sister. Worse, it was well known in England that she despised the Despensers who now held so much sway at her husband's court. At the moment she was sent to France she'd been more or less under house arrest.

The negotiations were tense, and made harder by the fact that the queen was under constant surveillance by her husband's handlers in Paris. But Isabella ultimately pressed her brother personally and achieved a breakthrough on the last day of March. The French would keep the lands they'd already swept up, but they would let the English keep what they had if they paid the French for what the war had cost them. More than that, Edward was required to come to Paris and personally give homage to the French king for the few lands he'd have left in Gascony.

In schoolyard terms, a bully had taken Edward's lunch money, and now Edward was going to pay the bully for his time – while publicly declaring the bully's superiority.

Or at least that's how the English saw it. To the French, this wasn't bullying at all. It was probably less than the punishment that Edward deserved for his defiance of his liege lord.

Edward, embarrassed on the world stage once again, tried to save face by giving Gascony to his eldest son, the future Edward III. He sent the teenaged boy to his mother in Paris to give the necessary homage so he wouldn't have to.

King Edward's pride may have been saved, but it came at a heavy cost. If Isabella hadn't already been planning to rebel against her husband, his decision to send their boy in his stead surely tipped the scales in that direction. She now possessed the heir to the kingdom, and – after September, when the young man did the necessary homage for it – *he* possessed Gascony.

So Isabella did not immediately return to England. That Christmas the queen met the exiled Mortimer. She soon, by all accounts, began an affair with him.

It may be that they'd already had a relationship in England. Regardless, her consorting with him now – when he stood in exile as a fugitive from her husband the king – was a point of no return. She had rolled the dice on an open rebellion.

She and Mortimer raised a small army to dethrone Edward, and Isabella promised the count of Hainaut that if he provided them with a fleet to sail it to England, his daughter Philippa could marry her son, Prince Edward. The agreement was struck. Aboard the Hainauter fleet, Isabella and Mortimer sailed for England and landed near Ipswich on 24 September 1326.

Their coming wasn't a surprise. Communications had run ahead of them. Many of Edward's subjects felt that his rule had been a failure, and they were more than ready to welcome and support the returning queen. The city of London opened its gates to her. The numbers in her army swelled.

Edward II fled, but in November he was captured in Wales. His favourite was captured with him, and Isabella and Mortimer oversaw a trial that ended with Despenser being sentenced to death. On the 24th of that month, Despenser was dragged naked through the streets of Hereford. He was hanged, but pulled down before death. Then, according to the chronicler le Bel, he was tied to a ladder and hoisted high so that the gathered crowds could see. There, his genitals were cut off and burned on a fire in front of him. He was disembowelled and had his heart cut out – all these being fed to the flames 'because it was a false and treacherous heart'[4] – before he was beheaded and his body cut into quarters.

Edward was secured in Kenilworth Castle while everyone tried to figure out what to do. He was still king, after all, and he was still married to Isabella. Eventually, it was put to him that if he abdicated the throne, the crown would pass to his son; if he refused, they would both be disinherited. In tears, Edward agreed to abdicate. His 14-year-old son was crowned as Edward III on 2 February 1327.

THE SOURCES OF OUR SOURCES

History books say that Edward tearfully agreed to hand over his crown to his son. This report ultimately derives from Adam Murimuth, a clerk in the court of Edward III in the 1340s.[5] But is this true? Who could have known it? How trustworthy is their report?

Let us say that Edward had in reality roundly condemned the lot of them as traitors and sworn to be defiant to the end, confident that his subjects would rise up to his aid: an entirely plausible position for the king to take. Even if this were so, the few individuals who were present for the meeting would surely report nothing of the kind. They were there not because they aimed to preserve the objective facts of history *for us*, but because they were invested in the success of Isabella and Mortimer's new regime *for themselves*. No matter what happened in that room, the report coming out of it would be very much the same: the king was saddened, contrite, and accepting. The realm would have a new king by the will of the old king.

Think about any celebrity break-up you have ever heard about. At first there are the grasping rumours: her husband went to Saint-Tropez without her! She changed her hairstyle! Is there trouble in paradise? Next comes the joint statement from their publicists: yes, the couple is breaking up, but everything is amicable, and everyone involved wishes everyone else the very best.

Sometimes, that's all we hear. Other times, a week later we learn that the husband has been spotted kissing a half-his-age model-slash-actress in Beverley Hills while the wife has entered a yoga-spa rehab with her previous boyfriend.

Even if a salacious story *doesn't* eventually come out, we would be well within our rights to suspect that the smooth statement from the publicists probably isn't the full story of the relationship's end.

This kind of scepticism is exactly how we should view the cooperative deposition of King Edward II. The report that we have is the statement from the publicists of those who deposed him. It's the story that best secured the present safety and future security of the realm.

That doesn't mean we know it's a lie – sometimes the celebrity couple really *does* part on the best of terms – but it does mean that we need to keep that possibility in mind. The story we have could be propaganda. For that matter, it could be that the story is true, but the real story is the unreported stage-management that happened behind the scenes and forced the king into making certain statements.

Writing history isn't a regurgitation of facts. It's instead a grappling with what the facts are most likely to be.

Take, for example, a poem written in Anglo-Norman – the French of England spoken by the royal household since William the Conqueror – that was long been believed to be from the pen of Edward II. Supposedly written while he was in captivity, 'The Lament of Edward II' begins:

> In winter harms overtook me,
> By hard Fortune thwarted:
> Now all my days stand ruined.
> My life often proves it true:
> None is so fair or so wise,
> So courteous or so praised,
> That, if Fortune revokes her favour,
> They won't be declared a fool.
>
> I cry out, but no one answers:
> When favour cannot be found,
> A man's love grows quickly cold.
> I have trusted men too much,
> Great honours granted to many
> Who now seek to damage me:
> Love me little, pity me less,
> In prison they abuse me.
>
> They torment me most cruelly,
> Though it is well deserved.
> Their false faith in Parliament
> Has struck me down from on high.
> Lord of Salvation, I repent!
> I cry mercy for all my sins!
> May the suffering of the flesh
> To the soul bring joy and mercy![6]

The identification of the poem's author as Edward II not only makes sense from the basic context of what the narrator is saying here, but it also fits with the fact that both manuscripts in which the poem was found were written before 1350. Plus, one of the manuscripts has a note before the poem literally telling us it was written by him.
    Except it wasn't.

More accurately, it's *very likely* that it wasn't. As I put it at the beginning of this book, history is shaving away what's not true in order to get closer and closer to the truth. History is probabilities.

So why, if one of the manuscripts says he wrote it, do we not believe it was?

For starters, nowhere in our sources is Edward regarded as a man of such artistry. This doesn't mean he couldn't compose poetry – if this poem was genuine, then we'd have evidence that he did – but it decreases the likelihood.

Also, it seems unlikely that the king who had done so much damage to his kingdom through his headstrong acts – with Gaveston, Despenser, and others – would now say that he deserved what was coming to him or that he had 'lost all honour', as he later confesses. This contrition doesn't fit well at all with what we know of the king's character from his actions and other reliable reports. Strange, too, is the outright resignation expressed in later lines. He writes that the time has come for his death – 'without delay' – and prays only for his own soul and for his son's success: 'God confound his enemies! / And make of him a king of great wisdom.'

How are we to imagine this poem even existing? Are we to imagine the king's jailers bringing him quill and paper to write it down? Why, if he wrote such a thing, would they allow it to get out, to be copied and read? Not only does the poem's opening speak ill of Parliament, but it later mocks their 'folly' at electing three rulers after him – that is, Isabella, Mortimer, and Edward III – but putting the crown only on the youngest of them. It even refers to the king's broken heart due to the actions of his 'faithless wife':

> Isabel the Fair, whom I ever loved!
> Extinguished now is the spark
> Of my love; by this my joy
> Is gone, as it is for many.

If it's hard to imagine Edward writing this poem, it's even harder to imagine that those jailing him for Isabella and Mortimer would have let it get out.

Edward II died in late September 1327 under rather mysterious circumstances; it's probable that in the face of continuing calls from the people to have him restored, Mortimer ordered his murder. After his father's death, Edward III's relationship with Isabella and Mortimer deteriorated quickly, and the king found himself under strict control. Then, in October 1330, just weeks before his 18th birthday, Edward and a small band of allies managed to have Mortimer arrested and declared a traitor to the crown. A month later, Mortimer was executed. The same group put Isabella under house arrest for a few years before Edward phased her into what can best be described as a retirement (she died a nun in 1358).

Edward III had, in effect, executed a *coup d'état* on those who'd had him crowned through a *coup d'état*. This would have been an ideal time for the 'Lament of Edward II' to appear: a poem from the dead king's hand, accepting his own fate, condemning the triumvirate rule, painting Isabella in a poor light, and conveying his prayers and blessings upon his son as the rightful king of England.[7] In all likelihood, the poem has nothing to do with Edward II's captivity and everything to do with Edward III's self-rule. Whoever wrote it did their work so well that it fooled the scribe who copied it into one of those manuscript copies, certain that, as he labelled it, the lament was 'About King Edward, the son of King Edward, the song that he made himself'.

Edward III, from 1330, ruled as his own man.

In just seven years, he would begin the Hundred Years War.

Wine, Wool, and the March to War, 1202–1337

Belgium may seem a strange place to find a reminder of medieval England, but there's an unmissable marker in the town of Ypres (Dutch: Ieper) today: an extraordinary building that stretches alongside the Great Market in the centre of town. The Cloth Hall, as it's called today, is a modern medieval building (Figure 6). In World War I, Ypres was the site of some of the most horrific fighting ever known. When the guns stopped shooting, the mustard gas stopped choking, the artillery stopped shelling, and the fires stopped burning, the hall was a ghostly ruin on a hellish landscape of death and destruction. Stone by stone, it was painstakingly rebuilt into its former glory. It stands today as a testament to resiliency and loss. When it was first built – in 1304, just four years before the marriage of Princess Isabella and the future Edward II – its ground level was the market space of the largest commercial building in Europe. Today, it houses the Flanders Fields Museum, a memorial to the countless lives lost in what was supposed to be the war to end all wars.

Ypres' Cloth Hall is a haunting place to visit, but it's also an inspiring one. Over 400 feet long, with a central belfry tower extending 230 feet into the sky, its size is matched only by its beauty. Arches line the building's sides, supporting two rows of still more arches above – hundreds of windows and niches once filled with statues. From its delicate stone lacework to its intricate rooflines, everywhere the eye looks the building announces fabulous wealth. And a great measure of that wealth came from England.

There are many reasons the Hundred Years War happened. Running through the 250 years of conflict over England's holdings in France, we've already seen several reasons for that strife. Cultural prestige was one. Pride and authority very obviously played a role: English kings didn't want to pay homage to the French kings to hold the land; French kings didn't want the English kings to hold the land without it. Both believed it was theirs by right and by blood. Winning was a matter of pride.

But, as with almost everything, it was also about money.

GETTING RICH IN GASCONY

Economics isn't the most exciting topic, especially in a book that's ultimately about one of the most remarkable wars in the Middle Ages. But war isn't cheap.

Why were the English willing to go to war to possess Aquitaine and later Gascony?

Because, in the parlance of our own time, these particular lands were *loaded*.

We don't know for sure the origins of the word *Aquitaine*, but it's a good bet that the Romans who named it *Aquitania* had in mind the many rivers that roll down from the Pyrenees to thread across the landscape. That water (Latin: *aqua*), added to the nutrient-rich soil and the beautiful skies of southern France, had made the region enormously fertile. Agricultural production of one kind or another – wheat, wine, and much else – had long been at the heart of economic activity in the area, along with everything else that good land provides, like livestock, fisheries, and forests for timber. Those weaving rivers were also ready paths of transport to move the abundance of the heartlands from one part of the countryside to another, enabling an expansion of trade that increased the value of production. Even better, those rivers ran to the Atlantic coast, where bustling ports of trade thrived. None of these ports was greater than the one found in the city of Bordeaux, at the mouth of five rivers, where business boomed for those merchants moving the goods from Aquitaine onto an international market. The movement of all this money – all ultimately tied to the land – brought great opportunities for income via customs. This income could support new infrastructure for trade or security or whatever else was needed to increase the amount of trade and the taxes that came with it.

And it wasn't just the fact that having lordship of these lands meant riches. The region's vast size and burgeoning prosperity brought another abundance, too: a fertile land tends to create a fertile people. Between growing cities and swathes of green countryside, Gascony's population could provide a significant amount of raw manpower. This was a useful labour force in peacetime – and a vital fighting force in wartime. In pre-modern conflicts, manpower could be one of the greatest determinants of victory in battle.

Plus, there's the wine.

As causes of war go, wine might seem an odd thing to kill for – no matter how much you like the fruits of the vine – but its importance to pre-modern Europe cannot be overstated. It was a way to have something to drink at a time when water sources could go bad. It was also, of course, alcohol. And whatever one's personal proclivities, the general human love of alcohol goes back at least to the Stone Age. Human beings like to drink. They like the way it lowers anxieties and inhibitions. They like the way it can ease pains and dull the senses. Then and now. But in the pre-modern world especially wine had additional qualities.

One was that it had some medicinal value to both the body and the soul. Doctors utilized wine to cleanse wounds and instruments, or to dull the patient's sufferings during treatment. And in Church, priests utilized wine to cleanse the wounds of the soul: wine was a necessary part of the sacramental rite of the Eucharist. No celebration was more central to the Christian faith than the breaking of bread and the corresponding drinking of wine.

Another reason wine was valued was that it wasn't universally available. Wine might be enjoyed everywhere, but it cannot be *made* just anywhere. The grapes from which it is fermented require a particular combination of climate and soil that limits its production. This is quite different from ale, which is made from grains with a far wider range of growth. As a result, while ale was by far the more widely used drink in the Middle Ages, wine was by far the more valuable trade commodity. It cost more. And as a result of *that*, the drinking of wine became a mark of class distinction. The commoners had ale. The rich and powerful – that is, the minority ruling class who were calling the geopolitical shots for *everyone* – had wine.

Which brings us to southern France. Because while England at this time was one of the places where grapes didn't do well, the climate and soil of France produced – as it still does today – some of the finest wines in the world. As the conflicts between the two kingdoms grew, however, England's elites were forced to become more and more reliant on a single source for their much-needed booze: Gascony. By 1250, three-fourths of the wine imported into England for the royal family was coming from its port at Bordeaux, and that number would only increase in the coming years.[1] In 1307, preparing for his wedding to Princess Isabella, Edward II ordered 1,000 *tonneaux* of the city's wine, which is the rough equivalent of one million bottles. And tax records show that in 1308 Bordeaux exported nearly 105,000 *tonneaux* – over 26 million gallons of wine – with the vast majority of it going to England.[2] Each barrel and bottle was taxed coming and going, only amplifying the wealth of Gascony.

If the English elite needed their wine – both for its comforts and for the riches it could supply – they needed Gascony. The French, on the other hand, were in no such straits. They had ample and ready sources for *their* booze.

GETTING RICH IN FLANDERS

For all its social and economic importance, wine wasn't England's chief financial engine. It isn't what helped build the Cloth Hall at Ypres.

That honour belonged to the sheep.

Sheep are remarkably resilient creatures. Unlike grapes, they can survive and indeed thrive in a wide array of climates and conditions. For good reason human beings have domesticated them for millennia. When they're slaughtered they offer up sheepskin and meat. Before that, they offer milk and – most valuably – wool. That wool grows in response to climate: in warm climates it's thin and loose; in cold climates it's thick and dense. So while the sheep could be grazed just about anywhere in Europe, the amount of wool that they supplied – and its quality – was unequal.

England's cold, wet climate might have made it incompatible with the wine industry, but for the production of wool it could hardly be more ideal. By the 13th century, sacks of wool were being funnelled from across the country, through an elaborate system of middlemen, onto the waiting looms of cloth-makers. Because of the lack of domestic cloth industry and the high prices that foreign buyers were willing to pay for the raw material, this system of exchange was, in large part, an export business: those port cities that could service this wool trade, and the merchants in them who facilitated this service, became quite wealthy. And by virtue of a heavy taxation on the trade, it is no exaggeration to say that in the late Middle Ages the king's coffers rested upon the back of the realm's sheep. When Eleanor needed to pay a literal king's ransom for the imprisoned Richard I, she was able to do so with wool subsidies. By the end of that century, wool production, trade, and taxation was responsible for half of the wealth generated in England.

A flourishing export implies a prosperous import. On the other side of this international trade, urban cloth-makers experienced a corresponding boom in their local economies. Nowhere was this relationship stronger and more profitable than between England and Flanders, a region with both excellent ports in close proximity to England and a burgeoning weaving trade: a potent combination that soon made Flanders one of the most prosperous regions in Europe – quickly exceeding French wool production. Flemish cities like Bruges, Ghent, and Ypres absolutely blossomed with wealth – the Cloth Hall at Ypres is an expression of precisely this economy – as the thick English wool, arriving by the shipload, was dyed and tailored into full cloth to be sold at still further markets. As long as everyone got along, seemingly everyone could get rich, so political ties between these cities on the Continent and the kingdom of England grew fast and strong. Unfortunately for England, Flanders was also – and had been since the ninth century – a nominal county of France. And while the French kings may have allowed Flanders to enjoy a relatively autonomous existence for long periods of its history, the lucrative wool trade between England and Flanders – along with a corresponding part of the Gascon wine trade that also ran through Flemish intermediaries into Europe – made the region a potential new front in the history of conflict across the English Channel.

We often focus so closely on the single axis of history between England and France that we can forget how much more intricately woven the politics of this period really were – and how much Flanders played a part in every move that was made between the two rival kingdoms. It's no exaggeration to say that exactly why and how so many thousands of men would die at Crécy – just over four decades after the Cloth Hall was first built – has a lot to do with the history of Flanders during this period. So let's step back for a bit and recall how Flanders moved in and out of the events we've been grappling with in the build-up to the Hundred Years War.

CATCHING UP WITH FLANDERS

Let's start with the story of Joan, the eldest daughter of Baldwin IX, the count of Flanders.

In 1202, Baldwin left his family to take the cross in the Fourth Crusade. Since Richard the Lionheart had failed to do it in the Third Crusade, the mission once again was to reconquer Jerusalem from the Muslims. Along the way, a portion of the crusading army diverted to the great Christian city of Constantinople, capital of the Eastern Roman Empire of Byzantium. The plan was to reinstall the deposed emperor and then reap the rewards of military assistance from the grateful allied ruler. It was sensible enough in theory, but in practice the whole enterprise quickly went pear-shaped:

the Byzantines resented the effective occupation of their city by the crusaders, and they despised the deposed king who was forced back upon them. They rose up and murdered the man. In response, the occupying crusaders sacked the city and then elected Baldwin as the new emperor in 1204: the Fourth Crusade had, in effect, conquered an ally rather than the enemy. Baldwin's short reign was beset with troubles both foreign and domestic. There were revolts to deal with. There were invaders at the door. His wife, having left their two daughters behind in Flanders, died on the journey to meet him. Then, only months after his coronation, Baldwin attacked the Bulgarian Tsar Kaloyan outside Adrianople in 1205. His army was destroyed. Baldwin himself was captured. He disappeared, assumed dead.

Back in Flanders, his eldest daughter Joan became the countess of Flanders. She was only six years old. Her uncle, in whose care she and her sister were placed, became engaged to the daughter of King Philippe II of France. In a corresponding move the two orphaned girls were sent to be raised in the royal court in Paris.

We've already seen Philippe's remarkable political acumen. He'd played the English royal family like a drum for years: egging Richard to attack his father, then egging John to attack Richard ... while plot by plot taking apart their empire. He'd done much the same to Flanders by deftly manoeuvring marriages and military actions. He'd frequently been at odds with Baldwin over the region of Artois in particular – a struggle that had seen the Flemish count turn to King John of England and the Holy Roman Emperor for support. In Philippe's eyes, the orphaned heirs of Baldwin were an opportunity too good to pass up: a chance to secure and expand his realm and his influence. Just seven years later, when Joan was 12 or 13, the king arranged for her to be married to Ferrand, the fourth son of the king of Portugal. He was in his 20s.

On their journey from Paris to Flanders, however, the newlyweds were attacked and captured by Philippe's eldest son, the future Louis VIII, who demanded that Artois be given to him in full. Philippe refused to help the couple, who were forced to sign a treaty surrendering the lands.

Enraged, Joan and Ferrand turned to her father's old friends, the king of England and the Holy Roman Emperor. An alliance was made, and a wave of anti-French sentiment swept through Flanders.

Philippe responded by putting Lille to the torch. Armies poured into the field. It all ended disastrously at the battle of Bouvines in 1214.[3] Ferrand was captured and would remain in prison for a dozen years, with Joan needing to raise a significant ransom for his release. He was among the lucky ones: huge swathes of the nobility in and around Flanders lost their lives or were hopelessly imprisoned after the battle.

The impact of the post-Bouvines social change was enormous. It's simplifying something much more complex, but if we imagine the feudal system as a rising pyramid of relationships – based on an exchange of allegiance and service – then at its highest levels there are nobles answering to a ruler up top. The Flemish loss in 1214 had blown enormous holes through these topmost parts of the pyramid, sending cracks down to its very foundation stones. The whole structure teetered in the middle of the 13th century, but it was stabilized when a new class of leaders filled the gaps. These were men and women whose power was built on the new and seemingly ever-rising wealth of the Low Country towns – a wealth that was tied directly to the wool trade with England. No surprise, then, that in the following decades anti-French sentiment smouldered, in constant threat of flashing into a white-hot blaze at even the slightest breeze.

At the turn of the century, the wind blew hard. After Edward I had abandoned his rebellious allies in 1298, Philippe IV of France not only forced the count of Flanders to renege on his agreement to marry his daughter to Edward's son, but he also came down hard on the population at large with taxes and restrictions. When the Flemish objected, French military forces carried out the king's will. On 18 May 1302, the oppressed Flemings of Bruges – set off by a dispute over the rights to trade in English wool – responded by massacring the French garrison in town, along with any they found who supported the king. The Matins of Bruges, as it came to be known, took perhaps as many 2,000 lives. The uprising spread quickly.

The king of France was enraged, and he sent an army to quash the spreading revolt. The Flemish rebels tried to draw together an army of their own. The opposing forces met outside the walls of Kortrijk on 11 July, where the Flemish obliterated the supposedly superior French forces (Figure 5). The hundreds of spurs that they collected from the slain knights gave the battle its name: the battle of the Golden Spurs. The heaviness of this loss was a big part of the reason that Philippe came to a peace agreement with Edward that involved the marriage of Edward II and Isabella.

It took two years for Philippe's army to recover its strength and return against the Flemings, but it finally came in 1304. This time, he led the army in person, and at the battle of Mons-en-Pévèle the two sides fought to a rough draw. A year later, Philippe signed a treaty that gained the cities of Béthune, Douai, and Lille for France, as well as a yearly Flemish payment to the French crown.

THE BATTLE OF CASSEL

That yearly payment ensured that the French were never far away in the minds of the Flemish. And the French, despite (or perhaps because of) the agreement, gradually encroached more and more on Flemish affairs. So it's not surprising that in 1323 an uprising began against the ruling class of Flanders that collected the money for France; it's only surprising that it took so long.

The French initially responded to the Flemish uprising with the application of political pressure, hoping that the count of Flanders could sort it all out and keep the money flowing. The situation changed, however, with the death of Charles IV – the last of Isabella's brothers – on 1 February 1328.

Charles died without a son, and the crown passed on 1 April to Philippe of Valois, who ruled as Philippe VI. There were questions about whether his succession was right and proper – we'll hear more about this soon – and Philippe saw the dispute in Flanders as an opportunity to solidify support for his reign. When the rebellion against the count showed no sign of slowing, Philippe went on the march.

As the French army approached, the rebels took position on Cassel, a stronghold atop a high hill in Flanders, recognized as a superbly defensible site long before Julius Caesar seized it during the Gallic Wars. This was a sound move. 'Fight from the high ground' is arguably the most famous and true adage in military history, something we learn even in playground games like 'king of the hill' – or in the fact that it's harder to walk uphill to school than downhill. The rebels knew this when they dug themselves into the heights.

Philippe, down on the plain, was no fool. He knew it would be unwise to send his knights charging uphill into the teeth of the defence. And so, wisely, for three days he tried to goad the rebels down to fight on even ground. After pillaging the nearby villages and farms to supply his army, he made a show of setting fire to them.

When rebel messengers came down to negotiate terms for battle, Philippe greeted them with scorn – the French message was that the Flemish were a disorganized rabble, unfit for diplomacy with the king. As if to show how little regard he had for them, Philippe's knights removed their armour in the heat of the day.

The rebels, both incensed and inspired, quickly gathered and made an assault downhill on the French camp. It was brilliance and folly. They succeeded in surprising the French, but they had also given up their advantage of high ground. After regrouping, Philippe personally led his knights in making a counter-attack on the Flemish rear. It was devastating. The rebels were cut off, then cut down. Thousands of them died. The French reportedly lost 17 knights.

Flanders was once more under the French thumb. And along the way Philippe had also proven himself a capable commander. In France, the question of whether he was the rightful king was settled.

In England, the question was very much still alive. It would start the Hundred Years War.

THE SUCCESSION CRISIS

All three of Philippe IV's sons had ruled as kings of France, as had one grandson, but they had done precisely what had been so inconceivable when Philippe had agreed to marry his daughter to the king of England so many years earlier: they had left an empty throne with Isabella's son, King Edward III of England, as the closest male heir to the throne of the king of France.

It was a remarkable twist of fate. Less than three centuries earlier, the childless death of Edward the Confessor had prompted William of Normandy's claim on the throne of England. Now, the childless death of Charles IV had given the throne of England claim over not just Normandy and Gascony but the whole of the French realm.

The closest thing to precedent was the death of Louis X in 1316. His only child at the time was a daughter, Joan, whom he'd had with his first wife, making it the first time since 987 that there wasn't an eldest son at hand to take the crown. His second wife, though, was heavily pregnant with a potential heir.

The king's brother Philippe, now the last surviving son of Philippe IV, made an agreement with Joan's uncle, the duke of Burgundy: if the unborn child was a son, he would be crowned king; if it was a daughter, Philippe would be regent until the crown could be placed with one of the two daughters by Louis's two wives. The latter situation would no doubt have been disastrous – a recipe for internal strife if not outright civil war – but none of it mattered when Louis's widow thankfully gave birth to a boy. In accordance with the agreement, the newborn was immediately crowned Jean I.

The infant died just five days after his birth. And Philippe, rather than letting Joan take the crown – which would have made sense given his earlier agreement – took it for himself as Philippe V. Joan's family predictably cried foul.

The king called an assembly of powers, the Estates-General, and charged it with adjudicating the matter – though in truth they were in no real position to make a free determination. They were called by Philippe to find a reason that the crown had to go to him despite his own earlier agreement that it could go to her. Not surprisingly, they found one: no woman could succeed to the crown.

A sexist judgment, to say the least, but it was irrelevant from the point of view of Edward's potential claim to the throne in 1328. Edward wasn't a woman.

The French would counter that since Isabella could not have taken the throne herself, then *any* claim descended from her, male or female, was likewise disallowed. Long after the Hundred Years War had begun, French lawyers would claim that this principle was part of an ancient 'Salic Law' dating back to the fifth century, but no one invoked this in 1316, and no one invoked it in 1328, either. Its application to the matter decades later was an after-the-fact effort to justify actions with paper.

The truth was far simpler: the French, who had struggled for so long to push back against the English holdings in France, were in no hurry to hand over the keys to the kingdom to them. Instead, they gave the crown to Philippe of Valois, who was the son of a son of Philippe III: thus the closest male relative through an all-male descent. He became Philippe VI of France.

Edward III had been king of England less than a year and was still subject to the oversight of Isabella, his mother, and Mortimer, her lover, when Charles died. In May 1328, a party of English bishops were sent to France to press his claim to the crown – no doubt sent by Isabella – but they were turned away. Beyond this, there wasn't much that any of them could do. They were still securing their rule after deposing King Edward II, including attempts to resolve the longstanding wars in Scotland. No one was anxious to go to war in France, too. Still, when Philippe summoned the latest Edward to do homage for Gascony, the English king tried hard to do homage for the lands that his ancestors had held *before* the War of Saint-Sardos. It didn't work, and the best Edward could do was to niggle with the ceremony to try to lodge his protests about the seized lands. This was done on 6 June 1329 (Figure 7).[4]

The French thought the new status quo was settled. The English, it was clear, did not.

ROBERT OF ARTOIS

A key player in what was to come was a man named Robert of Artois, who'd lost his father only a few years before he lost his grandfather at the battle of the Golden Spurs in 1302. Sadly, such a tragic circumstance was common enough at the time that it probably wouldn't merit mention except that his grandfather happened to be the count of Artois, and his late father had been his heir. Robert thereby had a claim on the region. Instead, it went to his aunt. At first, Robert wasn't able to put up much of a fight. He was only 15 at the time. In later years, though, he made multiple attempts to recover what he believed was the right of his inheritance. The newly crowned Philippe VI provided him with just such an opportunity, but in 1331 Robert overplayed his hand: it was discovered that he'd forged evidence to support his claim. Philippe exiled him in response. Robert made his way to England, where Edward III welcomed him into his court. Soon enough he was apparently encouraging Edward to push his claim on the throne of France.

How much Robert of Artois influenced Edward's aims isn't known for sure. Later writers certainly thought his urging was a big part of it. After the battle of Crécy in 1346, an anonymous poet composed a satire called *The Vows of the Heron*, which depicts a London dinner in September 1338 at which Robert produces for the meal a heron, a bird that symbolizes cowardice. Presenting it to the assembled court and Edward – called here 'Edward Louis' owing to his connection to the French crown through Saint Louis – Robert declares:

> And since the bird is cowardly, I proclaim my intention:
> That to the most cowardly of all those who lives or has lived
> I will give the heron. That is, to Edward Louis,
> Disinherited of France, that noble country,
> Of which he was the rightful heir. But his heart failed him,
> And for his slacking he will be dispossessed of it until death.[5]

The gauntlet, as it were, was dropped.

Blushing with both rage and embarrassment, Edward makes a vow upon the heron that he will declare his claim to the throne and then back it up with a force of arms. By 1346, he says – the year of the Crécy campaign, after which this work was composed – he will take an army to France to make war upon

'Philippe of Valois', the man who wears his crown. Robert then provokes further vows from those present. Many of them are, from the post-Crécy view, full of irony and biting satire of testosterone-fuelled bloodshed. The earl of Salisbury, for instance, vows never to open his eye until Edward has the crown of France; since the earl had already lost an eye in Scotland in 1333, this meant he would go to war blind – an analogy to the chaotic slaughter of war. Walter of Manny swears he will seize and burn Tournai. Instead, in their haste to strike the first blow of the war, he and a small band of followers would sneak into the nearby town of Mortagne-du-Nord at dawn in 1339, many of them disguised as women. Let into the initial gate, they found the castle locked up and retreated. Jean de Beaumont declares that he will be the one to lead Edward's armies; in fact, by 1346 he had switched sides to fight for the French king – it was his herald, Colins, whom we met upon the field in our opening chapter.

The oaths given in the *Vows of the Heron*, if it's not clear, have more to do with the later histories of these men than they have to do with the reality of what might have taken place earlier. If nothing else, we also know that Edward was on the Continent in September 1338, not in London. Regardless, it may be that something like this scene took place: Robert was pining for a war that would reinstate his lands, and this helped push Edward towards considering a claim for his inheritance – maybe even as early as Robert's arrival in 1331.

Even if so, Edward wasn't yet in a position to go to France. Scotland was on his mind, and it would give the English an opportunity to utilize and improve upon the very tactics that the royalist forces had used at Boroughbridge.

BEAUMONT AND THE LONGBOW BATTLES

We don't want to get too deep in the weeds of the wars between England and Scotland, fascinating though they are. We need to know just enough to understand the role played by a man named Henry de Beaumont.

Although hardly a household name today, Beaumont is the closest thing we can point to if we're looking for an architect of the war-fighting that would lead to so much English success in the coming years. Despite being born in France, Beaumont made his way into the service of Edward I when he was fighting in the Low Countries. When Edward returned to England, Beaumont went with him, and for his loyalty in fighting for the king at the successful battle of Falkirk he was given the earldom of Buchan in Scotland. Because he continued to fight for English interests in Scotland – including at the side of Edward II in the disastrous (for the English) battle of Bannockburn in 1314 – that earldom was stripped from him by the Scottish Parliament as soon as it had the power to do so. Beaumont would spend much of his life trying to get it back. He eventually hitched his star to the cause of Edward Balliol, a would-be claimant for the throne of Scotland.

It was this cause that brought Beaumont and Balliol to Scotland in 1332, at the head of a small army of supporters with English allies that was quietly supported by Edward III. After some initial skirmishes, they found themselves facing an advancing Scots army that was significantly larger at a place called Dupplin Moor.

Beaumont had been in the royalist lines at Boroughbridge. There, the royalist cause had been at an enormous advantage in numbers; here, his forces were instead overmatched by perhaps a staggering ten to one. Nevertheless, Beaumont knew the enormous effectiveness of using archers to funnel the enemy's approach and control the tactical dimensions of the field. In Scotland, the English would replicate and improve upon that example.[6] His first move was to choose ground that naturally hemmed in the enemy. Providing a smaller frontage for the fighting would naturally negate some of the numbers advantage possessed by the Scots. He found such a landscape in a tight valley among hills and dismounted his men. Across the valley bottom, the men-at-arms lined up on foot with fixed pikes. On the rugged hillsides to either side of the valley Beaumont ranged out a formidable number of archers. Their lines stretched forward like open arms, waiting to pull the enemy into the embrace of the weapons in the valley between them.

The Scots rushed towards them with the intention of breaking the line of men-at-arms immediately. This took them straight through the line of fire of the archers, who loosed down into them from both sides as they charged. The momentum of the Scots slowed. When they struck Beaumont's centre, the line of men-at-arms bent but didn't break.

The next wave of Scots, making its own headlong charge for the glory of killing Beaumont and Balliol, now piled into the first – truly piled, in fact, as it was said that a great many Scots died as they were suffocated or trampled in the press. All the while the archers rained merry hell on the disorganized jumble of the Scots. The victory was enormously lopsided.

The following year, Beaumont was present when the English army met the Scots at the battle of Halidon Hill on 19 July 1333 – this time under the command of King Edward himself. Here, the Scots were forced by circumstances to do exactly what Philippe had wisely not done at Cassel: they had to take the fight to an enemy. In their favour they had greater numbers, but their leaders surely knew that any topographical advantage of the English position could negate that in a hurry. Worse for them, the English followed the example of Dupplin Moor in deploying forward archers to funnel and thin the charging enemy. Once more, the victory was total.

According to the Auld Alliance, the French were bound to help the Scots if they were under attack from the English. Though his own treasuries were getting low, Philippe did what he could by encouraging the piracy of English ships and supporting the Scots with whatever he could afford. Dominoes fell fast, one into another, as the two realms hurtled towards the war that had been brewing for generations.

On the day after Christmas in 1336, Philippe demanded the return of the fugitive Robert of Artois, who was still safely ensconced within Edward's realm. Edward refused. Furthermore, he refused to do further homage to the king of France. The following May,

Philippe declared the English holdings in France forfeit as a result – the very move that had previously brought Edward II into line during the War of Saint-Sardos.

But just as Edward II hadn't been a mirror of Edward I, Edward III wasn't a mirror of Edward II. Rather than back down, the English king doubled down. He declared war on Philippe.

The Hundred Years War began.

4

The Hundred Years War Begins, 1337–46

Despite Edward's popular reputation as an aggressive king, it was Philippe who struck the first hard blows of the war. He was, quite frankly, in a better position to do so. His treasury was full. Edward wanted a war, and the French king was more than ready to give him one. As we've seen, the French and English had been squabbling for centuries now. But Philippe's first move signified how different and destructive the Hundred Years War would be.

When Edward declared war on Philippe, he and everyone else on the English side would have conceived of it as a war 'over there': the English Channel, then and now, does far more to separate the English people mentally from the Continent than it does physically.

Philippe was about to show what a false sense of security those waters were.

THE COASTAL RAIDS OF 1338–39

In March of 1338, a fleet of ships sailed out from the French port of Calais. Flying English banners, they cruised entirely unmolested and unchallenged into the harbour of Portsmouth and laid waste the unwalled and undefended town. Booty in hand, bloodied footprints on the docks, they reboarded their ships unhindered. Sailing back out to sea, the fleet then struck the Channel Islands, seizing much of Jersey.

Edward responded by sending a letter to Paris – probably received in May – declaring that he was the rightful king of France and would soon conquer France and defeat 'Philippe of Valois', as he addressed the man who wore the crown.[1]

They were strong words, but for the moment there wasn't much Edward could do to back them up. Not only was he facing conflict in Scotland, Gascony, and the Low Countries, but he now had to worry about his own coasts, too.

News of the enormous success of the Portsmouth raid spread quickly, after all. And under the flags of France, its allies, and the mercenary help anyone could hire – from Scotland and Scandinavia in the north to Castile and Genoa in the south – ships flooded the Atlantic and the North Sea. They were prowling, determined to attack and seize English ships wherever they found them, while making opportunistic raids on English ports wherever they could make them.

None of these attacks were unheard of in principle, but what Philippe and his commanders had initiated went beyond mere piracy. The aim wasn't the riches of any individual ship or port alone, but what totality of damages the collective effort could manage together. Philippe's strategy over the next two years was to command the seas that connected the island nation to the Continent. As Philippe's admiral, Nicholas Béhuchet, noted at the time, it was a campaign that could cripple the English ability to wage war not only by devastating England's fisheries and its trade routes but also forcing its crown to spend money on ships it didn't yet have.[2]

It was as effective as it was brilliant. England's economy suffered, and with it Edward's ability to wage war. In hindsight – as it was with the War of Saint-Sardos – it's astonishing that the English were so completely unprepared to be attacked. Nor did they respond quickly to the situation, as another devastating raid that autumn makes clear.

Sunday, 4 October 1338 was a special day for the people of Southampton. It was the feast day of one of the most well-known saints in Christendom: Francis of Assisi (d. 1226), who had founded the Order of Friars Minor and become popular in Christian art and stories for preaching to the birds, the beasts, and even the stones of the earth. He was the patron saint of nature and the outdoors, and in the wealthy town of Southampton this would have had special significance. Their prosperity, like that of so many coastal towns in England, came from the sheep whose wool filled their warehouses and their pockets.

The townspeople were probably in good spirits as they got up and followed their neighbours to Mass.

Many of them didn't have long to live.

Sailing up to their city, apparently unnoticed by anyone, was a fleet of dozens of ships from France and her allies in what would soon become the Hundred Years War. Just a month earlier they had hit the Channel Islands of Sark and Guernsey, which had both fallen.

Why no one had sounded the alarm at their approach is tough to understand. Later writers suggested that the ships were hidden by fog. Perhaps this is so, though it might be a convenient excuse told by the English authorities to cover up their utter failure to anticipate such an attack or even notice its imminent arrival.

The ships hit the port around 9am, disgorging soldiers ready to do battle. French sources say that the townspeople put up a strong resistance before they were overwhelmed. English sources suggest that there was hardly any fight at all: the militia, charged with the defence of the town, fled from the attack almost immediately, leaving the defenceless townsfolk to the enemy. When the church bells rang out the warning, other towns in the area didn't respond: they thought the priests of Southampton were calling their flock to prayer.

Those gathered to remember Francis and what the natural world had given them found themselves cut down by marauders seeking that same bounty. Women were raped. Families were hanged in their homes. Destruction was rampant. When it was done, roughly a third of Southampton's population was lost.

The raiders filled their ships with everything they could take – much of it Gascon wine and English wool – then set fire to the town and departed. English records hint that what was left was then further looted by the English themselves.[3]

Edward was furious at the attack, especially when it became clear that one reason the raiders had been so easily able to attack the city was that funds intended for its defence had been fraudulently shifted elsewhere.[4] Along the seaside, where walls ought to have been built, there was effectively no defence. Apparently, the town's wealthy citizens, living along the lucrative docks, wanted their barrels of Gascon wine unloaded into their cellars as efficiently as possible. To prevent another raid, the king personally ordered the construction of substantial fortifications, many of which can still be seen in the city today.

Of course, the construction of those walls and towers cost money, which such assaults were leaving in increasingly short supply. During the next year the French hit Harwich, Hastings, Plymouth, Sandwich, Rye, and other targets. The coasts of Devon, Sussex, and Kent were fair game for the enemy. And everywhere they prowled the waves.

EDWARD AND THE LOW COUNTRIES

What was Edward doing all this time? For the most part, he was trying to get help and money – especially money, since getting help often required a lot of it.

When it came to money, he was initially stymied by the fact that the wool trade was in disarray. The ruling count of Flanders, Louis of Nevers, had been placed in power by Philippe's victory at Cassel. Unsurprisingly, he, along with a wide swathe of the Flemish nobility, strongly supported the French king. So when Philippe had ordered a crackdown on English interests within his realms during the run-up to the war, Louis had complied. Edward had responded in turn, implementing economic sanctions in August 1336 by shutting down all wool exports to Flanders.

Economic sanctions inevitably harm both parties: it's simply hoped that the one putting them in place will be hurt less. It's true today, and it was certainly true in 1336. Shutting down the trade had an awful effect on England's economy – wool, as we've seen, was arguably its most powerful engine – but it was absolutely devastating in Flanders. Without wool, their cloth-making industries ground to a halt. This, in turn, halted other industries that relied upon cloth-making, which then touched off failures in yet another and another part of the economy.

The mercantile classes, who directly relied on the wool trade with England for their livelihood, were quickly ready to do just about anything to get it back, and they were furious that Louis put his duty to the French king over his duty to the citizens of Flanders. And each day, as the damage spread, more and more people were likewise enraged. Though in a war they'd be the first to die and the last to get anything for their troubles, the common folk were buckling under the crumbling economy.

In the last days of 1337, the resentment exploded into outright rebellion under the leadership of Jakob van Artevelde, a leading weaver from Ghent whose family had made its wealth within the wool trade as weavers and who was himself a wealthy brewer. Resistance collapsed in the face of Artevelde and his loyal band of what might charitably be called enforcers. Now in control of the region, Artevelde entered into negotiations with the English. He declared that Flanders would be neutral in the war and do nothing to help either side. This meant several things. Flemish ports would no longer be a staging ground for French attacks on English interests, and the Flemings would not resist the English king if he sailed up the River Scheldt to Brabant. In return, Edward agreed to reopen the wool trade.

If Artevelde expected that he could walk the Flemings along a line between their economic ties to England and their political ties to France, he was wrong. Philippe was furious. Flanders was nominally part of his kingdom, but now he had lost its support. For all his rage, there was little he could do for the moment. On 13 June 1338 he formally accepted the neutrality of Flanders.

The importance of the Low Countries to the English cause cannot be understated. We've already seen the economic ties that

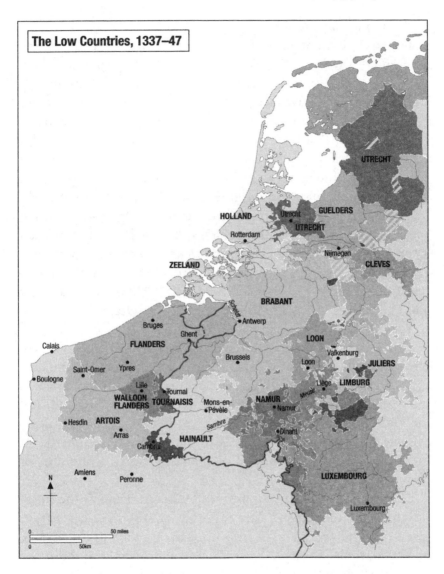

The Low Countries, 1337–47

bound Flanders to England, but we need to step back to get a bigger picture of what the Low Countries were – and why they were central to Edward's best hope of invading France.

Draw a line from the town of Étaples on the French coast to the River Meuse in the Ardennes. When the Hundred Years War began, this was essentially the frontier of France.

Beyond it was a jumble.

Just over that border, stretching up to Calais, was the county of Artois – the lands that Robert of Artois claimed, and which the English coveted for the massive port at Calais. Running up the coast, from Gravelines to the Scheldt, was the county of Flanders. Heading up the coastline from there were the counties of Zeeland and Holland. Further north was the see of Utrecht, centred on that city. The county of Guelders was built around Arnhem and Nijmegen, with the county of Cleves just beside it. The county of Brabant had the great cities of Antwerp and Brussels. Valenciennes was the centre of the county of Hainaut. Tournai was an island amid it all, called the Tournaisis. Lille and Bouvines stood in Walloon Flanders. Namur was its own county, and so was Luxembourg; between them, punched up to include the prince-bishopric of Liège, was the county of Loon. Beside it, Maastricht and Valkenburg were within the duchy of Limburg.

You get the point.

Though a few of these regions were eking out an independence of one kind or another – the see of Utrecht, for example, was ultimately under the control of the Pope but operated semi-autonomously – most were split up among the rival powers of France, England, and the Holy Roman Empire. In some cases, like Artois and Flanders, this meant they were held as fiefs to the king or the emperor. In other cases, the ties were bound by marriage, treaty, economics, or even culture.

Edward had the early support of Hainaut. Though the long-serving count of Hainaut – his wife's father, who had years earlier given him the fleet that got him his crown – died in the middle of negotiations, he made his son and heir swear to uphold the agreement to support England in the coming conflict. It cost the English some £15,000, but it was worth it. Guelders came for the same payment. Brabant followed: the duke was Edward's cousin, but more importantly he was interested in how his port city of Antwerp could take advantage of the profitable wool trade with England. That, with a £60,000 payment, was enough to settle it.

This was a good start, and the neutrality of the Flemish made it better. The English treasury might fill up with the taxation of the wool exports. The French offensive at sea would be hampered. More than that, the English presence in the Low Countries put the French into a defensive position. English forces could now sail up the Scheldt to Antwerp and other Brabantese or Hainauter ports. From there they could take bases in Valenciennes, ready to strike French-controlled Artois, Cambrésis – or even the royal realms of France itself. That pressure would prevent Philippe from putting all his strength into Gascony.

What Edward needed to be sure of was the Holy Roman Emperor, Louis IV. England had worked with the Holy Roman Empire in the past, and Louis had no great love for France. It was natural for Edward to turn in his direction at the outbreak of the Hundred Years War. At the very least, the English needed to ensure that the emperor wouldn't join forces with Philippe for any reason: their combined forces could potentially turn the port cities of the Low Countries into hostile ground. Edward needed the Low Countries corridor open at all costs.

And it *did* cost him. Louis supported the English in return for some £45,000. Worth it, though: if Edward lost the Low Countries, he'd lose the war.

The king was bleeding money he didn't have. Whether it was for alliances, ships, fortifications, outfitting, or everything else a war would take, fighting for the crown of France was going to cost him piles and piles of money. Scotland already had his coffers echoing. And although he'd more or less secured the lucrative wool trade now, there was only so much money to be made back from the sheep. Edward needed more, so to finance the war effort he made agreements to borrow massive sums of money from anyone who would lend it to him – principally, the Bardi and the Peruzzi banks in Italy. The terms he received were anything but generous. With staggering interest rates and ever-increasing shortages, Edward faced the 'dangerous and humiliating' prospect of bankruptcy, as he called it on 6 May 1339.[5] He needed success fast.

He had his safe harbour in the Low Countries, though, ready to serve as a beachhead for any raid or invasion he might conduct in the area – as well as a logistical conduit for everything he would need to pull it off.

Almost a year after the disaster at Southampton, he made his first offensive move.

EDWARD'S FIRST INVASION

On 20 September 1339, Edward marched out from Valenciennes, the capital of Hainaut, at the head of an allied force of English and men of the Low Countries – including men from the Holy Roman Emperor. They ravaged the countryside of the Cambrésis, which had allied with France. Soon, they moved to terrorize the Vermandois, too.

Philippe made his way to meet him: he knew as well as anyone that there was a wide road running from Cambrai to Paris.

Edward presumably wanted to goad Philippe to battle, to defeat him, and thus bring the war to a short and, perhaps more importantly, relatively cheap conclusion. He was, after all, in debt to his eyeballs. Philippe was in no hurry to oblige him: on 10 October, the French king joined his army, which was encamped at Péronne where the road between Paris and Cambrai crossed the Somme. He was a mere 18 miles from Edward, but he made no further move towards the English.

It seems probable that Philippe understood his enemy's plight: Edward's supply lines were stretched. He was heavily reliant on the foodstuffs he could pillage from the countryside – which rarely provides enough to sustain an army. The longer he stayed in the field, the hungrier and weaker his army would be. More than that, he was under financial siege. His creditors haunted him like shadows. The support of his allies in the Low Countries threatened to fray as their self-interests led them into competition for the meagre scraps that Edward was paying out of his promises to them. Like any siege, the longer this went on the more desperate the besieged would become. The damage

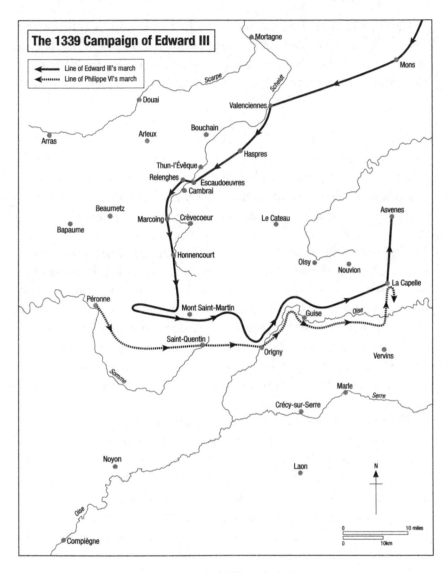

The 1339 Campaign of Edward III

← Line of Edward III's march
← Line of Philippe VI's march

Mortagne

Mons

Scarpe

Scheldt

Douai

Valenciennes

Bouchain

Arleux

Arras

Haspres

Thun-l'Évêque

Relenghes

Escaudoeuvres

Cambrai

Beaumetz

Marcoing

Crèvecoeur

Le Cateau

Asvenes

Bapaume

Honnencourt

Oisy

Nouvion

La Capelle

Péronne

Mont Saint-Martin

Guise

Oise

Saint-Quentin

Origny

Vervins

Somme

Marle

Serre

Crécy-sur-Serre

Noyon

Laon

N

Oise

Compiègne

0   10 miles
0   10km

the English were causing to the countryside as they ravaged and
ransacked for supplies was undoubtedly awful, but in the larger
picture of the war it was regrettably acceptable. France had the
means to repair and recover quickly. It is likely that Philippe
was prudently waiting for Edward's desperation to make him
stumble into a mistake.

On 14 October, Edward had marched to within a mile of the French at Péronne. But then, quite suddenly, he pulled back and retreated to Origny-Sainte-Benoîte, which he promptly burned to the ground. According to sources, he had barely avoided a pitched battle:

> And then the king [of France] decided in his secret council that the next day [14 October], in the morning, he would fight against the king of England. And he made each of his councillors swear that they would keep this quiet. Nevertheless, it was revealed to the English king, who immediately ... retreated.[6]

The French king wasn't a fool, but the English king wasn't one, either. Despite the military and financial stresses he was under, he didn't want to fight on unfavourable terms. The French outnumbered him – probably by two to one – and he'd nearly added to his troubles by fighting on ground of their choosing. Philippe had nearly made the blunder he was hoping to get from Edward. It might have been last minute, but the English had realized the situation, been spooked by it, and wisely manoeuvred away to find better ground.

The two kings were engaged in a deadly dance.

On 16 October Philippe moved to Saint-Quentin. A day later he sent a letter to Edward: let the English choose any open ground and the French would give them battle there in five days. Edward accepted and his scouts led him to La Flamengrie.

22 October came, but Philippe had yet to appear. Tired and hungry, the English prepared to retreat north towards the Low Countries. Finally, a message came from the French. Their king was just a few miles away. He would fight.

The next morning, Edward arrayed for battle. The field was about five miles from Philippe's encampment with, as the chronicler Jean le Bel describes it, 'open country, with no river or fortification to impede him'.[7] Their formation was built on the lessons the English had learned in Scotland: a line of infantry and dismounted knights at the centre, flanked by wings of archers that would funnel the enemy into them. A diary from the campaign describes units of Welsh spearman bristling at the tips of those wings.[8] These were a solution to the one weakness of the formation: the exposure of the archers to attack on their own flank – particularly via cavalry charges. At Dupplin Moor the archers on the wings had been protected by the rugged terrain on which they'd been positioned. At Halidon Hill they had been on high ground. Here, exposed in open space, Edward had improvised as best he could.

Nine days earlier it had been Edward who suddenly withdrew from the face of the enemy. This time, it would be Philippe. He pulled back and entrenched his forces behind a great ditch and other field fortifications.

Writing to Parliament after the campaign ended, Edward claimed he knew why. French scouts had captured one of his men – a German knight, the king says – who had seen the entirety of the English battle plan and divulged it to the enemy.[9] As we are learning to do with any of our sources, we might want to take this report with a grain of salt. It is an entirely self-serving spin for the king to provide: he would have fought and won, but when the French realized how *brilliant* he was, they ran away! Perhaps. But the French certainly saw it differently, with excuses ranging from it being too close to the Sabbath to their army being tired or hungry or even obstructed from the field. The variety here is telling: there wasn't a single clear reason that was well known, which might give more credence to Edward's claim that Philippe had thought better of the fight as soon as he knew what he faced.

The English were keen to view this as a sign of cowardice – though in reality it would hardly be more 'cowardly' than their own earlier retreat from the French. In both cases, the truth was that the kings were acting in the best interests of the men under their command. As le Bel reports, some of Philippe's advisors told him:

> it would be a great folly to do battle, for there was no way of knowing what everyone was thinking and if there was any danger of betrayal ... for if Fortune turned against him and he

was defeated, he'd lose both his kingdom and his life, and even if
he beat his enemies it wouldn't mean he'd won the kingdom of
England or the lands or possessions of the other English lords.[10]

These would be wise words. Running headlong into a
disadvantageous fight and wasting men's lives just because it was
close at hand or the prescribed time had come would be the very
opposite of good leadership. This wasn't a fairy tale: Philippe's
forces weren't going to turn into pumpkins if they didn't finish by
the chiming of the clock. He could afford to be patient.

But Edward could not. Low on food and money, he disengaged
from the field and retreated from France. From across the border
in Avesnes he made a show of challenging the French king to come
and fight, complaining about Philippe's unwillingness to fight
like a man. It was a face-saving bit of bluster, and Philippe wisely
ignored it.

Edward's first campaign of the Hundred Years War was over. It
had accomplished nothing of substance.

EDWARD'S SECOND INVASION

On 26 January, 1340, Edward at last made a public declaration that
he was the rightful king of France. No matter how much or how
little he'd been pushed to do it by men like Robert of Artois, in the
final act it had nothing to do with taking an oath upon a heron
or any other bird. It had everything to do with legal necessity. It
was deeply improper to fight one's sworn liege lord in the Middle
Ages, which is exactly what Edward had done. He'd given homage
to Philippe VI in 1329 and even affirmed it after he was ruling on
his own, as an adult, in 1331. An August 1337 broadsheet issued
by the king to justify his foreign war had even called Philippe the
king of France.

To make his acts of aggression against Philippe legal, Edward
could have renounced his homage to him, but doing so would also
have renounced his right to hold Gascony – the very basis of his
dispute. His only solution was to declare that Philippe had never

really been king of France in the first place – no matter what his own acts of homage had said before.

Edward didn't really have a leg to stand on in any of this, but the truth is often twisted to serve the interests of those in power.

Nor was this legal fiction helpful to Edward alone. Many of his allies – those in Flanders in particular – were in the same troublesome spot: by helping the English they'd been going against oaths and treaties that were owed to the king of France. But if he had never been king – if, in fact, Edward was really the king – they could claim they were fulfilling the letter of the law. In a likely corresponding move, Jakob van Artevelde publicly declared his support for Edward. Bruges, Ghent, Ypres, and other ports were now open to the English. The count of Flanders fled for Paris.

Beyond Flanders, the war hadn't been going well for England, but Edward finally got some good news with a massive victory at sea at the battle of Sluys on 24 June 1340 (Figure 10).

Because it doesn't pertain to the tactical decisions made at Crécy, we won't go into the details about Sluys here – but that shouldn't be perceived as a slight on the importance of the fight.[11] This fierce naval battle was the first major engagement of the Hundred Years War, and it was a major win for Edward and his Flemish allies in particular: in addition to the advantages of a typical military victory, the English defeat of so many ships meant the further easing of constrictions on the wool trade.

Not long after Sluys, Edward conducted his second invasion of the Hundred Years War: the siege of Tournai.

As he had the previous year, the English king used Flanders as a base to make an attack on lands controlled by the French king. This time it was the magnificent town of Tournai. Philippe once again arrived upon the scene to harry the English, but he otherwise refused to give battle. Edward, too, seemed disinclined to bring about a pitched battle, and meanwhile his own alliances were breaking down. In the end, both forces pulled back, agreeing to a cessation of combat formalized in the Truce of Espléchin, on 25 September 1340. The signing of this truce was not driven by a desire for peace on the part of the princes. Little had been accomplished. Nothing was settled.

To the contrary, the reason for the temporary reprieve from war appears once again to have been money: both kings had not just tapped out their financial resources, but were heavily in debt to foreign powers. Edward was to all intents bankrupt. His loans were coming due, and he had been unable to raise sufficient domestic revenues to cover these, much less his mounting costs to continue the war. The contemporary Florentine chronicler Giovanni Villani claimed that Edward was ultimately in debt to the Bardi family for 900,000 gold florins, and that he owed a further 600,000 to the Peruzzis. His default on these loans might well have caused these banking firms to collapse. Yet Villani is a biased source – his brother was a member of the Peruzzi family and he was himself deeply in debt to them[12] – and there are other questions about exactly how much Edward III's default can be directly linked to the problems of these banking firms.[13] What *is* certain is that the English use of and subsequent default on Florentine loans not only had a major impact on the economy of Florence, but also led to a keen Italian interest in Edward's campaigns. The existence of Villani's richly detailed account of the battle of Crécy is assuredly a direct result of the financial ties between the English king and the leading economic powers of medieval Florence.

CRÉCY APPROACHES

This brief interlude of peace was broken during the so-called War of the Breton Succession beginning in 1341, when England and France backed rival claimants to the duchy of Breton in northern France, leading to armed conflicts including the battle of Morlaix on 30 September 1342.

Once again, financial concerns won out, and the Truce of Malestroit was signed in January 1343. Though longer-lasting, this peace was hardly due to some idealized goal. As soon as it was viable, hostilities were resumed – most notably with a resurgent struggle for the English holdings in Gascony that soon focused on Aiguillon, a fortified town between the cities of Toulouse and Bordeaux, strategically situated at the confluence of two major rivers. The English had taken it the previous year, and now the French badly wanted it back. Beginning in March 1346, the eldest son of the French king, Jean the duke of Normandy – who would himself rule as Jean II – brought perhaps 15,000 men to lay siege to the Anglo-Gascon garrison at Aiguillon, which may have numbered as few as 1,000 men.

Remarkably, week after week, the beleaguered men at Aiguillon held out despite the enormous odds against them. Their success has yet to be given the focused attention it deserves.

Alas, this won't be the place to do it justice, either.

Because as the calendar turned to June, events in Gascony were about to be overtaken by events in the north.

PART TWO

The Crécy Campaign, 1346

Princes and Peasants lay together mixt,
The English Swords, no difference knew betwixt.

Michael Drayton, 1627

The Campaign Begins, 12–23 July

On a rise near the beaches of Saint-Vaast-La-Hougue, the 16-year-old prince of Wales knelt before his namesake father, the king of England. In coming years this younger Edward would come to be known as the Black Prince, and the legends of his actions would come to fill poems and songs and storybooks. But for now, as he bent his knee upon the French soil they'd come to claim, he was an untested boy no doubt hoping he could simply survive what was to come.

We can picture the scene fairly well. It was around midday on 12 July 1346. The sun was high and hot, but a good wind had carried the fleet over the sea from Yarmouth on the Isle of Wight. We can hope, for the boy's sake, that there was a breeze to stir the banners and pull some of the heat off his mail coat. We can imagine he looked something like the soldier pictured in the Westminster Psalter, drawn perhaps a century earlier and celebrating a young man being knighted as he prepares to go on crusade (Figure 9). Though the Black Prince would wear plate and helm in many of the battles to come, at this point he was probably wearing a simple chain shirt and leggings beneath a surcoat embroidered with his coats of arms.

The same breeze that cooled off the boy shook the furled sails of the massive fleet of ships that crowded the waters of the bay. They were 'a great multitude', according to the *Grand Chronicles* of France, 'estimated at a good 1,200 ships, aside from the small ships and other vessels'.[1] The English army was pouring out of them, coming ashore wherever they could along the beaches. If the young prince had stood and looked south, he would have seen those sands stretching away down the east coast of the Cotentin peninsula.

No one could have known it, but this wouldn't be the last invasion that this stretch of coastline would see. Almost 600 years later, the coastline south of La Hougue would be code-named Utah Beach during the D-Day Invasion. That invasion would be notorious for the blood that was spilled across the beaches of Normandy as thousands of Allied men lost their lives to establish footholds against the Axis forces of World War II.

This landing was entirely different. There were no coastal defences to be breached. When dawn revealed the thousands of sails riding the tide into the bay, the people of La Hougue fled. The heat wasn't the only reason the Black Prince probably wasn't wearing plate armour as he was dubbed a knight. There simply hadn't been a need to strap into the heavier gear. Their landing had been almost entirely unopposed.

How the king of England had managed to land his army in France with hardly a Frenchman in sight is a testament to his planning. In 1339, Edward had retreated when he heard that Philippe was about to attack him, supposedly prompting the king of France to exclaim 'Can I not speak quietly in my private room without the king of England listening? Must he always sit invariably by my side?'[2] We don't know how Edward had placed his spies so close to Philippe at that point – another testament to their good work, frankly – but it was impressively done. Unfortunately for the French, the reverse seems not to have been the case in 1346: Philippe didn't expect an English landing on the Cotentin at all.

To be fair, the French had no doubts that an invasion was coming. Philippe's intelligence gathering was more than adequate to recognize the men and ships that had been assembling in the south of England for many months. Public calls to arms had given no room for doubt that Edward was bringing an army to France.

Philippe just didn't know where they'd be landing. As a result, he had gathered forces in key locations, ready to respond once the destination was known.

In part, this seems to be because Edward himself wasn't sure. There are indications that he was first planning to set sail to Brittany, before he changed his mind in the late spring to aim for the south-west of France. Certainly this made the most immediate sense: the English army had ready ports there to disembark from, and once on the ground they could relieve besieged Aiguillon and counter the French army that was currently trying to push them out of Gascony.

In late June, though, Edward changed his mind again. He was going to take his army to the Cotentin peninsula in Normandy. The chronicler Jean le Bel suggests that this was on the advice of Godfrey of Harcourt, a French viscount who, like the now-dead Robert of Artois, had been exiled by Philippe only to join the English court and push Edward to war. Nicknamed 'the Lame' because of a limp from birth, Godfrey had held land, before his exile, in the middle of the Cotentin peninsula: he 'knew the whole region well'.[3] The king clearly trusted him: Godfrey was named one of the marshals of the invading army. On the same hilltop on which the Black Prince was knighted, the lame viscount knelt and paid homage for his holdings on the peninsula. This act, he said, was done to the true king of France.

As much as he was prized, however, it is doubtful that Godfrey alone was the reason for Edward's decision to invade the Cotentin. It had numerous other advantages. Foremost among them was the fact that the Normandy coast was the closest landing point for Edward's fleet. Few of us today think much about the dangers of the sea in a time of wind and sail. The ocean as Edward would have known it was unpredictable and unforgiving. To take the waves was to cast lots against death: the less time spent on them the better. Normandy was a straight shot across the Channel. That made the invasion easier, and it would also make future support easier, too: whether it was for reinforcements or escape, a direct line would be the best line.

The English also had good reason to think the region would be mostly undefended. The duke of Normandy – Philippe's son, Jean – was at the moment in the south, still trying to break the beleaguered English garrison at Aiguillon. The friendly ports of Gascony offered more assurance of a successful landing if the fleet got to them, but the bare beaches of Normandy were a close second.

The invasion force that hit those beaches must have been a terrifying sight to see. It might have been as many as 14,000 men strong, and half of them were archers. Recent work has revealed that the armoury of the Tower of London provided in two batches a total of least 5,518 bows, 30,126 bowstrings, and 11,206 sheaves of arrows for the initial campaign. Each of these sheaves contained 24 arrows, and a standard allotment was two sheaves per archer.[4] This was in addition to what other men and retinues provided for themselves. The arrows – 268,944 from the Tower alone – filled dozens of crates and barrels that were carried or rolled down off the decks of ships onto the shore to be loaded onto every wagon that the fleeing populace had left behind. There were hundreds of non-fighting men and women with the army, too: armourers, blacksmiths, bowyers, butchers, carpenters, cooks, engineers, masons, saddlers, surgeons, tentmakers, wheelwrights, and many more. All of them had their supplies and needed equipment. Everything was mobile. The army was a city on the move.

Trying to create discipline in this mobile city were the deputies of the constable and marshal of the army. They no doubt did their best, but the truth is that the vast majority of those who took part in the invasion didn't do so from any great sense of national pride or destiny. Either they'd been forced to come because they couldn't pay their way out of service or they'd volunteered in hope of getting rich off a share of booty taken in the campaign – or even just to get three square meals a day. In any case, the looting was rampant, unavoidable, and – insofar as it could feed the men without tapping into any of the campaign's closely guarded supplies – welcome. It didn't matter whose army it was, thousands of men marching to war was not something anyone wanted to be near.

The men gathered on the hilltop to witness the knighting of the Black Prince weren't here to pillage personally – though most of them would certainly take a cut of any looted goods they could manage – but they were still after their own kinds of profit. There was the social profit of proximity to the king and, they hoped, the glory of victory. The latter opened up avenues for profits deriving from new titles and lands. There was also the potentially extreme profit of taking hostages. It was common practice in medieval warfare not to kill men of title and rank, such as themselves. They had connections, and, as such, they had access to wealth. It was far better to capture them and hold them hostage than to kill them. A dead man had no value. A living man could be worth much indeed. Under such terms, war could be extremely profitable.

For the common man, of course, battle held no such luxuries. If captured, their names would not save them. And if by chance they captured some named lord, they could be certain that little of the ransom for his release would go to them: the lords on their own side would claim the glory.

And so, even on the first day of the invasion, the villages around the landing were looted. The next day, things got so far out of hand that La Hougue itself was accidentally set on fire and the king's encampment had to be moved to the other side of the bay at Morsalines. On 14 July, English raiders had reached the large harbour of Barfleur. It was there that William the Conqueror had boarded his flagship, *Mora*, bound for England in 1066. It was there, too, that the *White Ship* had sunk in 1120, carrying William Adelin with it to the deep; it was his death, leaving Henry I without a clear heir, that had precipitated the Anarchy between Stephen and Matilda.

Now, the English took the harbour to use it for disembarkation. The town was plundered, and any who resisted were killed.

FINDING SOURCES

In the Introduction I talked about the many erasers of the past. The last of them, I said, is ourselves: the extraordinary story of

Colins de Beaumont identifying the dead went unheard for so long not because it was unknown but because it was ignored. Colins spoke; generations of historians failed to listen. I suggested that one explanation might be that Colins' work is poetic, and that poetry scares a lot of people away. But there are plenty of other reasons that people might ignore a story.

One of these reasons is that a story doesn't match what a person believes – or wants to believe, or was told to believe – about the past. A story that contradicts the accepted understanding of events can be thrown out. Some of this, as we'll see, happened to the stories of Crécy.

Yet another reason why stories can be erased is that they don't match our expectations of what a story should look like. This is the category to which most of our 'new' sources for history belong. We don't find them by following treasure maps. There are no secret archives to raid, no dusty tomes held in the skeletal hands of long-dead writers. A great measure of the modern historian's work is instead done in a well-worn office chair, using search algorithms to comb through the catalogues and the digitized books and manuscripts from libraries around the world. Few medieval sources are truly 'discovered' in the sense that no one knew that they existed; they are discovered in the sense that someone finally took note of what they might mean. This is true, for instance, of a slip of parchment in the British Library, which Kelly DeVries and I located during a routine search of their holdings. Historians have long repeated the claim that no hostages were taken at the battle of Crécy, yet this scrap, written on 18 November 1350 by the French prince Philippe of Orléans, tells the story of the apparent English capture at the battle of the 16-year-old Frenchman Guillaume de Tournebu – and his father's efforts to secure his ransom afterwards. We didn't find this by fighting through spider-filled catacombs in London – exciting though that would be. We filled out a call slip, and a few minutes later a staff member brought it to us to examine. It was on their digital catalogue. The British Library knew they had it. They simply didn't know what it *meant*.

Another such story exists in a roll of parchment housed today at the National Archives in Kew. It's not a remarkable artefact at first glance. Rolled out, it has no striking illustrations or florid handwriting. The scribbled text reveals no astonishing narratives. The roll is, in fact, a sequence of receipts. What makes them of immediate interest to us is whose receipts they are, when they were written, and where.

The first question is easy to answer: the author's name was William Retford, the clerk in charge of the kitchens that fed King Edward III of England. Better still is the answer to the second question: the roll contains his receipts for the Crécy campaign in 1346. And that leads us to the answer to the third question: Retford wrote the *Kitchen Journal*, as we titled it, while on the Crécy campaign itself (Figure 11).

The story Retford tells us isn't one of blades and bows and blood – it's meat and wine and the monies to procure them. Day after day, camp after camp, in careful, patient writing, Retford dutifully records what stores the king's kitchens used, and how much cost had been incurred in using them. The roll is an entirely administrative sequence of receipts. If you're not interested in the daily food consumptions of the king and those closest to him, the story that Retford tells us is, in a word, *boring*.

I don't know if this is why William Retford, like Colins de Beaumont, was so long ignored. But I do know how tragic it was that he was ignored: because even a boring story can contain absolutely vital information.

Think of just about any receipt you've ever seen in your life. It tells you what you bought. It tells you when you paid for it. And it also tells you *where* you paid for it.

Retford's *Kitchen Journal* works the same way. Translate the Latin and sift through its many abbreviations, and the information is all there: a record – an eyewitness account – of where the encampment of King Edward III was established at the end of each day of the Crécy campaign. For all intents and purposes, it's a road map of where he went and when he went there. This is powerfully important information. By corroborating

this with another itinerary preserved in the British Library –
called the *Cleopatra Itinerary* – and the numerous narrative
accounts of chroniclers, we can build a detailed timeline of the
movements of King Edward III and his 14,000 men as they
moved across France.

ROADS AND RIVER-CROSSINGS

On 16 July 1346, Retford records that the king's kitchen was
'still' located near La Hougue on the Cotentin coast.[5] Edward
was overseeing the continued gathering up of his mobile city.
Other records tell us that the army plundered much of the
peninsula before putting it to the torch. Ahead of the English,
the countryside was emptying out. People hurriedly grabbed
everything that they could carry from their homes and poured
out onto the roads headed south. Most of them were on foot,
gathered into bands of tired, terrorized refugees scattering for
cover at the sound of approaching hooves. Death threatened no
matter which way they went. It was just more certain behind
them. So it is in every war.

Philippe was in Paris. Word of the crisis reached him quickly. He
now knew where Edward had landed, and he had to decide how
to respond. Much of his military strength remained in the south
with the duke of Normandy. The vacuum they had left behind, as
we've seen, was likely part of the rationale for Edward's landing
spot. So the French king immediately set about gathering a *second*
army from his remaining subjects and allies. Until they could come
together to face the English and defeat them, local forces would
simply need to delay the English march as best they could. To
this end, even with Edward still disembarking, the eyes of France
turned to Caen.

There were other towns between Caen and La Hougue, some of
them walled. But no one yet knew how quickly the English would
begin their march. If the French tried to form their battle-line too
close to the English army, it might be overrun before it could be
established. And not one of those towns, no matter how well it was

loved by its people, was as mighty and well fortified as Caen, long the capital of the dukes of Normandy.

Caen had something else going for it, too. If Edward planned to march on Paris, the city stood directly in his way.

To grasp this, we must remove ourselves from the modern world, with its paved roads crisscrossing a drained and gentled landscape whose wildness is fenced in by sweeps of earth tilled and levelled by tractors. The medieval military commander saw none of this. Even as recently as the D-Day landings, much of the Cotentin coast now greened by modern drainage was largely impassable marsh. Such was the case in numerous parts of Europe. And even where the land was relatively free of forest, swamp, or whatever else nature had wrought, it was very rarely *flat*. Open space meant farming, and farming in the Middle Ages meant ridges and furrows. As oxen pulled a medieval plough, the tilled ground was pushed to one side and built up, run by run, year by year, until it formed a ridge of earth rising up on either side of a ditch or furrow of deeper earth. Today, the weathered remains of medieval fields have ridges that are still a couple of feet high. In the Middle Ages, they were much higher. To cross a ploughed field was to go hiking: one had to climb over a line of earth some six feet high, every few dozen feet or so. And if one needed to pull a wagon – or, as Edward did in 1346, perhaps hundreds of them – to cross fields was no easy task.

To make good speed, to keep good order, and to not exhaust itself, a medieval army on the march needed roads.

Following game trails, finding routes through the wilds, people have long made natural paths across the landscape. Roads are something far more significant, the pointedly artificial result of an effort to ease travel between two points. There were roads before Caesar came to Gaul – what Rome called France – but there's no question that what the Romans built across the landscape were markedly different from what had come before. Roman roads were typically paved and drained, as wide and straight as their engineers could manage. Inevitably, then, these routes encountered rivers or streams. The Romans knew only too well that a handful of people could cross at a ford, but that even a mere couple of hundred men and wagons moving as a group could quickly turn a ford through the smallest of streams into a spreading morass of sucking mud. In modern military terms, these encounters constitute 'wet-gap' crossings, and in logistical planning they ought to be avoided – especially when operating in enemy territory or in close proximity to the enemy. The Romans, as a result, favoured bridging rivers and streams whenever possible.

Romans built roads for the rapid transport of goods and men, and they built them to last. As the centuries rolled on, new roads were here and there added to the existing Roman network, but the routes of the Roman system still underlie an astonishing portion of the modern freeway maps even today.

As the English disembarked, Edward and his commanders had a map of the roads at hand. They knew that a Roman road ran straight along the spine of the Cotentin peninsula, from the port of Cherbourg to the town of Valognes – the former estate of Godfrey of Harcourt – where it split. One route headed south towards Coutances on its way to Rennes. The other ran eastwards through Carentan to Bayeux and then Lisieux. There were roads from there to Paris via Dreux, but by far the best road available to anyone wanting to get to the capital of France was the wide, welcoming pavement on the other side of the Seine: from Rouen to Paris.

The French knew this. They also knew that an ideal place to stop the English advance along this route was between Bayeux and Lisieux, where the road crossed the River Orne. Almost as soon as Edward landed, the count of Eu, who had been stationed with his men at Harfleur in anticipation of an English attempt on the Seine, immediately headed there, gathering men and supplies to reinforce its castle even as the refugees from Normandy came flooding towards the safety of its walls.

Edward, meanwhile, was on the move.

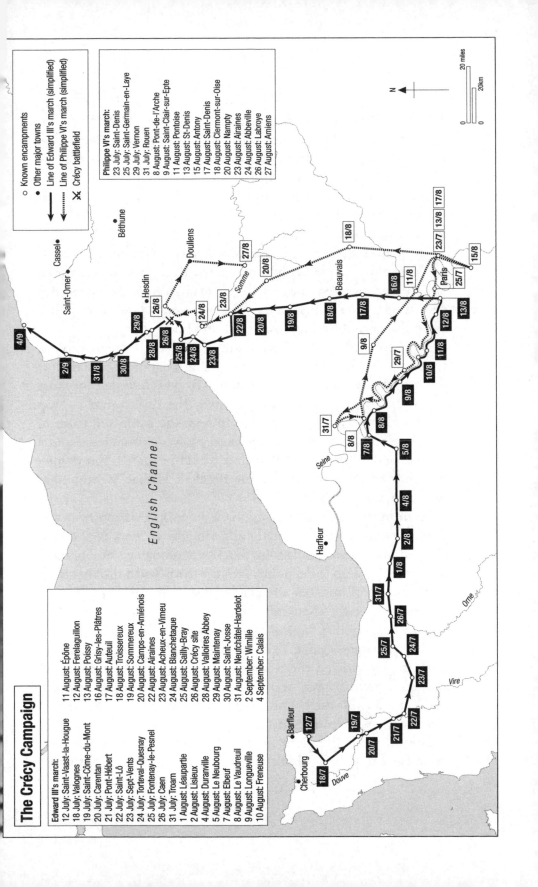

The Crécy Campaign

Edward III's march:
12 July: Saint-Vaast-la-Hougue
18 July: Valognes
19 July: Saint-Côme-du-Mont
20 July: Carentan
21 July: Pont-Hébert
22 July: Saint-Lô
23 July: Sept-Vents
24 July: Torteval-Quesnay
25 July: Fontenay-le-Pesnel
26 July: Caen
31 July: Troarn
1 August: Léaupartie
2 August: Lisieux
4 August: Duranville
5 August: Le Neubourg
7 August: Elbeuf
8 August: Le Vaudreuil
9 August: Longueville
10 August: Freneuse
11 August: Épône
12 August: Ferelaguillon
13 August: Poissy
16 August: Grisy-les-Plâtres
17 August: Auteuil
18 August: Troissereux
19 August: Sommereux
20 August: Camps-en-Amiénois
22 August: Airaines
23 August: Acheux-en-Vimeu
24 August: Blanchetaque
25 August: Sailly-Bray
26 August: Crécy site
28 August: Valloires Abbey
29 August: Maintenay
30 August: Saint-Josse
31 August: Neufchâtel-Hardelot
2 September: Wimille
4 September: Calais

Philippe VI's march:
23 July: Saint-Denis
25 July: Saint-Germain-en-Laye
29 July: Vernon
31 July: Rouen
8 August: Pont-de-l'Arche
9 August: Saint-Clair-sur-Epte
11 August: Pontoise
13 August: St-Denis
15 August: Antony
17 August: Saint-Denis
18 August: Clermont-sur-Oise
20 August: Nampty
23 August: Airaines
24 August: Abbeville
26 August: Labroye
27 August: Amiens

Legend:
○ Known encampments
● Other major towns
— Line of Edward III's march (simplified)
···· Line of Philippe VI's march (simplified)
✗ Crécy battlefield

N

0   20 miles
0   20km

* * *

The *Kitchen Journal* informs us that on 18 July Edward reached Valognes. Those of its citizens who hadn't fled met the king on the road and begged for mercy. Edward gave the order that they be spared, and their property with them. The king passed the night there, in a house belonging to the duke of Normandy. The next morning, despite Edward's promises, the town was put to the torch as the English marched out.

The following night, he was at Saint-Côme-du-Mont. The people of Normandy, Jean le Bel tells us, 'were in a state of shock: they'd never experienced war or ever seen a man-at-arms, and now they were seeing people slaughtered without mercy, houses set ablaze and pillaged, and the land laid waste and burnt'.[6]

To their credit, the small number of local French soldiers, retreating ahead of the invaders, were doing what they could to slow the army down. Under the command of Robert Bertrand, they tore down the bridge over the River Douve. The English had to stop to rebuild it, then they proceeded to seize the castle and town of Carentan on 20 July. As at Valognes, these were surrendered to the English under the promise that they would be spared. But despite the king's best efforts, according to his clerk Michael Northburgh, this town, too, was burned.[7]

From here, the English army made its first deviation from the Roman roads. Instead of marching straight to Bayeux, Edward directed his forces towards Saint-Lô. It was probably nothing more than greed. As Jean le Bel points out, the town 'had a thriving trade in cloth and all manner of merchandise, and many prosperous citizens: fully eight thousand men plied their trades there, both wealthy burghers [i.e. high-ranking citizens] and artisans'.[8]

When Bertrand's scouts reported the English turn, he raced ahead of them. He ordered the bridge across the River Vire destroyed and, for a night at least, seems to have thought to make his own stand in Saint-Lô itself. This may be why so many of its citizens stayed despite the coming danger.

Edward spent the night in Pont-Hébert on 21 July, while its namesake bridge was rebuilt over the Vire. It took a night and a day for the English engineers to reconstruct the bridge and allow him to proceed, but the crossing was inevitable. Seeing the speed of the English progress, knowing no one was coming to help him, Bertrand abandoned the town. Despite its walls, the leaderless Saint-Lô fell to the English army without a fight on 22 July. Jean le Bel describes what happened next:

> When the noble king drew near he made camp outside – he didn't want to take lodging in the town for fear of fire. But this great town was taken with little effort and sacked and pillaged from top to bottom. Not many alive would ever believe the wealth of booty plundered there, or the vast quantity of cloth they found – you'd have got a good price if you'd fancied buying: it was there for the taking! But few were interested in that: they were more intent on the piles of gold and silver they found – so keenly intent, indeed, that the city was spared the flame. But a great many of the wealthy burghers were taken prisoner and sent to England to be ransomed, and a lot of the common folk were killed when the town was first entered – and a good number of fair townswomen and their daughters were raped, which was a dreadful pity.[9]

On this same day, in Saint-Denis, 150 miles away as the crow flies, Philippe raised the Oriflamme – the battle-standard of the king of France. At this point he knew that it wasn't just the English army in Normandy that he had to worry about. Edward had dispatched Hugh Hastings to oversee the raising of an army in Flanders and invade France from the north-east. Hugh and the English with him had arrived in the Low Countries on 17 July. Philippe had to think that it wouldn't be long before whatever Anglo-Flemish army they managed to scrape together would be pushing at the border. The king accordingly split his gathering forces: one part would march to Amiens, where any invasion from Flanders could be stopped by the line of the River Somme.

Philippe, with the rest of his men, would march down the main Roman road through the Seine valley to Rouen, ready to resupply Caen if it held – or to serve as a backstop if it fell.

6

The Sacking of Caen, 23–30 July

As Edward left Saint-Lô and headed east, he cut a gash across the heart of Normandy. Bands of riders from his army ranged as far as they could manage every day, plundering with near impunity. Though it varied according to the local terrain, the path of total destruction, according to Jean le Bel, was six or seven leagues on either side of the route – up to 40 miles wide.[1] Even if the truth was only half that, the English bearing down on Caen were inflicting a horrifying amount of damage.

The historical irony is hard to miss. Only 280 years before King Edward III set his eyes towards it, his six-times-great-grandfather had left Caen in order to seize the throne of England – all because another Edward had died. William's victory at Hastings changed the course of history, and it enriched Caen beyond all measure. The city where he'd been buried – just one more indication of the duke's relative feelings about his kingdom-by-conquest – was the largest city in Normandy after mighty Rouen on the Seine. Outside London, there were few cities in England to rival its size.

Caen is where the French hoped to stop the English advance. Understanding what the city looked like in 1346 makes it easy to see why.

The city was built where the River Odon met the much larger River Orne in a wide valley. These watercourses mingled through a number of little islets and one large island at their confluence called the Île Saint-Jean. The road to Rouen – the road Edward needed – ran over beautiful stone bridges to and from the island before heading east. What had been the centre of William the Conqueror's Caen was nestled up against the north bank of the Odon, astride the first bridge to the island, flanked by abbeys that could also serve as fortified defence-works. This oldest part of the town was huddled around a strong castle on a hill between them. William had been the one to begin building the castle and its impressive keep, just six years before he invaded England, and subsequent kings both English and French had expanded and updated the original construction. It was a formidable sight.

The entire circuit of the old town was walled, but this was less impressive. The castle's keep and walls had seen regular upkeep. The town's walls had not. They had fallen into significant disrepair in several places. Some of this negligence was likely due to the fact that the wealthiest of Caen's citizenry had moved out of the old town and into a newer, bustling suburban enclave that was flourishing upon the Île Saint-Jean. By 1346, large and lavish homes were packed into the land between the waters that served as the beautiful island district's primary defence. No one seems to have given much thought to the idea of marring its loveliness with walls: it was, after all, an island between the rivers.

The mood in Caen was tense as the English marched closer. The city's streets were full of refugees. The wind carried the smoke of the destruction of their homes.

In charge of the defence was Raoul II of Brienne, the 31-year-old count of Eu and one of the constables of France (essentially one of their chief military officers). With him was Robert Bertrand, the man who had bought the city at least two extra days to prepare by destroying the bridges behind him. Bertrand was able to tell the count exactly what he was facing: the English army outnumbered their soldiers by roughly ten to one. Still, the commanders had reason to feel good about their chances. The city's walls wouldn't allow the full numbers of the English to attack at once, and Raoul had worked hard to use the time Bertrand had given him to conduct emergency repairs of the areas where prior neglect had left those fortifications in disrepair. More than that, the whole of the city seemed ready to fight to defend their lives and homes. If they were all put into the field, they might well outnumber the coming enemy.

By the night of 25 July, an English messenger brought a letter from Edward: if the people of Caen surrendered the city to him, he promised to spare their lives and personal property.

It had been exactly one week since Edward had made much the same promise to the good people of Valognes and even less time since he had made the promise to Carentan. Those towns were now in ashes.

Bertrand's brother, the bishop of Bayeux, tore Edward's letter to pieces. The messenger was imprisoned.[2]

That night, the English king encamped in a Cistercian priory at Fontenay-le-Pesnel, just ten miles west of Caen. With his newly knighted son leading the vanguard, Edward had thus far swept through Normandy with stunning and confidence-building speed. Across perhaps 100 miles of foreign territory they had met with precious little resistance. But the king had every reason to believe that Caen would be different. His scouts and spies made it clear: the city's gates were shut and its storehouses were full of supplies to withstand a siege. Caen knew that the English king was coming, and it had every intention of resisting him.

Edward was determined. Caen was one of the wealthiest and most important cities in Normandy, and seizing it would be a significant victory. Not only would it serve as a much-needed propaganda triumph to his people back home, but looting the riches of the city might well produce enough booty to cover the financial burden of the whole campaign for his creditors abroad.

Early on the morning of 26 July – exactly one month before Crécy – the English army arrived before the walls of Caen. What Edward saw surprised him. Aside from the suburb on the island behind the city, there were suburbs in front of the city's fortifications, too. Raoul would have been expected to sacrifice this part of the city in order to mount a defence within the old town, trusting its walls and castle to hold the attackers at bay. He had ready access to water from the rivers at his back, after all, and he no doubt had significant stores of food and arms to supply the fighting men who had been pulled from the surrounding region to gather and halt the English advance. Edward's plan had surely been predicated on this assumption.

Instead, Raoul, his men, and thousands of the townspeople had issued out from the walls to stand between the English and the outer suburbs. They weren't going to abandon those parts of the town. They were going to fight the English on the open fields. 'They marched out,' le Bel says, 'and deployed before the gate to face the English line of approach, giving every sign of being ready to put their lives on the line and mount a valiant defence.'[3]

For all we know, the day might have brought another battle of the Golden Spurs – where the Flemish militia at Kortrijk had defeated a seemingly superior force before the gates of their city – except for the fact that when they saw the approaching columns of English, the people of Caen lost their nerve. The French *Grand Chronicles* say that they stood their ground until the English 'assailed the town in four places, and shot arrows from their bows as dense as hail'.[4]

The first few townspeople slipped away quietly, but soon many were fleeing loudly. In seconds, a trickle of desertion became a flood of panic. With the enemy in sight, the defensive lines fractured and collapsed.

Raoul had lost tactical control.

Chaos erupted on both sides.

The front lines of the English, seeing their enemy in flight, broke ranks and chased after them. Later accounts would say that these were units under the command of the earl of Warwick, the earl of Northampton, and Richard Talbot. Even if that's so, we can't imagine that these men of title had any more control over what was happening than King Edward did at this moment. The undoubted truth is that the lower ranks of English men on foot – mostly archers, we suspect – recognized the confusion of the enemy and, eager to pillage the city's wealth, abandoned their formations to attack in their own confused fashion.

This only hastened the terrorized rout of the French.

As his lines hurtled back into the city, Raoul did his best to form up a new defence and save the city. He ordered a small force of 300 men to defend the castle under the command of Bertrand's brother, the bishop of Bayeux. He tried to send everyone else to man the walls and gates of the old town. If the gates could be closed before the English got in, then perhaps he'd have a chance.

The wealthy citizens were having none of it. A defence centred on the castle might leave their estates and riches on the island exposed to the English torches. And while Raoul had been able to make repairs to the city's walls, a few days was scant time to undo decades' worth of neglect. What if those old walls fell? What then? Wouldn't the island, with its surrounding waters and choke-point bridges, be more defensible in the long run? They certainly thought so. They bolted straight through the old town and out the other side onto the Île Saint-Jean. Most of the city followed them, grabbing whatever they could. As they crossed the bridge over the Odon, they hastily attempted to barricade it behind them. It was a terrible miscalculation, and it would have disastrous consequences.

Things were happening faster than anyone could assess in the moment. It was utter chaos.

Raoul, probably trying to close and defend the city's main gate, was overrun by the marauding English. Trapped in the gatehouse with some of his knights, he could do nothing but look down and witness the lower ranks of the English 'slaughtering defenceless people without mercy'.[5] In the midst of it all, he spotted the surcoat of a man he recognized – a man of wealth who might be more interested in taking a ransom than a life. Raoul called out and surrendered to him. He would go to England as a prisoner.

English boots, meanwhile, were still pounding ground, pouring into the city. They seem to have had nothing better than a mob mentality. Edward certainly had no idea what was happening. He signalled for a retreat to try to re-establish command of his forces. No one listened. The loot-lust of the first wave of men who'd broken ranks had infected a second wave of men, then a third. Seemingly the whole mass of the army was streaming forward into the open gates of the city (Figure 12).

The first of the men were now crashing against the simple barricades that had been so hastily thrown across the bridge to the Île Saint-Jean. The melee was hard and heavy. It was the first real taste of battle that the English had seen since they had arrived in France and no one was in command. Today the road the French were defending is the Rue Saint-Jean. To stand beside the Église Saint-Pierre – it was there in 1346 – and then look down the street to the south-east is to see where it happened.

The Genoese crossbows were busy, shooting bolts into the English, but their ammunition was beginning to run out.[6] Meanwhile, some attackers seized boats that had been left behind on the riverside embankment, and they used them to push over to less-defended parts of the island. Still others saw how the midsummer drought had lowered the waters of the river enough that a few men here and there could wade across. In short order, the French trying to defend the bridge found themselves cut off from behind. They fought to the last man. It was all for naught.

Even before the last of the French were slaughtered at the bridge – long before King Edward figured out what the hell had happened – the rage-fuelled looting of the island behind them had already begun.

It would last four days.

* * *

On 29 July, the king of England sent a letter from Caen back to England, probably accompanied by rich hostages like Raoul. Of the sacking of the city, Edward reports little:

As soon as we had made encampment at Caen, our men commenced to make an assault on the town, which was well defended and filled with perhaps 1,600 men-at-arms, as well as 30,000 militia and townspeople, and they defended it very well and boldly, so that the fight was very fierce and prolonged. But, praise be to God, the town was at last taken by force, without losing any of our men.[7]

As in his report of the results of Crécy, the king gives no figure to what he accounts only as 'a great number of nobles, knights, gentlemen, and militia [who] were slain' on the French side. Most modern historians, though, estimate that at least half the city's population died during the initial attack and in the days following during which, as the English king put it, he rested 'to provision and refresh our army'.[8]

Many thousands were dead. It is royal hyperbole to imagine that no man was lost in the English army: what the king means is that no man he considered worthy of notice had died. It was nevertheless true that it was a lopsided and unexpectedly swift victory. Through no effort or brilliance of his own, Edward had quickly and decisively stumbled into the capture of a major city in France.

The sacking of the city was also far more violent than Edward cares to describe. Jean le Bel calls it a 'great slaughter': 'it was pitiful to see the townsmen and their women, daughters, children: they didn't know which way to turn, and had to watch their wives and daughters raped, their houses smashed open, and all their belongings plundered.' The abbeys were razed to the ground. The nuns – 120 of them, along with 40 lay sisters – were all viciously raped. The king's ears must have been ringing from the cries that rolled through from the ancient streets. His nose must have been full of the stench of the smouldering fires. His eyes must have had their fill of the ravaging search for war booty. 'But,' le Bel concludes, 'these things happen in war and they have to be accepted'.[9]

The chronicler speaks what many believed. Warfare is and always has been brutal. Nothing about the bloody fighting between armies or its horrific aftermath could be called glorious. Nothing about what happened at Caen could be called noble. There's a reason Edward didn't go into the details. At the same time, he no doubt thought it all necessary. Men had to be paid one way or another. If they could have their fill from plunder, all the better for the king's coffers.[10]

EDWARD'S PLANS

In that same letter to England written on 29 July, Edward asks that monies be raised for the continuance of the war effort – his men, though rich from plunder, were still demanding their actual wages – and that a resupply be prepared: 'as many bows, arrows, and bowstrings as you can'. Furthermore, he requests that these all be sent, with more men-at-arms and archers, on ships to the French port of Le Crotoy, at the mouth of the River Somme, over 150 miles away to the north-east, near Flanders. He expected these to be in place by 20 August.[11]

These were new orders. Edward had clearly changed his mind about what he was doing. This begs two questions: what had been his plan to this point, and what had it changed to now?

In all honesty, historians haven't been sure. These questions have been at the centre of a long-standing debate among scholars.

On one extreme is the idea that 'Edward's conduct of the campaign of Crécy shows no proof of any rational scheme' – that the English king had, in effect, no plan at all.[12] This is highly unlikely. Edward's campaign was an enormous undertaking. Just getting all the men to France was a staggering feat, not to mention the further logistics of keeping them supplied for war. And Edward remained painfully short of money. Attacking Philippe had England teetering on the edge of bankruptcy. And of course there were the human costs of war – not likely to touch him and his son, but in war anything could happen. So the idea that he sailed to France, as one famous historian put it, for 'a chivalrous adventure' just doesn't hold an ounce of water for me.[13]

On the other extreme is the idea that Edward's plan was so detailed that 'from the start of the campaign' he was planning to stand and fight Philippe on the exact eventual battlefield at Crécy.[14] The draw of thinking that Edward was playing some kind of three-dimensional chess during the Crécy campaign is understandable. With the benefit of hindsight, we know that he marched across France and made his stand at Crécy. We know he won a major victory there. For those who laud him for this victory, especially those keen to view the events through a nationalist lens, it is only natural to assume that he meant to do what he did. Edward's court was surely engaged in this very same kind of after-the-fact reasoning. Jean Froissart, who received most of what little 'new' information he had here from Edward's court decades later, tells a story about Harcourt convincing Edward to have mercy on the people of Caen for fear of losing some of his men in the process: 'you still have a long way to go before you shall arrive before Calais, where you are aiming to go'.[15] In other words, Froissart's English informants had told him that the target was Calais from the start. And, well, *of course* Edward and his court would push such a tale: Calais was the one place the campaign actually conquered, so saying 'I meant to do that' was to put the best spin possible on the entire affair.

But I doubt it very much. The plan to go to Crécy alone would require (1) that the English king knew the exact hilltop in France, (2) that he knew of no better site for a battle, (3) that his chosen route to get there was a 250-mile march through enemy territory despite it being near the Flemish border, (4) that he had sufficient mapping to do this, and (5) that he expected the French to play along and fight on the ground of his choosing despite the fact that his entire history with Philippe in the field showed his refusal to do exactly that. If Edward truly thought such things – if this was his *plan* – then he was out of his mind. 'It's so crazy it might just work' isn't a good military command strategy: even if it does manage to work, it's still bloody crazy.

But the king of England wasn't crazy. He knew damn well there were too many variables out of his control to plan such a thing. If he'd planned to make for Crécy or Calais from the beginning, he surely would have put such plans in place long before he was engaged in hostile territory where his communications could be cut off at any moment.

Look back at what happened when Edward made his first invasion into France in 1339: he and Philippe danced around each other and never gave battle. The same thing happened when they later met outside Tournai. And the same thing would happen on this very campaign: the English king would ultimately have several opportunities to bring his forces to bear against Philippe, but Edward consistently chose not to do so. The only exception is the climactic battle of the campaign, when Philippe had made it impossible for the English king to retreat further.

Sure, Edward loudly complained each time of how he was totally ready to give battle and he totally would have done it if Philippe hadn't been so cowardly and all that ... but when we set aside any of those nationalistic lenses and look at the situation objectively, we see that none of this was ever quite true.

What Edward wanted – and what Philippe wanted, too – was to *win*.

We often equate body counts with victory, thinking that winning a battle means winning the war. And it's not just us. Those to whom Edward's boisterous complaints were directed probably thought likewise. It's easy to think this, especially given the weight of myths and stories that define the ideal of heroic masculinity in arms, where lethality becomes synonymous with superiority. Hollywood loves its grand battles and waving flags. Medieval people did, too. *Most* people are fascinated with battles. That's not necessarily a bad thing, but it can be a problematic thing when as historians we become too focused on the battles and miss the bigger picture of the war. The very historical concept of the decisive battle is itself greatly over-imagined. We will see that this is especially so when viewed against the very real results of the eventual battle of Crécy itself, which could hardly have been more decisive in favour of the English and yet decided very little.

In part our battle-focus is due to our relative safety. When we watch the dance of Edward and Philippe, we're a bit like spectators at a car race, waiting – in a rather twisted sense, *hoping* – for a crash. That's where the action is! But from the point of view of the drivers in that race, the *last* thing they want to do is crash. They're in the car. We're not. So it was with these kings.

Both men had seen battle. Both men knew how chance could tear apart the most careful plans. What happened at Caen is a microcosm of this. For the English, the taking of the city didn't happen because of anything Edward planned or ordered; it happened *despite* those things. For the French, the loss of the city didn't happen because of anything its defenders planned or ordered; for all we know, what set their defensive lines into rout might have been the screaming flight of a single random tradesman. Broken down into the scales of personal experience, war is never the ordered majesty of pushing coloured blocks about on a great wooden map board. It's ever and always the utter chaos of uncertainty.

If any battle, no matter how good the odds are, is still a roll of the dice, wise military commanders won't seek it just to seek it: they'll seek it because they have no choice, or because they firmly believe it's their best chance of winning.

Again: it's the *win* they're after. That's all.

So when Edward arrived in France, *that* was his objective. Not winning a battle on some hilltop hundreds of miles away. Winning a war. Everything he did flows from that.

Seen through this lens, his actions since he'd landed make complete sense. So does every action he took afterwards.

His initial plan was not too dissimilar from that of the D-Day landings so many centuries later (or what William the Conqueror had done in 1066, crossing the sea in the other direction): he was going to establish a beachhead in France. He'd establish himself on French ground as efficiently and effectively as possible, securing both a port and local support. He'd prepare with an expectation that his enemy would come and meet him as soon as possible. That's what Philippe had done when the English had invaded before. This time, though, Edward would land in such force, making such a bold claim on the very soil of the kingdom, that there might be no dance of armies. They'd line up and fight – *if* Philippe came, and *if* the field favoured Edward's position. Remember: winning, not fighting, was the goal. That's why both sides hadn't met in pitched battle before.

Edward knew that killing Philippe would be the fastest way to winning, of course, and speed was very much on his mind. Not because he was impatient (though he was), but because the one thing that had bogged him down – the one thing that had stymied his war effort again and again – was money. A cold war was expensive, a hot one more so. He needed to win or he needed to get money. Either one. Quickly. He couldn't win the war if he went broke.

He'd landed successfully, probably more easily than he'd dared dream. He'd made his claim to the ground as rightful king of France. So far so good. From the first days he was even accepting homage from French nobles like Harcourt for Norman lands. These lords of Normandy, who had a far better ability to gauge Edward's actions than we can manage, clearly thought the English king had come to stay. According to the *Acta Bellicosa* – an anonymously written and unfortunately fragmentary contemporary campaign diary[16] – Edward even issued orders to underscore his posturing as the true protector of the realm beginning on his very first night in France:

> no house or manor was to be burnt, no church or holy place sacked, and no old people, children or women in his kingdom of France were to be harmed or molested; nor were they to threaten any other people except men who resisted them, or do any kind of wrong, on pain of life and limb.[17]

This edict was immediately and repeatedly ignored: from La Hougue to Caen, no one was listening. Most of Normandy was on fire. The dead were everywhere. Either Edward didn't have full control over his men, or the edict was a public relations ploy. A cynic might favour this second case, but what happened at Caen favours the first: his army was so vast, and so inexperienced, that Edward and his commanders failed to control it. It may only have been, as *Acta Bellicosa* says, a small number of 'some evildoers [who] left the army who were not afraid of breaking the king's edict' who were making the king a liar at Valognes and other places,[18] but the hard truth is it didn't really matter. The damage was done. As soon as the lands he'd said he was saving were going up in flames, any plans he'd had of holding tight onto his beachhead went up in flames, too.

And Philippe was nowhere to be seen.

So Edward shifted his plan.[19]

After all, the one good thing the looting was doing was making him the money he so desperately needed – especially when he reached wealthy Saint-Lô. The booty was already enough to start slowing down his advance, but then he took Caen and was suddenly and unmistakably loaded.

And so Edward shifted his immediate goals *again*.[20] His many days of delay in Caen gave him time to thoroughly ransack the place. Less obviously, it gave him time to offload the results of all the ransacking. The *Acta Bellicosa* tells us that his fleet was paralleling his track along the Normandy coast from La Hougue. He sent his enormous amounts of war booty to these ships from Caen, so they could take them back to England for safe-keeping: at this point 'they could not transport all the spoils' they had acquired by the roads.[21] With them went the captives. As Jean le Bel reports, 'truly, their ransoms equalled what the king had spent in mounting this campaign and in gifts to his men'.[22] Philippe hadn't shown up to fight yet, but at least the economic side of Edward's needs was being fulfilled. And even if the bounty was enough to pay for *this* campaign, the English crown still had past debts to pay.

And the Crécy campaign wasn't over.

So Edward wrote his letter home: raise more money, and send more supplies and men to La Crotoy.[23]

Does this mean he had his eyes on Calais now? Despite its problems, does Jean Froissart's story hold some kernel of truth?

I still don't think so.

With conquest proving untenable, Edward's strategy had evolved into a massive *chevauchée*: a fast-moving raid designed to cut a gash across the countryside both gathering plunder and terrorizing the inhabitants. The king of England intended to burn a line across the north of France from Normandy to the mouth of the Somme, pillaging, destabilizing the local French economy, and causing a general panic that might force Philippe to withdraw the duke of Normandy from Aiguillon, or – even more ideally – provoke him personally to meet at last under conditions favourable for a decisive battle for the crown of France. Why was Edward sending troops to the mouth of the Somme? Because the mouth of the Seine was too heavily defended. So the Somme was his next chance for a port where he might be able to offload any of the goods he hoped to seize in the coming weeks. Whether that would be from the town of Saint-Valéry-sur-Somme on the river's south bank or from La Crotoy on the river's north bank would be something he'd figure out when he got there. Was Calais a possible target after that point? Absolutely. But it needn't be the only or necessary target.[24]

So from Caen, Edward was marching to the Somme or to Philippe – whichever came first. And if his Flemish allies and Hugh Hastings were able to press south to meet him, all the better.[25]

Whether due to his awareness of the French forces still far to the south in Aiguillon or his low opinion of Philippe's capabilities – Edward had been in France for two weeks now and encountered little enough opposition – the king of England appears to have anticipated little difficulty in making his *chevauchée* towards the mouth of the Somme.

Everything so far had been easy, so he might have thought this would be, too.

It was a serious underestimation of the French king.

The Long Road to Paris, 30 July–16 August

Philippe was east of Paris at the chateau of Becoiseau, near Mortcerf, when Edward landed with his army in Normandy. We don't know how quickly the news of the English landing reached the French king, or how accurate the initial reports of the invading army were, but within a week he had moved to Vincennes, just outside Paris. And by the time Edward was leaving Saint-Lô on his march east towards Caen, Philippe was already at the ancient seat of royal authority in Saint-Denis. He was flying the flag of war, and he was raising an army as fast as he could.

It was a difficult task. Edward had prepared for his invasion for months. Philippe had only days to field his response. And he had to do it with a significant number of the fighting men of France – including what would have passed for his regular army – already engaged to the south in Gascony under the command of his son, Jean.

The French king was 43 years old, and he was as veteran a warrior as Edward was. Both men had fought in significant battles before they would come to blows at Crécy. Edward had beaten the Scots at Halidon Hill in 1333. Philippe had destroyed a Flemish militia at Cassel in 1328. Both had a host of battle-experienced advisors at hand, too. In sum, neither man was a caricature, and in retrospect we can see how both men made choices that were both wise and foolish. No matter his brilliant success in the end, the English king's assumption about his ability to cross France betrays a deeply misplaced confidence. And no matter his total failure in the end, the French king's basic strategy in the campaign was simple but effective.

After hastily raising sufficient forces – knowing that even more would be streaming in – Philippe marched with all speed north out of Saint-Denis, tracing the eastern bank of the Seine. This was the old road to Rouen, itself one of the greatest cities in France then and now. The road, which was wide and well maintained from Roman times, allowed his army to move with the speed he so desperately needed if he was to cut off Edward's march.

ROADS, AGAIN

Travel today is so easy that we can forget how significant a factor roads were in the pre-modern world. It was for good reason that an army of the Roman Empire was both an excellent fighting force and a supreme corps of engineers: building and maintaining a road as they marched gave them a vital path for the logistics of a campaign that are often ignored by modern scholars (and omitted by Hollywood). In truth, the success of an army in war depended as much on logistics officers, or rear echelon personnel like William Retford who toiled away in the kitchens of king and commons, as it did on the front-line nobles whose deaths Edward would be so anxious to record. Leadership was all well and good, but without the logistical effort of food, funds, and transport, an army simply could not function.

The networking of supply lines and the roads they relied on was central to that often invisible effort, but Edward was attempting a *chevauchée* after Caen – a campaign in which supplies were gathered on the march rather than along defensible logistic lines. This didn't diminish his reliance on roads. If anything, it increased that reliance. Edward's army required speed, not just to stay ahead of any hostile response, but also to drive itself into new territories to exploit for its necessary supplies. And the appetite for those supplies would have been staggering. Edward had landed with some 14,000 men. How many he lost in stops along the way we don't know. He was anxious to proclaim that it was zero, which is obviously ridiculous. Still, it's safe to say that even after men were sent home from Caen – either to accompany the booty and captives or because they were ill[1] – he had more than 10,000 men on the march all the way to the battle of Crécy. To feed so many, plus the animals that carried them or their supplies, was a staggering logistical effort. Jean le Bel says that across the long distance of the English march, 'along a front at least a day's ride wide, that whole rich land was laid waste' as the men seized everything they could.[2]

Roads also meant tactical mobility: both for attack and retreat. Tens of thousands of men were moving in the armies of England and France, with wagons of supplies, thousands of horses, and, for the English after Normandy, vast herds of stolen livestock that the English king planned to feed to his forces or potentially drive to Flanders and sell for further profit.

For these and so many other reasons, commanders sought to stay close to roads. This fact would have significant ramifications for Edward III's Crécy campaign.

When the English army left Caen on 31 July, only two days after Edward wrote home with a confident plan to reach Le Crotoy within three weeks, Philippe had already used the French roads to full effect. He had sped north from Paris to Rouen, his army stretching out behind him on the east bank of the River Seine. He now stood between Edward and his goal.

For the moment, the bridge at Rouen was still up. Edward, still hoping to provoke his rival to battle, marched east along the roads towards the city, setting enough fires to keep the sky glowing red at night. On the night of 31 July, the *Kitchen Journal* records the English king's encampment at Troarn. On 1 August, he was at Léaupartie, heading east. The following day, he reached Lisieux, where he was met by two cardinals sent by the Pope. The next day – all day – they tried to convince Edward to make peace, conveying that he could have his lands in Gascony, as well as his mother's lands in Ponthieu, if he would do homage to Philippe for them.

This would necessitate an admission that Philippe was the rightful king of France. Edward refused.

For at least the first few days in August it seemed that Philippe might be willing to give battle and end the whole thing once and for all. But on the same day that Edward was listening to the bishops' sermons and arguments, Philippe heard that Hugh Hastings' Anglo-Flemish army was on the march, bound for his northern border. The French king realized he was on the verge of being pressed on two sides. He pulled his forces back over the Seine at Rouen, breaking the bridge behind him. He also sent word to the duke of Normandy to abandon the floundering siege of Aiguillon. He needed the reinforcements.

Edward marched on, reaching Elbeuf, on the south side of the Seine, on 7 August. With the bridge broken, messengers were sent by boat across the river. Edward challenged Philippe to fight. Philippe refused and offered peace if Edward would do homage. Edward refused.

PHILIPPE'S PLAN

Because Philippe refused to give Edward his desired battle, English writers would go on to accuse him of cowardice over the next weeks, but the French king's actions were sound thinking. What he was doing, in military terms, is called a Fabian strategy. Named for Quintus Fabius Maximus Verrucosus, the Roman leader who had used it to great success against the Carthaginian general Hannibal during the Second Punic War (218–202 BC), a Fabian strategy relies on an often-neglected point of strategy: time. Instead of taking the hasty action of direct confrontation, the Fabian strategist fights the enemy through delay, harassment, and a lingering war of attrition. Philippe knew that he gained strength over time. He was still gathering his men, and he had safe supply lines through the country. Edward, on the other hand, was liable to lose strength over time. A *chevauchée* survives through the despoiling of territory, parasitically destroying the very thing that gives it life. It cannot long remain in one place. Edward and his men had to keep moving, and the French king laboured to weaken the English forces by denying them passage to the unravaged lands to the north of the Seine and instead trapping them within an increasingly barren Normandy. Doing so meant a short-term cost in terms of sacrifice from the civilian population there, but it also meant a long-term victory against Edward's invasion. It was the exact same thing that he had done so successfully when the English first invaded in 1339.

The English king knew what Philippe was doing, which is precisely why he was so desperate to fight immediately. His fleet had been sent home with all his riches, so a full withdrawal was not on the cards. His men had so thoroughly pillaged and burned the countryside that neither retreat back the way he had come nor entrenchment where he was were good options. He was facing a long and humiliating suffocation in Normandy.

His only other option would be to march south up the Seine towards Paris. This would bring new lands to pillage, along with the desperate hope of finding an open crossing of the river so he could either fight Philippe or make his *chevauchée* towards the Seine. Such a march, though, would also bring him deeper and deeper into foreign territory, where Philippe could choose the time and place of a final battle with his enemy under conditions most favourable to his side.

Philippe could see the same writing on the wall. It's why he not only didn't fight at Rouen, but also gave orders that the bridges over the Seine from there to Paris were to be burned, dismantled, refortified, or garrisoned. Though he was organizing on the fly, Philippe was effectively dictating Edward's choices.

Predictably, Edward turned south, towards Paris, hoping to find a way across the river.

The first major bridge up the Seine from Rouen was at Pont de l'Arche. The town was on the south side of the river, but it was walled – and there was a castle on the north bank, too. The English tried to storm the town anyway, but they failed. And soon enough Philippe's army was on the other side of the river, prepared to send reinforcements over the bridge if needed. Edward had to abandon the assault and head further up river.

The scene was repeated again and again. Philippe closely tracked the English on the opposite shore, ignoring the taunts that were supposed to insult him into making a tactical error. Winning was what mattered, and he was ensuring that the English couldn't cross. The further up the river they went, the closer they were to being trapped between it, the great walls of Paris, the ravaged lands of Normandy, and what might be the duke of Normandy's army arriving from the south. News of the duke's abandonment of the siege of Aiguillon was surely met with mixed cheer in the English camp. Their attack on Normandy had at least in part been intended to force the relief of Aiguillon, but that success was now threatened to be overshadowed by their own potential defeat and capture.

'We found all the bridges broken or fortified and defended,' Edward later wrote of his march up the Seine, 'so that in no way were we able to cross over to our adversary; nor did he desire to approach us, although he followed us each day upon the other bank of the river, and this greatly annoyed us.'[3] However annoying it might have been for the English, it was a sensible and effective strategy for the French. There were skirmishes here and there where small groups of glory-seekers on one side or the other managed to get into a fight. The English secured boats for small raids across the river. The French made sallies from walled bridge towns here and there. It was all small potatoes.

To stave off resentment among his men, Edward no doubt pushed hard on the line that Philippe was a simple coward. It would have been an easy sell. From what we can tell, the less wise among the French – probably those who had never seen battle – were starting to whisper the same. But for the time being, Philippe's prudence was the way forward.

FIGHT OR FLIGHT

By 12 August, the citizens of Paris could see the smoke of the English camps on the horizon by day, and the glow of the fires they were setting along their march by night. Shops were boarded up.

Philippe had to commit men to keep the peace and ensure that a general panic didn't break out.

Outside the city walls, there were three bridges over the Seine. Along the line of the English approach these were at Poissy, Saint-Germain-en-Laye, and Saint-Cloud – all towns on the south side of the river. Philippe ordered the towns emptied, then broke the bridges behind the evacuees.

The loss of Poissy was especially painful for the king. In 1304, his predecessor Philippe IV had founded a Dominican priory there to honour his newly canonized grandfather, Saint Louis. In short order, the institution had become enormously wealthy and lavish. Around 100 years later, the poet Christine de Pizan, visiting her daughter there, would describe its wonders as nothing short of paradise. It was no less impressive for the English who entered it on 13 August:

> It had a very fine church, that seemed as if built in one day, ornamented with most splendid altars and images. Even the outbuildings were built of squared and planed beams and quarried stones. Nowhere in the world would you find a finer priory than this, and indeed I confess that the workmanship of it was better than the palace in which the king stayed.[4]

It was around this time that Philippe was joined at Saint-Denis by King John of Bohemia and his son, Charles. John was the son of Holy Roman Emperor Henry VII, who in 1310 had married him into the throne of Bohemia at the age of 14. Just three years later, he had added the title of count of Luxembourg. In subsequent years John had been all over Europe. Soon enough, he had an international reputation as both an able diplomat and general. He had supported Philippe when the Hundred Years War broke out, and the French king had accordingly made him the governor of Languedoc from 1338 to 1340. Although he was now just 50 years old, he had been losing his eyesight for about a decade. He was, it was said, nearly blind. But he was nevertheless another respected and experienced leader to help advise the king and calm the city.

The French position described to John would have seemed a strong one. In terms of the sheer number of available men, the odds were stacked in Philippe's favour. So, too, was the fact that his men were generally more rested: Edward had been in France for a month, during which time his forces had marched roughly 400 miles and had fought numerous engagements beyond that which they had faced at Caen. Philippe's Fabian strategy had worked remarkably well. It had forced the English nearly to Paris, where Edward could be caught between the hammer of Philippe's amassing strength and the anvil of the city's massive walls. Everything was going perfectly.

And then, disaster.

Though the French had taken down the bridge at Poissy, its stone supports still stood in the river. Edward's builders had begun work building over them at once. They had just set one beam across the broken span – the *Acta Bellicosa* says it was 'sixty feet long and a foot wide'[5] – when French troops appeared on the other side. English soldiers danced across the beam under the cover of archers. There was a hard fight, but the French were driven back. A few hundred of their number lay dead. Work continued through the night, and by the next morning the bridge was wide enough for carts to cross (Figure 13).

Edward was no longer pinned down on the south side of the river.

The very geography that had been such an ally to Philippe suddenly became his enemy. The Seine makes a series of long looping bends between Poissy and Paris, such that the distance between them on the south shore is substantially shorter than it is on the north shore. If the French army marched out to meet Edward north of Poissy, the English army could attack Paris sooner than the French army could get back to it. If the French army marched out to meet Edward south of Poissy, the English army could use the bridge they'd built to escape Philippe's trap and bolt north towards Flanders.

On 14 August, Philippe sent a letter to Edward, challenging him to battle. Given the strength of his position he might have been planning to do so anyway, but at this point he had no choice. It had to be now. He didn't dare let Edward march so close to Paris and then get away, and he didn't dare let him burn the south bank to the ground while he himself was strategically paralysed on the north bank.

Philippe's challenge was brought to Edward by the bishop of Meaux. The English king had been chomping at the bit to fight, and now he would get his chance. Philippe would leave the city, marching out onto the open fields south of Paris, near Antony. There would be a battle. To the winner would go France. All that Philippe asked in return is that the English stop their destruction until the appointed hour.

Edward's exact reply is uncertain, though his men did stop their destruction. The English would later claim they had done so merely in observation of the Feast of the Assumption of Mary, which was celebrated on 15 August. If this is true, it's certainly not the impression that the French got: they clearly believed that Edward had accepted Philippe's challenge to do battle. Accordingly, the French king decamped from his position in the north, marched through the streets of Paris and over the Seine. He left the city. He reached Antony. He waited.

Edward didn't show.

The English never ceased their repair work on the bridge at Poissy. As the French were settling in at Antony, the English slipped across the Seine under cover of night – breaking their new bridge behind them for good measure. Without Philippe's army to stop him, Edward now marched north with all possible speed.

No matter what spin the English tried to put on the situation, there can be little doubt that Edward and his forces, after the crossing at Poissy, were essentially on the run. But to where? Jean le Bel, with the benefit of hindsight, says he was now aiming for Calais.[6] Another chronicler, Gilles li Muisit, says he was trying to reach his Flemish allies.[7] And there was also, in either case, his possible reinforcements at the mouth of the Somme.

He had probably had no contact with England since he'd left Normandy. He had sent his letters asking for ships and resupply to go to Le Crotoy, but since the moment he'd begun marching up the Seine he had been moving deeper and deeper into French territory.

The odds of messengers reliably getting through would have been small. All Edward could do was trust that his orders from Caen had reached England and that they had been obeyed. If he could reach the mouth of the Somme, he hoped to find his ships waiting for him there.

For the same reasons, he also probably hadn't been able to maintain regular communications with Hugh Hastings and the Anglo-Flemish army up north. The news from there, if he'd received it, would have been mixed. Part of their force had been defeated in a skirmish at Estaires on the River Lys around 10 August, but by around 14 August the army as a whole had crossed that river at Merville, burned Saint-Venant, and then begun a siege of the walled town of Béthune. That put them about 56 miles from where Edward hoped to find reinforcements. Was this where Edward had ordered them to go? Or was Béthune merely a target of opportunity? We don't know.

Finding out that his prey had escaped, Philippe was furious. He gave a public speech at Saint-Denis accusing the English king of being a treacherous liar on top of being a traitorous lord. Then his fastest riders hurtled north, along roads that would swing around the English route. Their destination was the Somme. Philippe didn't know Edward's plans any more clearly than we do. What he *did* know was that the Somme lay between Edward and wherever he was going – Béthune? Flanders? Calais? – and that the river was a line he could therefore use to cut him off. The orders the riders carried were simple and direct. The bridges across the Somme were to be fortified or cut. The English were not to cross the river.

Other riders reached Rouen. A couple of thousand Genoese crossbowmen who were there – mercenaries contracted by Philippe to help patrol the French coasts but now summoned to provide military aid on land – were ordered to join Philippe's army, which he quickly reassembled in Paris and began streaming north in pursuit.

Like a clever fox, Edward had managed to slip from the hunter's trap. By the singular engineering feat of rebuilding the bridge he had crossed the Seine at Poissy. It had worked. He'd got away. But for all his bravado and exultations, Edward had to know the truth.

The hounds were on his tail.

The Battle of Blanchetaque,
16–25 August

The English *chevauchée* had become a chase.

This was clear enough from the way Edward scurried over the Seine and ran. His first night on the north side of the river was spent at Grisy-les-Plâtres on 16 August. The next night he was at Auteuil. Heading away from Paris he was travelling over 16 miles a day, a pace ahead of what he'd averaged along the good roads beside the Seine approaching the city.

It was at Auteuil on 17 August[1] that Edward wrote a letter to 'Philippe of Valois' – though pointedly distributed among the members of his own army, too[2] – in which he states that he would have welcomed battle with the French at any time. His three days spent in Poissy, he says, were more about waiting for Philippe to fight than they were about rebuilding the bridge. The claim is, at best, half-true: the English probably expected the French to attack at almost any moment, but we certainly know they were quite desperately rebuilding and defending the bridge during those days and used it to escape the first moment they could. Edward also claims that he continues to welcome battle even now: 'at whatever hour you approach you will find us ready to meet you in the field'.[3] This is rather blatantly at odds with the fact that he was currently fleeing from Philippe's offer to give just such a battle, but it still makes sense. The prioritization of winning over fighting discussed above meant that Edward would fight if battle was presented *and* if it favoured him: 'But we shall never be dictated to by you, nor will we accept a day and place for battle on the conditions which you have named,' he says.[4]

He sent his letter. He made his usual boasts about it in camp.

He sure as hell didn't slow down.

The next day – 18 August – only underscored Edward's urgency.

On that day, the English army reached Beauvais. The vanguard – the foremost part of the English march – was under the command of the Black Prince. As he looked out at the rich city, the young man was certain that it could be stormed. The English had won so very many riches taking Caen, and here was a chance to do it again. He sent a message back to his father, asking for the go-ahead.

Edward refused the engagement. Looting and burning was still occurring all along his line, but it was all being done at speed. They didn't have time to slow down as they had at Caen, no matter the potential prize. This wasn't about getting rich anymore. They were being hunted. It was about surviving.

Nevertheless, despite Edward's orders that the English continue their march with all due speed, there were those in the vanguard who couldn't resist the temptation to plunder and burn. They'd been doing it for weeks now. It must have seemed natural to them.

As the king rode past the abbey of Saint-Lucien, 20 of these men came rushing out of it, loot in their arms and smoke billowing out behind them. Edward was apoplectic. He'd given clear orders. They'd clearly been disobeyed.

It wasn't anything new. But the circumstances of the army were dire now. The fate of the campaign – perhaps even of the war and Edward's crown – depended upon maintaining good order. Commands had to be heard and obeyed.

The men were summarily executed. Their bodies, hanged alongside the road, served as a warning to their countrymen marching by.[5]

That night, the king made his camp, the *Kitchen Journal* tells us, just beyond Beauvais, at Troissereux.

Philippe was at Clermont-sur-Oise, roughly 20 miles to the east.

The next day, Edward had reached Sommereux, and then on 20 August he camped at Camps-en-Amiénois. Philippe passed that same night at Nampty. Less than 15 miles now separated them.

THE SOMME LINE

The next day, 21 August, must have been a nightmare for the English.

Philippe was close at their heels. With the freedom of movement on his own roads, better supply lines, and an army that wasn't distracted by greed, the king of France had been steadily gaining on his prey. And now, the Somme lay ahead. Despite its easy, steady flow, that ribbon of water might as well have been a wall of rock: Philippe's commands had been obeyed. As they'd done at the Somme, the French had fortified or broken every bridge over the river.

Once again, a wet-gap crossing threatened to be Edward's undoing.

The king set himself up at Airaines, about midway between the walled towns of Amiens and Abbeville on the Somme. From here he threw detachments down into the river valley, trying to find a way across. All day, these tired and hungry forces probed in vain: at Pont-Rémy, Fontaine-sur-Somme, Long, Longpré-les-Corps-Saints, and Picquigny – in total, a more-than-14-mile stretch of the river. In every instance, the French turned the English back. Worse, the fact that King John of Bohemia and Jean de Beaumont were seen making the defence of the bridge at Pont-Rémy meant that parts of the main French force from Paris were now ahead as well as behind.

Even as his men continued trying to find a way across the river, Edward prepared to withdraw west, further from the most immediate danger.

It had to be frustrating. He'd fled one near-disaster only to be faced with another, as he was once again hemmed in by the forward-thinking French strategy. Philippe had barred, burned, or broken the bridges of the River Somme, and this time there were no abandoned bridge supports as there had been at Poissy. Edward was pinned between the converging enemy forces and the unforgiving sea. He knew well the danger, and he had scouts and riders trying to find any way out they could.

The next day, the earl of Warwick threw himself at the French guarding the river at Hangest-sur-Somme. Some of the scouts thought they had seen a weakness there, probably due to the shifting of men in the French defence.

It wasn't what they thought it was. Warwick was turned back.

All the while, the massive French army was getting closer. When his scouts reported that he was about to be overrun on 23 August, the English king bolted west. He had to leave so quickly, we're told, that the French were able to eat a meal laid out for him.

The road ahead of the English ran through the town of Oisemont. The people there issued out, intending to block his advance. As had happened at Caen, they were put to flight as soon as the English archers formed up and sent arrows hurtling into them. The English cut them down and quickly pillaged the town as they passed through.[6]

The king now encamped at Acheux-en-Vimeu, the *Kitchen Journal* says – less than ten miles from Saint-Valéry on the southern side of the mouth of the Somme. Philippe controlled everything behind him, including the well-fortified city of Abbeville, which commanded the last of the bridges over the Somme. The French lines were so very close.

Edward must have had scouts ranging as far as the walls of Saint-Valéry – gauging the defences there, but even more importantly watching the mouth of the Somme. Every hour he must have hoped to see the English ships on the horizon that might rescue him. His letters from Caen had ordered them to be in place off Le Crotoy by 20 August. Surely, he thought, they ought to be there by now.

They weren't.

He couldn't know it, but they hadn't even left England.[7]

What was bearing down on him was a frighteningly large force. The kind of material records that make estimates of English troop numbers somewhat reliable at this point are unavailable to us for the French side. The sources we have are all over the place. Richard Wynkeley, writing a week after the battle of Crécy, claimed that the French had 12,000 men-at-arms, 60,000 infantry, and 6,000 Genoese crossbowmen.[8] We're confident this is an exaggeration, since it's about five times as many men were available 'for the defence of the whole kingdom' in 1340.[9] More likely, the French force was something like the size of the one that had campaigned in Flanders just six years earlier: 22,500 men-at-arms, 2,500 infantry, and 200 crossbowmen. Judging from the additional arrivals of John of Bohemia's men and the newly arrived Genoese crossbowmen, the French force might have had around 26,000 fighting men in total. It was a massive army. English losses between their arrival at Normandy and this moment are unknown, but previous historians' estimates of 1,000 men seem suitable, leaving them around 13,000 men.[10] If so, they were outnumbered by at least two to one. And beyond the sheer numerical advantage, the French tactic of delaying engagement meant that while Edward's army was haggard and hungry, Philippe's army was relatively well rested. Edward had said that he was ready to meet the French in battle whenever they approached, and this is surely what he continued to tell the men of his encampment in order to keep their spirits up, but the truth was that he was being run to ground.

In the Introduction to this book we met Colins de Beaumont, the French herald who wrote such a moving account of the Crécy dead. There were such men on the English side, too. Among them was a man who served as the herald of John Chandos, a close adviser and friend to the Black Prince. So close was their relationship that the Chandos Herald, as he is known, wrote a magnificent 4,000-line poem honouring the Black Prince's life and deeds. The poem is worshipful: it suggests that at this point in the campaign, with the English on the ropes, King Edward put his youthful son in charge of finding a way across the Somme. To accomplish this last-ditch effort, the Black Prince took with him 100 chosen knights from the vanguard.[11]

No matter how highly regarded the 16-year-old boy might have been – though, in honesty, he hadn't really done much to this point – it's hard to imagine the king doing anything of the sort. If the Black Prince was leading this expeditionary force, it was in name only. Finding a way across the Somme was the only way to save thousands of men and potentially salvage the campaign itself. For all Edward knew, it might be the only way to save his crown.

BLANCHETAQUE

If Edward's escape at Poissy was remarkable, his crossing of the Somme must have seemed nigh on miraculous: on 24 August, the English found a low-tide ford over the river between Saint-Valéry and Abbeville.

How this path was found depends a great deal on who is telling the story. Many historians have been eager to proclaim a wide range of awareness of the ford among members of the English host from Bartholomew Burgersh to even King Edward himself.[12] The closest one can get for evidence that something like this *might* be so would be Jean Froissart's later claim that Godfrey de Harcourt knew a ford existed but just didn't know exactly where it was. Attempts to go further than that and portray the English use of the ford as something planned ahead of time by a calm and collected king – rather than the desperate act that it was – are doubtful in the extreme.

Instead, we should surely listen to the contemporary sources here, which insist that Edward heard about the ford from local informants. Jean le Bel says it was one of the king's prisoners of war who told him about the secret way out, and that Edward was stunned and overjoyed at the news.[13] Michael Northburgh, who made the crossing, wrote on 4 September that before they took the ford that day 'no man had previously crossed it'.[14] Heroic embellishment this might be, but it certainly doesn't fit well with the idea that the crossing was so generally well known that 'the English would likely have found it even without assistance', as one historian has claimed.[15]

The ford was called 'Blanchetaque' (i.e. 'white stain'), supposedly on account of the bed of white chalk that marked its path under the water. We suspect that it crossed through the marshes and then the river somewhere near Petit Port – which is about five miles from the bridge in Abbeville – but exactly where it was, we don't know and probably can't know. It wouldn't have much of a path even at the time: the crossing could only be managed for a short window twice a day, whereas the stone bridge just a few miles upstream was available all the time. Now that the canalization of the Somme has altered the landscape between Abbeville and the sea, the site might never be rediscovered. This is too bad, because the battle of Blanchetaque on 24 August might well be remembered among the great military escapes were it not overshadowed in our collective memories by the battle of Crécy just days later.

With the French army bearing down upon them, the English pretended to bed down for the night on 23 August, still in place at Acheux-en-Vimeu, about six miles from the river. Around midnight, Jean le Bel reports, Edward ordered his trumpets sounded. The army rose up, and with everything they could carry they marched for the river. The Italian chronicler Giovanni Villani, writing within two years of the battle, says that Edward left watch-fires burning at the site of his camp in an attempt to trick any French scouts or spies into thinking he was still there rather than plunging out into the half-moon dark.[16]

Led by their local informant, the first English reached the water's edge as the sun was coming up on 24 August. By just after 6am the whole army was there.[17]

Even at low tide men would be waist-deep to cross at the ford, and it was a narrow path: some of the sources speak of it being wide enough for only a few men moving abreast, while others talk of enough room for maybe a dozen. Regardless, we've already talked about how dangerous wet-gap crossings are and why commanders avoided them at all costs. Between the salt and the sands and the sea, so much could go wrong. Edward trying to press his army through the waters was a truly perilous undertaking even under the best of circumstances.

Only Edward wasn't going to do it in the best of circumstances. He was going to have to do it in daylight, with the enemy awaiting him on the opposite bank. It was reckless, but Philippe had left him no other choice. Reckless was the only move left.

The French defence was led by Godemar du Fay, who had, according to Michael Northburgh, 500 men-at-arms and 3,000 infantry waiting on the other side – most of them probably local militia.[18] Two days later, Richard Wynkeley described the French force as 1,000 men-at-arms and '5,000 or more' infantry, no doubt showing that the need to exaggerate one's glories starts early.[19] Ever seeking a good tale, Jean Froissart tries to tell us that these men were specifically assigned to guard the ford, but this isn't terribly likely. What they were assigned to do was to prevent any crossing of the river anywhere between Abbeville and the sea. As Jean le Bel describes it, the waters were still too deep when the English first arrived, so they had to wait for the tide to draw out. The French only appeared as the English were anxiously running out this clock: 'But before it was fully out, Sir Godemar du Fay appeared on the further bank with a great body of troops and men of the region who drew up in line of battle, ready to defend the ford.'[20] They hadn't been there the whole time. They were reacting to the English presence.

The Chandos Herald unsurprisingly puts the Black Prince at the literal forefront of the action when the English king sent the first hundred men into the river: 'And all the hundred, to a man, / Into the water, lances couched, / Were borne upon their coursers,' he writes, directly into the French on the other side.[21] Far more likely is the eyewitness report of Wynkeley, who records that it was the earl of Northampton and Sir Reginald de Cobham who led the first attack as soon as the water would allow it, commanding 100 men-at-arms and a company of archers.[22] King Edward and his son, according to the account of an anonymous citizen of Valenciennes, crossed together after the baggage had been pushed, pulled, and floated across.[23]

The initial charge must have been a sight to see. The mounted men-at-arms plunged into the river, their horses kicking spray.

The archers bravely splashed in, trying to keep their bows dry. When they reached range, the bowmen took what stands they could in the river and loosed.

The volley of arrows rained down into the French. Some men went down. Everyone was shouting over the sound of the horses crashing through the river. Crossbowmen on the French side loosed bolts into the English in the water – 'a good few were killed and wounded in the river,' le Bel writes[24] – but the first wave kept coming. Edward probably ordered a second wave into the water the moment the first wave hit the French on the opposite embankment. The dark waters of the Somme churned to pale froth as more and more men surged across.

The French fought hard against the surge, but the English, their backs against the wall, were ferocious. Step by step they pushed out of the river. Body by body they seized a landing on the embankment.

French reinforcements poured in to try to shove the enemy back into the water, but the English beachhead held. Sir Hugh Despenser[25] organized the vanguard as soon as it had the shore, and behind more and more volleys of arrows they slammed into the French defence until it finally snapped. The French, routed, were chased to Abbeville's walls (Figure 15).

The English had crossed the Somme.

ANOTHER BATTLE LOOMS

Philippe's army had advanced on the abandoned English encampment in the early hours of the day. They'd tracked them to the shore. They arrived just after the tide had risen and the last of the English wagons had managed the crossing. The English were shocked to see them so close at hand, but neither side could reach the other over the rising waters.

The French king was enraged.

With just hours to spare, the English had once more escaped a well-designed trap. Even worse, Philippe guessed that Edward's intention was to gain strength by meeting up with the Flemish allies who were besieging Béthune. When the king was stuck on the south side of the Somme, this couldn't happen. Now that he'd crossed the river, all bets were off. Wisely, Philippe immediately sent 300 men north along the road to Hesdin, the largest fortified town on the way to Béthune. It was an advanced force, something like a down-payment: just 300 men wouldn't stop Edward's thousands, but they could begin preparations for the city's defence and the arrival of the main French army should it be required.

No one knew it yet, but at that very hour Edward's allies – Hugh Hastings and the Anglo-Flemish army – were abandoning their siege and beginning to retreat north. They were seemingly unaware of the proximity of the English king. Whatever plans they'd had at the start of the campaign had apparently fallen through.

Back at Blanchetaque, the two kings faced each other over the river, watching the water levels. Edward and his men made lines as best they could, probably on the rise in the landscape just east of Port-le-Grand today. The fact that Philippe was apparently contemplating his own charge across the river shows how profoundly enraged he was: Edward had done it out of sheer desperation; to do it voluntarily would be breathtakingly foolish.

Edward was in no position to be smug. He needed supplies and he needed them badly. The speed of his march from the Somme had left him without an opportunity to fully resupply. And just in the past days he'd had to abandon supplies at Airaines, with a decent chance that he'd abandoned still more when he hustled out of Acheux at midnight. His men had started the day tired and hungry, and now they'd just rampaged their way through a river.

So, with the incoming tide preventing an immediate attack from Philippe, the English king sent out raiding and scouting parties as far as Le Crotoy to the west and Saint-Riquier to the east. He needed to know where the French were, what roads he had at hand, and, most pressing of all, final confirmation of whether the supplies and reinforcements that he'd ordered to meet him off the coast of Le Crotoy were there or not. The reliable Sir Hugh Despenser was put in charge of this most important task. He took a raiding party west along the north bank of the Somme. Meanwhile, the army hunkered down in place for the night, setting lines and establishing what field fortifications they could manage. The *Kitchen Journal* says they were encamped 'beneath the Forest of Crécy'.[26]

The next day, 25 August, Despenser returned from Le Crotoy. He brought grim news. The supply ships that Edward had ordered from Caen were nowhere to be seen. Despenser had nevertheless managed to seize much-needed victuals from a small Genoese garrison in the town – including a herd of livestock that would satisfy some rumbling stomachs – but it was hardly a fix for the king's tenuous position. The English still needed a way out: it was only a matter of time before Philippe came upon them with all his gathered strength.

That night, the *Kitchen Journal* says the king was camped 'in the Forest of Crécy'.[27] Most historians have assumed that this was the same spot he was at the previous night, beside the Blanchetaque ford. It wasn't. As the *Cleopatra Itinerary* points out, they were now 'at another edge of the forest'.[28] This makes sense. Edward was under a constant threat of attack at this point. Philippe could show up at any time, and the English needed to be in the best position possible when that happened. The river bank surely wasn't it.

This new camp couldn't be far from the river. As Edward himself explained in a letter on 3 September, his army had maintained its defensive position at Blanchetaque from the moment it had made the crossing on the morning of 24 August. They were there 'the whole day and the next day, until the hour of Vespers' (i.e. around 6pm), when they eventually realized Philippe had gone back to Abbeville earlier in the day – the French king having finally abandoned the idea of a making a wet-gap crossing against his enemy.[29] This afforded only a few hours for the English to make a move to a more defensible site. It was probably under the eaves of the Forest of Crécy, somewhere near Sailly-Bray, about three and a half miles away.

* * *

Edward's crossing at Blanchetaque had been a near-miraculous escape, but the terrain into which it had deposited him severely limited the king's options if he was going to stay ahead of his enemy and reach the relative safety of the Low Countries. Then, as now, the dominant feature of the land here was the Forest of Crécy, a wide swathe of deep woods spread across the high ground between the valley of the River Somme and the valley of the River Maye to the north. Going directly through the Forest would slow him down far too much – if it was even possible to do so with over 10,000 men and their wagons, packhorses, and a herd of livestock in tow! – and that day's scouting had surely included questions about whether he would attempt to find a path around the Forest to the west or to the east. The former meant crossing dangerous (and delaying) marshland. The latter meant faster travel along established roads and an earlier attachment to his Flemish allies (if indeed he knew of their siege at Béthune through rumours or earlier communications) – but it also meant closer proximity to Philippe and his army at Abbeville.

By the morning of 26 August, Edward had decided his path: the English would march east around the Forest of Crécy. As with so much else that he had done, it was a throw of the dice, but probably the best throw. Philippe was also on the march north that morning, no doubt determined to get ahead of Edward and cut off his path to Flanders.

It was a race, and though history would count him the loser in what followed, Philippe won it. The exhausted English had no chance of outrunning his forces, who were moving over native soil. At Blanchetaque the English had managed yet one more improbable escape, but it was short-lived. The armies were too close now. Edward had run out of time, and by noon it was clear that open battle could not be avoided.

It is a tribute to the abilities of Edward and his advisors that the battle of Crécy – which began later that afternoon – was not the English disaster that it might have been. Our sources are clear that the French were confident of victory – proudly overconfident, so many later chroniclers would say in hindsight – but probably Edward feared the worst. He did what he could to prepare. His scouts might well have identified the ultimate place of the fight within hours of crossing the Somme. Even so, no one could possibly have predicted the incredible turn of events that would bring such a total victory to the English crown.

The losses at Crécy were astonishing. By the time the killing was done, the dead included a king, a duke, dozens of counts, and thousands of other men. Even those who survived would forever carry the scars both upon the body and within the mind.

Exactly how many knights and nobles died that day, the Chandos Herald would later write, 'I do not know. And it is not right to count them.'[30] Others nevertheless tried. Edward III reports 1,500 dead knights in the first attacks.[31] As for the remainder – the 'common' men without title who followed the banners to their deaths – their number is as lost to history as their names are. As we have already seen from the report of Colins de Beaumont, so thick were the corpses upon the field that three days afterwards wounded but still living men were being dragged from the piles of the dead.[32]

The explanation of how this happened – how it is that the tired and outnumbered English so thoroughly defeated the French forces – is complicated, as it will require us to find the earth under which the mangled dead would find their final rest.

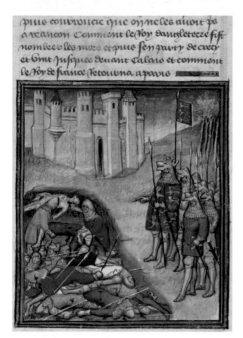

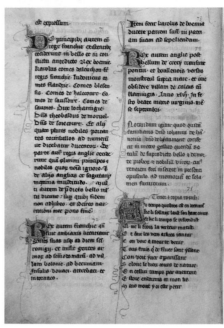

Fig. 1: King Edward observes as the dead are searched after the battle of Crécy. Note the naked man in the background, whose armour has already been removed from his body. (Den Haag, Koninklijke Bibliotheek)

Fig. 2: Colins de Beaumont's remarkable poem, *On the Crécy Dead*, begins at the lower right of this copy of Gilles li Muisit's chronicle. (Rijksarchief Kortrijk)

Fig. 3: King Harold is the man being struck down on the right in this image from the Bayeux Tapestry. Note the stripping of the dead in the lower margin.
(Myrabella/Wikimedia Commons)

Fig. 4: The homage performed by Edward I of England to Philippe IV of France in 1286 is depicted in this 15th-century illustration. (Bridgeman Images)

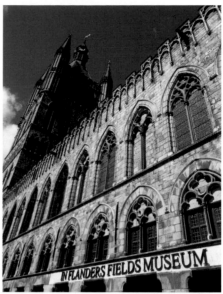

Fig. 5: Though rather imaginative in its armaments, this 15th-century image captures the fact that the battle of Golden Spurs outside Kortrijk in 1302 featured men on foot decisively beating men on horseback. (Getty Images)

Fig. 6: The Ypres Cloth Hall, destroyed in World War II, was rebuilt to its medieval glory as a monument to the wool trade that flourished between England and the Low Countries. (Getty Images)

Fig. 7: Edward III does homage to Philippe VI in this 15th-century illustration. (Getty Images)

Fig. 8: In 1340, Edward III quartered the arms of England with those of France – a visual declaration of his political claims. This new coat of arms appears here in a stained glass piece made a decade or two later. (Philadelphia Museum of Art)

Fig. 9: A crusader kneels to be knighted in this image from the Westminster Psalter. (Getty Images)

Fig. 10: The battle of Sluys, 24 June 1340, brought England one of its first victories in the Hundred Years War (Getty Images)

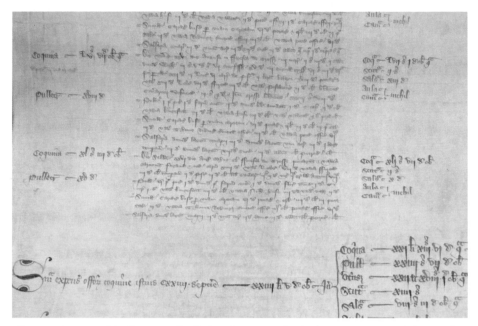

Fig. 11: A page of William Retford's *Kitchen Journal*, which was maintained during the Crécy campaign in 1346. The day of the battle begins eight lines up from the bottom of the main block of text. (Michael Livingston)

Fig. 12: The English attack on Caen was far more chaotic, and far bloodier, than illustrations could ever show. (Getty Images)

Fig. 13: The English make their way across the Seine at Poissy in this imaginative scene from a 14th-century manuscript in the British Library. (Bridgeman Images)

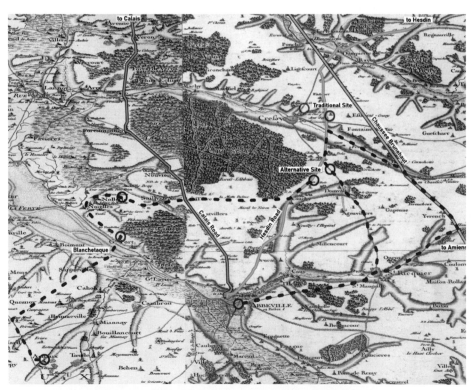

Fig. 14: Cassini's 1757 map of the region, overlaid with information discussed in the text. The red dashed line traces the likely route of the English to the battle site. The dashed blue line does the same for the two approaches of the French: the vanguard following the route to the north along the Chaussée Brunehaut. (Michael Livingston)

Fig. 15: Edward and the English fight their way across the Somme at Blanchetaque in this imaginative 19th-century illustration. (Getty Images)

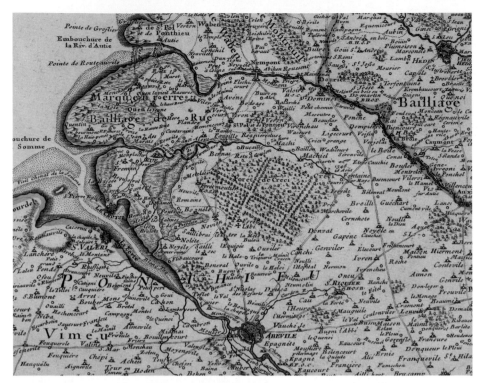

Fig. 16: A close-up of Guillaume de l'Isle's 1704 map of Artois: the earliest map to mark
the battle of Crécy in its traditional location. (National Library of France)

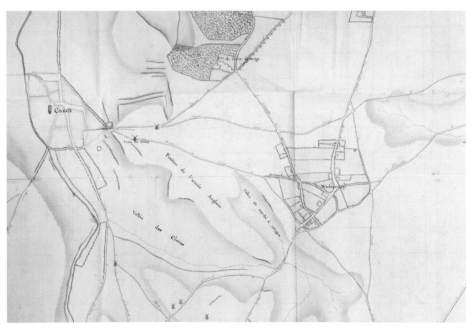

Fig. 17: Hilaire Picard's 1818 map of the traditional site of the battle of Crécy, showing
place-names that were then associated with the battle.
(© Bibliothèque municipale d'Abbeville)

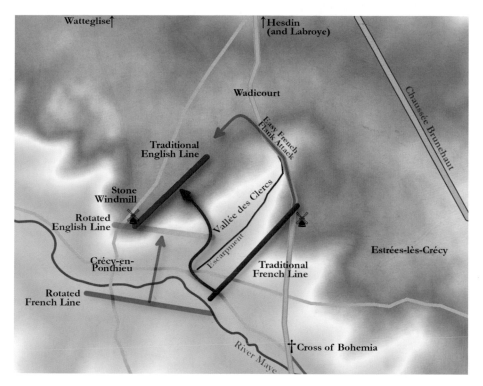

Fig. 18: The current interpretation of the battle of Crécy on the traditional site, overlaid on the topography: the French must sweep to the south, off high ground and through a choke-point to avoid the escarpment on the east side of the Vallée des Clercs. A sweep to the north across high ground following the roads (faded arrow) would make more sense. An alternative, rotated interpretation is shown in faded lines: here, the French fight across the river, ignoring the presence of the bridge in town. (Michael Livingston)

Fig. 19: Lower reach of the embankment at the traditional location, down which the French knights are imagined to charge. Its horse-maiming steepness, even blurred out by the vegetation, is apparent. (Michael Livingston)

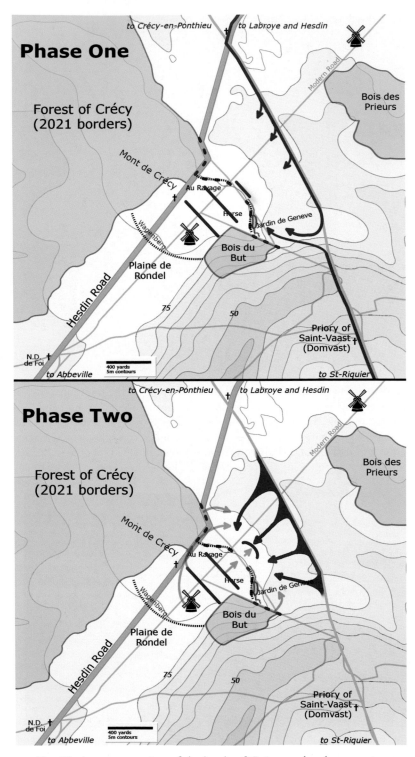

Fig. 20: A reconstruction of the battle of Crécy on the alternate site.
(Michael Livingston)

Fig. 21: The so-called Cross of Bohemia that stands on the former junction of roads east of Crécy-en-Ponthieu, from a postcard purchased in 1913. The base upon which the cross has been mounted is modern. (Kelly DeVries)

Fig. 22: The crossbowmen at Crécy needed good balance to pull this off, and muddy ground did them no favours. Neither did the fact that they were sent forward into longbow range without the shields that would protect them while doing this. (Getty Images)

Fig. 23: The stone-built windmill that formerly stood beside the traditional battlefield above Crécy, from a postcard purchased in 1913. (Kelly DeVries)

Fig. 24: The author on the proposed field of battle, from the Bois du But, looking north. The land called the Herse is on the Mount of Crécy to the left (i.e. the English position); the bowl called the Jardin de Génève extends to the right (i.e. the direction of the first French charges). A deep ditch is hidden in the trees in the right centre. (Michael Livingston)

Fig. 25: Looking west from the French lines towards the English position, with the Forest of Crécy in the far distance. The 'bowl' of the Jardin de Génève lies hidden at the foot of the taller trees at right centre: the wagenburg stood on the high ground of the Mount of Crécy behind it. (Michael Livingston)

Fig. 26: The initial moments of the battle of Crécy, as pictured in the late 14th century. Note that the illustration is missing the English wagenburg completely. (Getty Images)

Fig. 27: Though the man firing it is out of proportion – he should be perhaps twice as tall – this image of a hand-cannon from 1405 is otherwise a good approximation of the artillery fired at Crécy. (SUB Göttingen)

Fig. 28: The remains of John of Bohemia's body within his tomb in Luxembourg, published by anthropologist Emanuel Vlček in 1993. (Vlček)

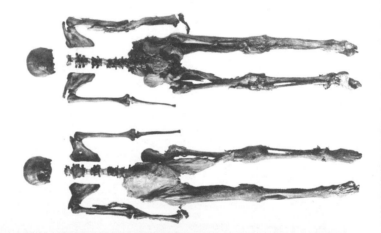

Fig. 29: The remains of John of Bohemia as they appeared when his tomb was opened in 1980. (© National museum of history and art – Luxembourg)

Fig. 30: Nearly everything about Julian Russell Story's *The Black Prince at Crécy* (1888) – an imaginative depiction of the finding of the king of Bohemia – is inaccurate, but it is nevertheless a magnificent testament to the lasting memory of Crécy. (Telfair Museum of Art)

Fig. 31: This casting of Auguste Rodin's The Burghers of Calais (modelled 1884–95, cast 1985) is housed in The Metropolitan Museum of Art New York. (The Metropolitan Museum of Art, New York)

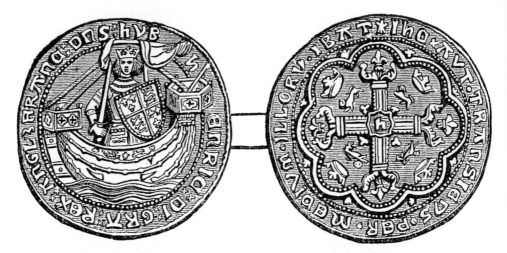

Fig. 32: Edward III is depicted as a Channel-spanning king in this coin issued after his conquest of Calais. (Getty Images)

Fig. 33: Edward III's effigy atop his tomb in Westminster Abbey. (Getty Images)

PART THREE

Reconstructing Crécy, 26 August 1346

Men hunted there all so bitterly;
No man wished to give way to the other;
Men split many a helmet,
So that the entire brain and blood
Out of the head must fall.
Of the bitter battle we cannot describe,
For it was so horrible and so ghastly.
Eight helmets sprang from four.

The Rhyming Chronicle, 1347[1]

9

Reconstructing Battles

We're about to reconstruct the battle of Crécy. This is no easy thing, and it's important to understand the hurdles we face and the tools we use to overcome them.

You already know that finding the truth about the past is hard. I've lost count of the number of times I've had to say some variant of 'we don't know'. I've talked about many of the reasons for that, like the erasers of our past and the biases of our sources. All of them are a problem pretty much all the time.

Battles, though, have always stood out to me for their particular thorniness. It might be one of the reasons I'm drawn to them.

To start with, battles aren't rational. That could be taken to mean that battles aren't generally an intelligent thing to engage in. And while that's certainly true at times – we've seen both Edward and Philippe wisely avoiding engagements when they weren't ready – it isn't what I mean here. I'm instead talking about how the people involved in battle tend not to behave rationally. Whatever forethought and planning a person might have taken from the outside looking in, the reality of being in the thick of warfare – heart pounding, nostrils filled with the stench of death, gasping for breaths that might be the last, feet stamping through blood-soaked mud – well, at that point all actions boil down to split-second decisions based on reactive instinct and past training.

None of this is new. There's a reason that militaries around the world drill, drill, and drill some more: they are doing everything possible to shrink the gap between instinct and training by endeavouring to make those reactive instincts fall into patterns of behaviour that are as predictable and effective as possible.

But soldiers aren't automatons. When it comes to the moment, it's an individual making those split-second decisions to charge or cower, to strike or retreat.

There were thousands upon thousands of men at the battle of Crécy, making thousands upon thousands of individual decisions.

Battles aren't rational.

That said, when we pull back the lens far enough, an order begins to appear in the chaos. Patterns of behaviour begin to emerge. An individual may have chosen to cower, but the majority of the force on the field chose to charge. This fact is about the only way we can hope to understand a battle and it's why we use big blocks of colour rather than thousands of tiny dots on our battle maps. We don't know the full story of a single person's experience at Crécy, but we can at least begin to understand the big picture of what was happening to the people who fought there collectively.

Whenever I approach a battle, trying to figure out what happened and why, I bring with me my handy dandy Reconstruction Toolkit. It doesn't have every tool that I'll need to understand every battle, but it certainly has some initial go-to tools of conflict analysis, whether I'm looking at the battle of Thermopylae in 480 BC or the battle of Towton in 1461.

ARCHAEOLOGY

Given how much time I've spent talking about the problems in trusting too much in our written sources, you can imagine what excitement there is for me when there is actual physical evidence that can be touched and tested. Human lives are so ephemeral in the grand scheme of things that they don't often leave such marks behind, but when we have them they're simply magic.

Unfortunately, despite their work being magical, archaeologists aren't wizards. They're subject to real-world constraints of personal availability, project funding, site access, and much else. So one of the problems with archaeology as a tool for understanding the past is that even if we think we might have physical remains available, we often don't have the ability to access it.

Still, when archaeologists are able to get on site their findings can be vital. And when we speak of findings, it should also be noted that non-findings are, paradoxically, a finding, too: if we've been told something happened somewhere – say, something that should leave lots of material evidence, like a bloody *battle* – it's a really important clue if archaeologists can find no shred at all of that evidence.

As it happens, this will apply to Crécy.

MULTI-SOURCE AUTHENTICATION

I've been quietly doing this a lot as we've been going through our story so far. Recall the question of whether or not the English knew about the ford at Blanchetaque ahead of time: Jean le Bel says no; Jean Froissart says yes. One reason to favour le Bel is that he's writing earlier. Theoretically that means there's been less time for accounts to be shifted by outside forces, though sometimes a later account is better because it had access to more information than the earlier one, or its writer could see things more clearly from a more objective distance. Another reason to favour le Bel is that other sources say much the same thing he does, while nobody else says what Froissart does. When multiple accounts line up – and are doing so in apparent independence from one another – our working assumption is that this information is more likely to be true than the outlier account.

This kind of processing isn't a *rule*. Sometimes the minority report is the correct one. But, generally speaking, the more sources we have telling us something, the more likely we are to believe it's true. This makes finding sources – as many sources as we can get, of whatever kind we can get – an essential task of the historian.

TECHNOLOGY AND TACTICS

Under this section of the toolkit we find all the stuff we know about warfare typical of the period in question.

On the technology, things can quickly get quite technical and specialized, but that doesn't mean it isn't absolutely vital: how far the longbows at Crécy could shoot, for example, is really important for determining how far apart the lines were at first contact – it's also a fairly testable question.

On the tactics, our understanding of how two combatants fought in a prior engagement can be tremendously valuable for understanding how they fought in the next one being studied. That said, we do have to be careful about turning the past into a limitation on possibility. Just because a general never did something before doesn't mean he won't do it later as a result of pressure or progression.

So when talking about 'the stuff we know' it's important to remember that it's really 'the stuff we think we know' at this point.

THE FOUR MAXIMS OF BATTLE

The tools so far have been essentially pools of knowledge. But these next ones are more akin to principles. Like all the above, these aren't hard and fast rules. Exceptions to them exist, but those exceptions are rare enough that I've come to consider my 'four maxims' a starting point for any given battle: I assume they're operative until proven otherwise.

Follow the roads. We've already seen this maxim in action throughout the Crécy campaign. Armies can't function without mobility of march and the availability of logistical support. Moving thousands of men and all their supplies – wagons, pack animals, herds of livestock – is a massive undertaking, and, in the pre-modern world, it all but requires roads. So when we're trying to find a battle, we'll always have an eye towards the roads that probably brought the armies into contact with each other. Find the roads and you'll often find the battle along them.

No man is a fool. Historians will often ignore the problems with their interpretations by waving them away with the excuse that one party or another didn't know what they were doing.

It's true that stupid happens. We all know that. But a battle reconstruction that requires one side to be stupid is, frankly, probably pretty stupid itself. Commanders want to win. Their soldiers don't want to die. These ideas shouldn't be surprising or terribly debatable, and they certainly can't be ignored. A reconstruction should be considered suspect if it doesn't have all parties making decisions that a reasonably intelligent person would have also made if they were subject to the same constraints of information. Those decisions might in retrospect have been tragically incorrect, but in the moment they must have *seemed* correct. Explaining how what seemed right was really wrong is an essential part of a working battle reconstruction.

A battle is its ground. Terrain stands at the centre of war. What forces can be brought to bear, how they can get there, what weapons they can utilize, where they can stand and fight, what they're driving towards or backed up against, what tactics are possible, what sight lines or sound-spheres they had to understand what was happening, where they could get their water ... all of it (and so much more) is fundamentally tied to the physical lie of the land on which conflict takes place.

This means that we have to *find* the ground. Reconstructing a battle in a featureless vacuum serves little purpose if the goal is to understand what happened in reality.

Once we have a battle-site located, we need to do our best to reconstruct that ground as it was, not as it is or as we would like it to be. As with finding roads, this can require a host of skills that we don't need to go into here – hydrology and geology, for starters – but doing so can answer a whole host of questions about what happened and why.

Men move like water. Human energy is a finite resource. So just as water follows the path of least resistance, human beings will tend to do so too. Recognizing what this means requires a thorough understanding of the ground. While it's usually the case that the easiest path to travel is downhill, local terrain conditions might dictate otherwise.

* * *

These are hardly all the tools we have at our disposal in battle reconstruction, but they're enough for us to get started on reconstructing Crécy. As we start to do so, it's important for us to remember the most basic principle to *all* of this:

History is a hypothesis. It's our working theory of the past, subject to revision if new information disrupts it. If that new information means that everything we thought was wrong ... well, so be it.

The Armies Approach, 26 August

In 1757, César-François Cassini de Thury published a map of the region north of Abbeville as part of his family's multigenerational atlas of France.[1] Cassini's rightfully famous map is a fascinating, detailed look at that country in the mid-18th century: roads and towns, windmills and shrines, drainages, and even the small tracks through the nearby Forest of Crécy all appear to be remarkably accurate to what modern surveyors can map on the ground. And clearly marked upon it, in the Vallée des Clercs beside a small hill rising to the north-west over and immediately adjacent to the town of Crécy-en-Ponthieu, is the location of the battle of Crécy on 26 August 1346: this was long thought to be the earliest map to mark the site of the battle of Crécy (Figure 14).

Cassini's map tells us a lot about the landscape. The 411 years between the battle and the publication of the map weren't static, but they also pre-date the Industrial Revolution and the development of the kind of modern technologies that have so dramatically reshaped our landscapes today. In other words, the landscape we see on Cassini's map is more or less what the two kings would have seen the night before the battle: Edward from the vicinity of Noyelles-sur-Mer, and Philippe from Abbeville.

This landscape dictated the choices they would make over the next 24 hours, and it was dominated – then and now – by two natural features.

The first major feature we can see on the map is the Forest of Crécy. This dense wood is today the largest forest for 60 miles in any direction. Roughly rectangular in shape, it covers over 15 square miles of high ground today, and it's shown even larger on Cassini's map. In 1346, with four centuries' worth of fewer cuttings along its margins, it was in most areas probably larger still.[2] One substantial road bisects the Forest today, running between the towns of Forest-l'Abbaye on its southern side and Crécy-en-Ponthieu on its northern side. Other smaller paths cut the woods in a rough grid. The Cassini map shows something like this in the form of a few north–south paths through the woods and two east–west ones. We don't know if these were in place 400 years earlier, but they can't have been anything substantial if they were. Even Cassini's maps shows them meandering through the thick trees. They can't have been much wider than a cart at most.

The other major landscape feature that Cassini emphasizes is the marsh that filled much of the space between the Forest of Crécy and the sea, from the banks of the River Somme in the south to the banks of the River Authie in the north. Cassini depicts a thin stretch of non-inundated land, with a road upon it, running along the edge of the Somme, from Noyelles-sur-Mer westwards to Le Crotoy. On either side of this, the land was otherwise, before it was drained, a changeable maze of marsh and little streams. How wet it was is recorded in the various water-related place-names around and within it: the *bray* of Sailly-Bray comes from the old Gallic word for 'marsh'; the *pont* of Ponthoile comes from the Latin word for 'bridge'.

THE LOST ENGLISH CAMP

As we've already discussed, Edward's camp on 25 August couldn't have been far from the Blanchetaque crossing, because Edward himself informs us that he didn't move from his initial defensive position until around 6pm. Retford's *Kitchen Journal* records this night's camp as being 'in the Forest of Crécy', whereas the previous night at Blanchetaque was 'under' the Forest.[3] We probably shouldn't put too much weight on the difference in the prepositions here, but they could imply that the army had moved inside the border of the Forest as they perceived it rather than remaining merely under its shadow. Since the Forest dominated the landscape north of the Somme, and Edward wanted to back away from the Somme, this would make good sense. It is likely that most of the wooded areas north of the riverbanks were generally considered part of the Forest of Crécy even if they weren't fully attached to its great block.

Writing just a few days later, Michael Northburgh reports much the same thing that Retford records: they were first camped 'in the Forest of Crécy, on the same river [i.e. the Somme]', then they moved to a camp 'in the same Forest of Crécy' for the night of 25 August.[4] The *Cleopatra Itinerary* seems to suggest that the camps were being made near the trees themselves: at Blanchetaque the king was 'beside the Forest of Crécy', and then the night before the battle he was at 'another edge of the Forest'.[5] Geoffrey le Baker, who was there but didn't write his account until around a decade later, agrees that the king was 'in his quarters on the banks of the Somme' on 24 August. He's less helpful about the next encampment, saying only that they moved towards 'the field of Crécy' where the battle would eventually happen.[6] Like le Baker, many of our other sources give a similarly unspecific impression of this crucial pre-battle movement. In their field dispatches, for instance, Wynkeley and Edward himself say only that after the ford they marched 'towards Crécy', which is rather unhelpful.[7] Crécy could be the Forest of Crécy or the town of Crécy-en-Ponthieu, after all – or even the *region* of Crécy, as it appears on many early maps, like Nicolas Sanson's 1741 map of Ponthieu – and in any case 'towards' says nothing about the actual *route* to any of these destinations.

These early witnesses aren't giving us a lot of information to work with, but – to look on the bright side – at least they're giving us roughly the same story.

The anonymous Citizen of Valenciennes says the king of England stayed at Noyelles-sur-Mer after his crossing at Blanchetaque – the town is about three miles down the riverbank from where the ford was probably located. It was, the Citizen says, 'surrendered' to him by the lady of Aumale, the sister of Edward's friend, the late Robert of Artois.[8] Jean Froissart agrees about the surrender – he specifically notes that 'the town and the countryside' was spared as a result of this connection – though he insists the army didn't stay there: instead, it marched further to lodge at 'Labroie'.[9] Though differing on the lodging, the Citizen also talks about Edward passing through such a place: the army 'rode towards Crécy, travelling through and pillaging Le Crotoy, Rue, and Waben on their way': they met Philippe after marching 'across La Braie and across Crécy' (making both sound like regions). Whether Rue was sacked is uncertain, but the sacking of Waben is very clearly in error: no one else has Edward reaching the mouth of the River Authie until after the battle of Crécy; if he'd reached it beforehand he would have needed to *backtrack* over two dozen miles to fight the battle!

The 'La Braie' business is interesting, though. There *is* a place called Labroye that we know to be associated with the battle: a castle of that name, on the banks of the Authie north-east of Crécy, is the place to which Philippe fled after his defeat. But that Labroye is at least 16 miles from Noyelles-sur-Mer. There's no indication Edward ever went there, even after the battle, and the chances that he did so *before* the battle – as our sources are saying – is exactly zero.

In fact, the Citizen of Valenciennes says, Philippe himself went to La Braie during his chase of the English, at which point he was 'between one and two leagues' (two and three-quarter miles and five and a half miles) from Edward, who was at a wood.[10] We get much the same information from the *Grand Chronicles* of France (written around 1350), in which Edward was camped 'near to a forest which is called Crécy' after crossing the Somme, and that on the day of the battle Philippe went to 'La Braie, a town that was beside the Forest of Crécy, and there it was said that the English army was around 4 or 5 leagues from him' – 11 or 13.75 miles – though this report wasn't true since there 'was not more than a league between the town and the forest, or around that'.[11] No one could possibly claim that the town of Labroye was next to the Forest of Crécy.

So where is the *Braie* that Edward passed through before the battle? Is it a region (as the Citizen has it) or a town (as the *Grand Chronicles* have it)?

The answer to the second question is 'both'. As we've already seen, the *bray* of the town Sailly-Bray refers to the forbidding marsh, now largely drained, that previously smothered the land west of Noyelles-sur-Mer. Despenser had crossed this marsh to get to Le Crotoy (and Rue, if that happened), and it would make sense for Edward to have moved closer to its edge after he initially pulled away from Blanchetaque. He wanted to open up space between his forces and those of Philippe at Abbeville. In addition, at this point he was still hoping that a resupply – or an escape – was waiting for him on the other side of that swamp.[12]

An encampment in this area might also help make sense of the information that Giovanni Villani provides. After the English crossed the ford, they continued to march:

> hungry and greatly discomforted, on Friday 25 August through the day and the night they advanced twelve Picardy leagues [33 miles], with no rest, tormented by hunger and anguish until they arrived at a village and place bordered by a forest called Crécy, six leagues [16.5 miles] from Amiens. And having to cross a narrow but deep stream, they found it expedient to ford it one or two at a time, and managed to cross unopposed. Discovering that the king of France was following them, they pitched camp outside Crécy on a small hill between Crécy and Abbeville in Ponthieu.[13]

Those arguing for the traditional site of the battle would want to argue that this must refer to the River Maye, which runs through the town of Crécy-en-Ponthieu and bordered the supposed site of the battle. But there are problems with such an identification. That hill isn't 'between Crécy and Abbeville', as Villani clearly says it must be, and the Maye is hardly 'narrow but deep', requiring a treacherous ford: the Maye had a bridge at Crécy-en-Ponthieu.[14] What Villani *could* be describing, however, might be a tributary running out of the Forest of Crécy and into the great marsh. One of these streams, Le Dien, passes beside Sailly-Bray today. Another, running just a quarter mile alongside, is the Rivière des Îles. Either could fit Villani's description quite suitably.

On the other hand, do we even trust Villani's topography here? The mileage he gives us is totally wrong – the Forest of Crécy is at least 30 miles from Amiens as the crow flies; the distance from Blanchetaque to the traditional site of the battle a mere ten. The same question hangs over the Citizen, given his false report that Waben was burned before the battle. Do these errors in one part of their narrative negate the whole? Or do we accept that specific details like the 'narrow but deep stream' on the way to the battle would be more likely to be accurately preserved than a specific mileage would be? Though we don't know exactly how Villani, writing in Florence, actually got his information, we know it was through a sequence of information exchange one way or another. Numbers are particularly likely to be garbled that way.

We must continually ask these kinds of questions – and understand these kinds of negotiations – as we try to understand our sources. The ideal is to find an explanation that fits all the data, but it can happen that we must resort to the best fit to the best data. In the present instance, for the English camp on 25 August, the eyewitness accounts give us the best data. And an encampment between Noyelles-sur-Mer and Sailly-Bray is the best fit for that data. That this might account for Villani's stream is an added bonus – but that doesn't mean that the identification of the encampment *relies* on Villani's stream. This is a very important distinction when it comes to how one handles the evidence. Think of it as explanation versus application. There's an explanation why the English encampment was there: that explanation can be *applied* to explain other sources.

At any rate, all things considered, Edward likely slept near the marsh as night fell. It cannot have been comfortable.

The next day, he would fight the battle of Crécy.

But before we get too far ahead of ourselves, let's return to the French king, Philippe. He had not been idle.

ROADS AND THE PLANS OF KINGS

Philippe was in Abbeville on 25 August. Cassini's map shows six main roads that he could take when he left that city. The easternmost road runs along the Somme itself down to the great city of Amiens. Moving counter-clockwise, the next is the road to the fortified city of Doullens. The next road, running through the nearby town of Saint-Riquier, ultimately leads to Arras. After that comes the Hesdin road, which I've highlighted in green on Cassini's map (Figure 14). It runs along the eastern side of the Forest of Crécy, then slips past the town of Crécy-en-Ponthieu (but not through it), before passing Labroye on the way to Hesdin. To the west of this is the road that bends around the western side of the Forest of Crécy and crosses the River Maye at Bernay-en-Ponthieu – this is the road to Calais, and I've highlighted it in red. Finally, there's the road that parallels the Somme downstream to the west, running through Noyelles-sur-Mer before making its way through the wide marsh beyond in order to reach Le Crotoy.

These roads would have been very much on the minds of the two kings.

Edward, beside the marsh, had hoped to find his ships at the end of the Crotoy road. There were none. His next most immediate option would have been the road to Calais. By the early modern period this was the main artery between that port city and distant Paris: a 1632 map produced by Nicolas Sanson shows it as a wide and well-travelled postal route connecting the capital to the whole region.

We've seen already that there are many historians – and a few of our sources – who think that Edward was planning to go to Calais all along, or at the very least had been planning to do so since Caen or Poissy at the latest. I've already expressed my doubts on this, and what Edward did now is the nail in the coffin. The road to Calais was the closest road to Edward. It was fast. It lay open to his march.

But on the morning of 26 August, instead of taking it, Edward marched his army *across* it.

He wasn't going to Calais.

That meant he was aiming for the *next* road, the one that passed along the eastern side of the Forest on its way to Hesdin. Philippe had dispatched 300 men to help defend that city the moment the English had crossed the Somme. So often painted the fool, the French king actually guessed Edward's plan exactly: the English king was marching towards Béthune, which was up the Hesdin road.

From Le Titre on the Calais road a smaller and slower local path ran eastwards across the landscape through Lamotte-Buleux before joining the Hesdin road at Canchy. Not substantial enough for Cassini to record, it was nevertheless passable for the wagons. This was apparently the route that the English took.

It was a bold move. There was a chance that the French could come upon them at any time, and if they were caught out in the open it might be a disaster. But if Edward wanted to reach the Hesdin road – the road that he thought would lead to his allies – then he had little choice but to take this path along the southern side of the Forest of Crécy before he could turn north-east around it.

I've mentioned before that there are historians who think that Edward planned, from the moment he landed in Normandy, to make his stand on the (traditional) site of the battle of Crécy. I've argued that this is nonsense.

What I *could* buy, though, is that on this day he had a potential battle-site in mind.

This isn't to say that he *wanted* to fight Philippe on 26 August. If he was set upon a fight he could have taken his time to build a perfectly defensible position using the arms of the marsh to prevent Philippe from surrounding him. Alternatively, he could have backed his entire force to Le Crotoy and defended the narrow marsh paths while still hoping for reinforcements by sea. If he wanted to fight, just about anything was better for his tired army than forcing it to march across hostile terrain within easy striking distance of the enemy.

The only thing that makes sense – the only thing that makes Edward not a fool – is if he broke camp that morning thinking he could reach the road and fly to his friends. It was a chance worth taking.

If the French screwed up that plan, though, he damn well was going to have a back-up plan. He would fight. So his scouts would have been tasked not just with keeping tabs on the French, but also with finding advantageous sites for battle if they were caught out.

Edward would get the credit for victory at Crécy, but one hopes that the scout who found the battle-site got an increase in pay. Where the English ended up was a brilliant match for the tactics they had perfected.

The reason a back-up plan became the actual plan was because the French king moved faster than Edward anticipated. On the same morning that Edward set off from the area of Noyelles-sur-Mer, Philippe set off from Abbeville.

We already know that he'd guessed Edward was headed for Hesdin, and his own scouts had surely told him of the English movements that confirmed exactly this. So taking the Calais road wasn't an option for him: he'd end up behind Edward, which is where he'd been ever since Poissy. If he took the Hesdin road instead – and he moved fast enough – there was a chance that he could reach Canchy before Edward did and so meet him there.

Philippe had to be thrilled at the idea of having Edward and his tired men rounding the corner of the Forest of Crécy to see the French army across the road before them, their banners high and their knights ready to charge across the open plain.

But if his history to this point tells us anything about the French king, it was that he was a careful man. Others would confuse this caution with cowardice, but the truth is that unchecked aggression and recklessness would be excellent ways for a king to get his people killed and himself captured or worse.

Caution meant that Philippe decided not to risk the Hesdin road. He wasn't going to chance Edward reaching it first and getting ahead of him. He was done chasing his enemy. He wanted to cut him off and put him to the sword.

So when he left Abbeville – after praying for victory at the priory of Saint-Pierre – Philippe marched up the Arras road to Saint-Riquier.

He was aiming for the Roman road called the Chaussée Brunehaut, which ran from Paris to Amiens to Boulogne-sur-Mer. The many bridges that the Romans had built along its path had given the region the name Ponthieu, and it remained usable for centuries. You can see it on Cassini's map – I've highlighted it in purple – running through Noyelles-en-Chaussée, to meet the Hesdin road just north of Wadicourt before continuing on to the north-west. It was there, at the junction, between Labroye and the Forest of Crécy, that Philippe could perfectly cut off the English advance.

But as Philippe was marching, his scouts spotted the English far closer than he expected. The English scouts probably spotted them, too. Edward knew the jig was up. If he was caught out on the open road his men would be run down. So he took the best position his scouts had found.

Philippe had been chasing Edward ever since Paris. He was exhausted, frustrated, and determined. But at last he'd cornered his enemy. There'd be no slipping away.

As soon as he learned that the English had stopped, Philippe angled down the road through the Maye valley towards Crécy-en-Ponthieu: it was a short-cut to the Hesdin road. He must have been ecstatic when he knew he'd reached it before the English. He turned south, heading up the road towards his enemy. From here, the Hesdin road ran up towards a rise called the Mont de Crécy, upon which the Forest stood.

And there, at long last, was Edward and the English army, waiting for him.

Finding Crécy

This will be a long chapter. It's also going to be a fairly dense one.

I'm going to discuss – and then discard – the traditional site of the battle of Crécy. Then I'm going to put another site in its place. Miles away. On the other side of a river.

This is an explosive claim to make, because so much is at stake in it. If *a battle is its ground*, the fact that folks have been looking in the wrong place would mean that nearly everything that's been written about this famous event might well be wrong.

In other words, I'm about to overturn a lot of scholarship that's been long believed by a lot of people. I want to get it right. So this is going to take time.

If you want to just trust me and skip to my reconstruction of the fighting itself, please proceed to the next chapter. But if you find the detective work of history fascinating – as I certainly do – then read on.

THE TRADITIONAL SITE

There are so many stories about the battle of Crécy. I remember hearing the story of King John of Bohemia's death there in my second year in college. A history major, I'd been given the opportunity to study abroad in Maastricht for a semester, in a programme that had lots of free time available for travel throughout

Europe. One day, the professor in charge of the program – the late Dr James Vardaman – took me aside and suggested that I visit nearby Luxembourg. I needed to tour its remarkable fortifications and pay my respects at John's tomb.

He then told me how this blind king, fighting for Philippe at Crécy, recognized that the French and their allied forces – which by then included two other kings, the king of the Romans and the king of Majorca – would lose the battle. Instead of fleeing the field in pursuit of safety, John asked two of his most loyal knights to attach their steeds to his. He took his sword in his hand. He smiled at its familiar weight. He wished the rest of his men well and asked that they keep safe his son, the future king of Bohemia. Then he was led forward to where the battle raged most desperately. Better to die in battle than in bed.

He got his wish. He died with his sword in his hand. Thousands of others died, too, but because they weren't kings their fates were forgotten.

The tale I told in the last chapter – of where these men met on the roads – is shown on my overlay to Cassini's map: the circles and the solid lines between them show what I've just described: the English encampments at Acheux, Blanchetaque, and near Noyelles-sur-Mer, and then the site of the battle on the eastern side of the Forest of Crécy; their blue counterparts show the French advance to the same point from Abbeville through Saint-Riquier.

This is not at all the typical story of Crécy.

Still today, a journey to the town of Crécy-en-Ponthieu will reveal little doubt about the location of the battle. Signposts along the road helpfully point to a prominent hill immediately north of the centre of town. A little car park near the summit there beckons tourists to an observation tower said to be built on the site of the windmill from which my professor said that Edward directed the battle.

Cassini's map tells us the same story: it very clearly marks the site in the traditional valley location north of the River Maye, triangulated by the towns of Crécy-en-Ponthieu, Estrées-lès-Crécy, and Wadicourt. I have placed circles to mark the traditional encampments there (Figure 14).

Cassini's map was long thought to be the earliest unequivocal map of the battle-site. I said as much in the *Crécy Casebook*. I'm happy to report that I was wrong: a student of mine located a map of Artois and its regions made by Guillaume de l'Isle in 1704 (Figure 16).[1] This map was clearly used by Cassini.

So we can be certain that 358 years after the battle, at least some people thought that Crécy had happened on the site that has subsequently become the traditional site. This is the *vulgato*, repeated so often that everyone has simply assumed it to be true.

Let's step through what we know, starting with what we can observe about the traditional site and what the battle there would require.

First, as Cassini's map shows, it would require that the English nipped past any French attempt to stand in their way. Marching from the vicinity of Noyelles-sur-Mer, they had crossed the face of Abbeville, reached the Hesdin road, and then veered off that road to cross the River Maye. Edward had seized the town of Crécy-en-Ponthieu, and then he'd taken up a position on the hillside to await the trailing Philippe.

Some scholars have suggested that they managed at least part of this feat by taking a cart path through the Forest itself – one of those routes that may or may not have existed in 1346 – but this has to be considered unlikely. Edward wasn't out for a lively trot alone. He was at the head of some 13,000 men, with an enormous number of wagons and a herd of livestock. Going through the Forest would be a logistical nightmare that would slow him down at the very moment he needed speed. It's true that the road along the southern edge of the Forest also wasn't much more than a cart path, but at least there his men could spread out along the route. They wouldn't be hemmed in by the crowded trees and brush.

Still, let's accept that the English could make it to Crécy-en-Ponthieu – by marching either secretly through the Forest or speedily around it. I've shown both possible options on the overlay.

Philippe, trailing his enemy, would have seen that they had taken a position on a high hill beyond the town of Crécy-en-Ponthieu. According to the traditional story of the battle, he marched up the Hesdin road near Estrées-lès-Crécy, towards the Chaussée Brunehaut, the Roman arterial road through the region. He took position facing the English on the opposite side of what's called La Vallée des Clercs today.

PLACE-NAMES AND TRADITIONS

Baron Seymour de Constant undertook an investigation of the battle of Crécy in 1832, including a military analysis of this traditional battlefield location. In doing so he first rebukes the famed historian François Eudes de Mézeray (1610–83) for supposing that Edward had utilized a forest to protect his left flank, thereby putting the backs of the English towards Abbeville and the oncoming French – 's'il eût seulement examiné la carte' [if only he had examined a map], de Constant writes – before mentioning that there are some who favour an alternative site south of the city: 'D'autres historiens ont pensé qu'Édouard avait mis sa droite à la forêt, et sa gauche à la Maye, à hauteur de Cressy' [Other historians have thought that Edward put his right flank to the forest, and his left at the Maye, across the height of Crécy].[2] These other historians go unnamed, and I haven't been able to locate them. Their proposal is quickly dismissed by de Constant since, in his view, a position on the south side of the River Maye would have been less militarily advantageous than the traditional site on the north side of the river – which was the vulgato, after all.

And so it was. In July 1818, an Abbeville surveyor named Hilaire Picard produced a map of the Vallée des Clercs, showing the English position on the ridgeline and a number of battle toponyms in the area (Figure 17).[3] First among these place-names is the Croix de Pierre [Stone Cross], a cross, which in other sources is called the Croix de Bohéme [Cross of Bohemia], that is said to mark the place where the blind king John of Bohemia

died. This monument sits at what was previously the intersection
of two main roads in the area: the one running between Crécy-
en-Ponthieu and Fontaine-sur-Maye and the other running
between Wadicourt and Marcheville. The location is just over a
mile away from the traditional site of the battle (some writers
quite erroneously claim a distance of a mere 700 paces), and it
may well be that the marker itself is actually 'a boundary marker',
which some have suggested pre-dates the battle.[4] Other battle-
related place-names on Picard's 1818 map are the *Ancien Chemin
de l'Armée* [Ancient Road of the Army], a path running from
the location of the Bohemian Cross across the head of the Vallée
des Clercs to Wadicourt, north of Crécy-en-Ponthieu, and the
Marché à Carognes [Path of the Dead], a small side valley at the
head of the Vallée des Clercs beside Wadicourt. Some of the later
lithographs based on this same map additionally include the
place-name *Moulin Edouard III* [Mill of Edward III] on the site of
a windmill above Crécy from which the English king supposedly
directed the battle, but Picard's 1818 map labels the windmill in
this location – where the viewing point for the battlefield stands
today – as the *Tour de Crécy* [Tower of Crécy].

It's fruitful to compare this toponymic evidence with the
Napoleonic cadastral maps of the area. These detailed maps were
the result of Napoleon's overhaul of the French fiscal system,
which required the establishment of a new procedure for property
taxation. As a result, an official department was instituted to
create a parcel survey of the lands of France beginning in 1807,
with the maps carrying various subsequent dates as the work of
the surveyors was completed. On the cadastral map of the Vallée
des Clercs (dated 1824)[5] the windmill in question is labelled
the *Tour de Pierre* [Stone Tower], the Marché à Carognes does
not exist (nor does anything like it), and the Ancien Chemin
de l'Armée is labelled instead the *Chemin de Marcheville* [Road
to Marcheville] – only further south, after leaving the Vallée
des Clercs and nearing the *Croix du roi la Boheme* (as they label
it), does this road appear to take up its military place-name,
which it carries for the entire route south to Marcheville.[6]

These Napoleonic maps do not mark the site of the battle or otherwise give any indication that the French and English fought in the Vallée des Clercs.[7]

To be fair, although it does not appear on the Napoleonic cadastral map of 1824, an area at the northern end of the Vallée des Clercs does seem to have been called by some the *Marché à Carognes* in the 19th century. Picard's map of 1818 associates it with a side valley or slight ravine running east–west beside Wadicourt, while Henri de Wailly connects the name instead with 'the traces of at least two pits' where he claims that 'the carcasses of hundreds of dead horses were buried', though there is no evidence that this ever occurred.[8] Leaving aside the fact that we have no historical precedent for such a practice of burying dead horses en masse after a battle – to the contrary, one suspects that the horses were instead stripped and sold for meat and hide – the closest possible distance between the proposed locations (the southernmost of Wailly's 'two pits' and the slope of the traditional field where the horses surely died) is well over half a mile. It's hard to imagine the efforts required to haul so many equine carcasses so far *uphill* across the fields in order to dispose of them. And even if we should postulate that this site was the burial point only for those that died in some kind of attempt on the English left flank (a speculation that would itself necessitate English lines stretching along almost a mile of ridgeline), it is striking that such a burial site should be memorialized on this spot rather than somewhere across the English front, which would have seen far greater loss of life and thus more burials. There's also something of a romanticized element to all such identifications, as demonstrated in a short touring account that appeared on 18 May 1878 in *Chambers's Journal*, a weekly popular magazine published in Edinburgh. Here it is reported that:

> walking over the ground [near Crécy] the spots where the carnage was most terrible may be traced by the names given to tracts of land, such as the Marche à Carognes, meaning 'The Pathway of Corpses'. In the morning, when the fields are covered with

dew, the deep ditches where the victims were buried may be distinctly traced, for there, curiously enough, the earth remains damp much longer than in the other furrows.[9]

All this 19th-century interest in the battlefield is assuredly tied to the Grand Tour, which brought with it an increasing 'interest in cultural visits to places of historical repute', as Philip Preston has put it.[10] Writing in 1861, George M. Musgrave illustrates the commonality of the site upon the Grand Tour when he rebukes his fellow Englishmen for not doing more than observing the great Forest of Crécy to the south: 'a passing look at this land-mark has generally sufficed for our countrymen to come home and say, "We saw Crécy on our way to Paris." This, be it respectfully observed, is folly.'[11] De Constant himself later notes that since at least 1814 there were tourists making '*pèlerinages au champ de bataille*' [pilgrimages to the battlefield].[12] It shouldn't surprise us that enterprising minds in and around Crécy should attempt to build on the notoriety of the site, to tell the story of the dead across the landscape of the living.

In this respect, one must admit that the traditional location makes for a dramatic scene. It is conveniently close to town – good for tourism – yet its hilltop location also imbues it with a powerful presence. Looking out today from the supposed location of Edward's windmill, one has a commanding view east and south, across the breadth of the approaching roads to Crécy.

The view is so commanding, in fact, that it's hard to imagine how the French army could essentially stumble upon the English position, as several of our sources indicate.

But that's the least of its problems.

THE DIFFICULTIES OF THE TRADITIONAL SITE

It was two decades after I visited the tomb of King John of Bohemia that I finally visited this place where everyone said he died. It was 2013, I was now a professor myself, and I'd come to northern France to test a hypothesis that English battles in

Wales had directly influenced the English victory at the battle of Agincourt in 1415.

With me were two extraordinary colleagues – Kelly DeVries, a medieval military historian from Loyola University in Maryland, and Robert Woosnam-Savage, a curator at the Royal Armouries – and it didn't take long walking the fields at Agincourt for us to conclude that my hypothesis didn't test well at all.

Fair enough. Whether we're inventing the light bulb or investigating our history, finding out what doesn't work is a key step in finding out what does.

On the same trip, we decided to visit the nearby site of the battle of Crécy in order to test DeVries' hypothesis about *that* battle. When we first arrived, we dutifully followed the signs through town, parked our rental car near the summit, and climbed to the top of the tower. Then we proceeded to erase the modern landscape from our minds. The paved roads, the metal-sided buildings, the more recent plantings – all of it we pushed away to try to picture the fields as they might have been on the fateful day that the battle began.

It's hard to do this for many medieval battles. The site of the remarkable battle of the Golden Spurs, for instance, has been swallowed up by the growing city of Kortrijk. A simple monument stands amid the grass of a small city park near the presumed site today, but around it loom the shadows of stone buildings and the swarms of noises of cars that render the past almost untraceable.

Not so for Crécy. The site we visited that day is still sloping farmland. The sight lines of hill and valley are little changed after more than six and a half centuries.

Signage in and around the observation tower invites this kind of interpretative imagining. It identifies the approach of the French forces from the east, originating near the hamlet of Estrées-lès-Crécy today. It shows how they swept down from that parallel ridgeline and crossed the Vallée des Clercs. It shows how they then charged uphill, attacking the English position on the higher ridgeline, where those who survived a withering barrage of

English arrows fell onto the English swords in bloody and senseless slaughter.

It doesn't take long, looking out from the tower, to begin to see the problems with several aspects of this story.

From the start, since *no man is a fool,* one wonders what could lead the French to make an attack on such a strong defensive position. On Figure 18, I've shown these traditional lines of the English (red) and French (blue) on today's topography. Arranged thus, Philippe could, if he wanted to do so, easily and quickly manoeuvre around the head of the valley through Wadicourt – this is shown with a faded arrow – in order to carry his attack across level ground directly into the English left flank. Looking back to the Cassini map, one can see that such a movement would be not only tactically advantageous but strategically sound: the English were attempting to flee north, and this would completely cut that line of retreat. The English could have their hill. Philippe could just hold his position and watch a tired enemy grow weaker by the day as supplies dwindled. Odds were good that the English would eventually have to descend from their high ground to attack him on his own strong position. That's exactly how he'd beaten the Flemings at Cassel.

From the French perspective, this kind of plan would be so perfectly obvious that one could almost imagine Philippe's glee on seeing its availability.

According to the traditional story of Crécy, though, he didn't do anything like this. Instead, he sent his Genoese crossbowmen rumbling down off his own high ground instead. They marched across the valley bottom, then laboured uphill to get the range to shoot up into the established English lines. The English hurled down a volley of arrows in response. Just as it had at Caen, this sent the enemy running. Seeing the Genoese retreat, the *vulgato* says that Philippe hurled a line of his choicest knights down after them. This cautious, careful king was now so furious at the failure of his paid allies that he was planning to overrun them to get to the enemy – despite the fact that a line of horses meeting a scrambling line of fleeing crossbowmen could only result in a collision that would send countless riders tumbling and the whole jumble of them subject to the same hail of arrows that had turned back the crossbowmen.

Which is exactly what happened.

Philippe threw yet another line down from his high ground, through their dying countrymen, and then up at the enemy. It met the same fate, crashing and breaking like a wave against unrelenting stone. So he sent another. Then another.

Wave after bloody wave.

For *hours*.

All this time, as all the bodies piled up – the entirety of this unfolding tragedy plain as day from the French position on the other side of the valley – apparently not one person tried to stop the king's madness. And in the weeks and years to come, not one person on either side mentioned what a fool he was.

It gets worse.

Walking down from the supposed English position reveals a literal stumbling block: a retreating glacier from another era has cut a steep embankment along the foot of the eastern ridge that the French are meant to be charging down. I've marked it as a dark grey line across the topography on Figure 18. As tall as a man – as tall or taller than this six-foot man, for sure[13] – this scar in the landscape would have spelled doom to the French horses coming down (Figure 19). Leaping from the embankment, countless steeds would have fallen in a chaotic heap, their front legs broken, their bestial screams mixing with the shouts of their thrown riders.

Wave after screaming wave.

It's a sad testament to how few historians walk the battlefields they study that this prominent geographic feature – and the massive impact it would have had upon the traditional vision of this famed battle – only came up in the past couple of decades. In a lengthy investigation of the site in 2005, Sir Philip Preston noted that:

> This impressive topographic feature, hitherto either ignored or unobserved, would have been a potentially fatal barrier to massed

cavalry attempting to charge into and across the valley from the east. No less significantly, to those within the valley, the bank would have presented an obstacle to retreat or escape. While similar obstacles feature in equestrian eventing, descent of this particular bank by literally thousands of horses and armoured men, in the heat of attack, as proposed in a frontal advance of the French cavalry across the valley towards the English lines, would surely have ended in awful disaster.[14]

As a result, the standard story of the battle was at last reconfigured – though without questioning the validity of the traditional site. Recognizing that the French could not have made such a direct charge, scholars now suggested that they rode around the obstacle, through a narrow passage between the end of the ridge and the River Maye beside which the town of Crécy-en-Ponthieu is built.[15] This gap is roughly 300 yards wide today, but it was probably narrower when the river's edge ran boggier. In 1346 probably only a couple of hundred men could get through at a time, far fewer if they were on horseback. And the weight of their steps would quickly push the embankment in, narrowing it still further. It's the kind of choke-point that military strategists love to see.

To preserve as much of the *vulgato* as they could, historians suggested that the French *voluntarily* marched through this choke-point. Immediately after exiting this severe bottleneck, they made a 90-degree turn, riding north-east up the valley floor until they were situated below the English position. There, they wheeled through another 90-degree turn, re-formed their ranks, and charged up the hill at the enemy.

That way they could die in the proper position dictated by the *vulgato*.

It's a complicated and strange set of manoeuvres. It's quite unlike the tactics we see in any other battle of this kind. And not a single witness or later account on *either* side of the battle mentions the embankment, the closeness of the river, an unparalleled S-turn, or anything even remotely like it.

That said, given the terrain of the site, there was little other choice in light of the generations of assumptions about the battle's location. I've marked this S-turn manoeuvre with a blue arrow on our map.

When we visited the site, my colleagues and I talked over these various problems. We walked along the embankment at the edge of the valley. We absolutely agreed that it was a mortal impediment to the traditional French charge from the east. We could also see that the proposed S-turn might have been undertaken while under the reach of English bowmen who shot first into the flanks of the French and then, after their second 90-degree turn, into their faces. This made the implausible border on the impossible, since the pinch points at the river would have been choked still further by arrow-riddled dead.

The S-turn also made the fate of the Genoese crossbowmen incomprehensible. If, after making their final turn to face Edward, they'd been forced into flight by the English arrows, they wouldn't flee back along the same S-turn. It was every man for himself now. They'd go as directly away from death as possible. That meant they'd clamber up the escarpment that the horses couldn't descend, or even fly towards the head of the valley. Either way, they wouldn't have been overrun at all.

DeVries suggested that if the English position was rotated into a more southern-facing arc facing the Maye, we could at least eliminate one of the turns in the serpentine assault. That way the French coming from Estrées-lès-Crécy would only be making a single 90-degree turn after the choke-point before meeting their required deaths.

It didn't take us long before we were finding issues with this, too. For starters, the English line at that point would be extremely uneven, as it would need to stretch down the slopes into the valley. That's not impossible, but it's definitely not the best position for the maintenance of line cohesion. Worse, solving the S-turn problem made the French actions even more bizarre. The French were staring at the English flank, but they rode around to die at the English front ... despite the fact that the English backfield was visibly open to a quick march up around the valley at Wadicourt. In the original *vulgato* construction it had only been Edward's left flank that would have been threatened by such a move. Turning the line towards the Maye left *everything* exposed.

The only other suggestion we could come up with on the spot was that the English position indeed faced the Maye, but that the French weren't at Estrées-lès-Crécy: they were across the River Maye, in front of them. I've shown this reconstruction on the topography as Figure 18. This would make the most sense ... except that no source described the French charging the English literally through a river. The Maye is admittedly not as wide as the Somme, but it's nevertheless a wet gap. There's a reason it was bridged at Crécy-en-Ponthieu about 1,000 feet downstream.

Rotating the battle-lines this way also made little sense when it came to what happened after the fighting: as we'll see, most of the defeated French didn't retreat to Abbeville – which was literally a straight-shot on open, familiar roads behind them here – but to more distant Amiens. Stranger still is Philippe's retreat to Labroye. This was already uneasy on the traditional configuration – the road there ran up past the head of the valley, in easy reach of English pickets – but it makes zero sense on the rotated configuration, which would have the French king fleeing to a castle *directly behind* the enemy lines!

It didn't matter which way we tried to situate Edward and Philippe on the traditional site. Nothing added up.

And then there was this:

There have been repeated major archaeological investigations of the site, each vying to find definitive traces of one of the most famous battles in history. It shouldn't be hard. The valley isn't that large. Thousands of men supposedly fought and died there. Thousands upon thousands of arrows plunged into the ground. Artefacts should be numerous.

Yet *not one* has been found.

Excuses have been made, of course.

Soil conditions have been blamed for eroding iron, though many of the objects that a 1995 survey *did* find were iron objects that pre-dated the battle. Barring that, it was speculated that the field was simply stripped for useful materials. This does absolutely occur, but systematic surveys at the site of the battle of Towton have revealed that the very act of stripping corpses leads to a proliferation of artefacts, not an absence of them.[16]

The other option, the one that apparently no one wanted to consider, is to conclude that archaeologists found nothing because there was nothing to find.

They were looking in the wrong place.

WHAT THE SOURCES SAY

Let's take away our assumptions. Let's take away the traditions.

If we started from scratch, what would the sources tell us about the location of the battle of Crécy?

There are a *lot* of sources. So famed is the battle of Crécy that when William Shakespeare imagined the Archbishop of Canterbury using Edward's 1346 victory to argue in favour of the young Henry V staking his claim to the throne of France, he did not even need to cite the battle by name:

> Go, my dread lord, to your great-grandsire's tomb,
> From who you claim; invoke his warlike spirit,
> And your great-uncle's, Edward the Black Prince,
> Who on the French ground play'd a tragedy,
> Making defeat on the full power of France,
> Whiles his most mighty father on a hill
> Stood smiling to behold his lion's whelp
> Forage in blood of French nobility. (*Henry V*, *I*.ii.248–55)

For Shakespeare and his audience, Crécy clearly served as a kind of perfection of a golden age of grand heroism. The triumph was most associated with the Black Prince wading through the blood of the enemy dead and then, after the battle, finding the body of the blind king John of Bohemia. The legend as Shakespeare knew it had the noble English according the corpse all honours, and the

Black Prince himself so moved by his enemy's chivalrous spirit that he adopted the three feathers of the Bohemia crest into his own, along with the German motto, *Ich dien*, meaning 'I serve'. Thus was formed, they thought, the crest and motto of the prince of Wales to this day.

For the *Crécy Casebook*, we gathered and translated – from Latin, French, Italian, German, Dutch, Czech, and Welsh – every known source for this battle that we could find: chronicles and poems, administrative reports and letters, *anything* that might provide information on what had happened.

The result was so massive that we had to limit our published book to those sources from the 14th century alone. That *still* left us with over 80 documents. Those sources told us much that surprised us, like the fact that the Black Prince, rather than foraging in the blood of his enemies, was probably captured by them and barely rescued during the battle. Prince Edward's 'most mighty father' didn't smile down upon the 16-year-old boy who had nearly cost him the war; he publicly berated him. Nor was the blind king's body well honoured by all: an examination of the remains held in his tomb in Luxembourg revealed horrendous post-mortem wounds. The Genoese crossbowmen long blamed for the French defeat were exonerated. The French king traditionally assumed to be a fool had made far better strategic decisions than historians had credited to him.

Another early discovery was just how strong a hold the *vulgato* has had on the thinking of historians: scholars were so convinced that the traditional site was correct that they would actually change our sources to conform to it. The chronicler Henry Knighton, writing almost 50 years after the battle (*c.*1390), is thought to have had access to lost primary documents related to the Crécy campaign, including perhaps a more complete version of the *Acta Bellicosa* – our text survives today only in a fragment that breaks off on the eve of the battle of Crécy. In his account that may use the missing pieces, Knighton states that the battle occurred as the English marched on the road '*ad pontem de Cressy ... in campo de Westglyse iuxta Cressy*' [towards the bridge at Crécy ...

in the field of Westglyse near Crécy].[17] The acceptance of a battle location north of Crécy has led scholars utilizing this source to claim that Knighton records not just an approach towards the bridge over the River Maye at Crécy (which he does) but an actual crossing of the bridge (which he does not). Worse, Knighton's identification of the battle-site as *Westglyse* (*Westglise* in the one variant manuscript) has undergone significant alteration. Because this place-name cannot be shown to have any connection at all to the traditional location – which was not itself subject to scrutiny – previous scholars have suggested that Knighton was in error: he ought to have written *Watteglise*, they say, which is a nondescript area one and a half miles north-west of the traditional site. Some writers have even gone so far as to *change* his text to read *Watteglise*, literally hiding the truth of what the manuscripts really say. Further, because Watteglise is so far from the traditional site, they claim that Knighton is locating the site of a much smaller, post-battle skirmish. To the contrary, Knighton is quite clear that Westglise is the site of the main event: at the battle 'were killed 2,000 men-at-arms and 32,000 other soldiers, for they fought well into the dead of night on the field of Westglyse near Crécy'.[18]

In a remarkable feat of circular reasoning, this reconfiguration of Knighton's evidence – I'm putting this in the most charitable way I can – has subsequently been taken to support the very location that forced its reconfiguration in the first place. One historian writes that Watteglise is 'consistent' with the English position north of Crécy (it's not) and the concept of the 'battle decaying into pursuits and skirmishes' (it's the actual battle-site), and that 'this specific mention' (which 'Watteglise' absolutely is not) thereby 'support[s] the battle having been fought' at the traditional location.[19]

It turns out that the *vulgato* tortures both logic and even the facts themselves.

PUZZLE PIECES

Some of the many documents we have give us more information than Knighton does about the site. A great many give us far less.

All of them are listed in Appendix A. Jan van Boendale tells us only that the conflict happened 'in the land of Ponthieu', a maddeningly vague regional location that also shows up in other sources, like the *World-chronicle of Köln*.[20] The *Polychronicon Continuation* claims it instead happened *'apud Crescy in Picardia'* [near Crécy in Picardy].[21] It may be that Thomas Bisset is simply following the popular *Polychronicon Continuation* when he likewise reports the battle was in Picardy, but the same can hardly be said for Heinrich Taube von Selbach, who simply locates the battle 'in Pychardia' [in Picardy].[22]

These conflicting details are confusing at a glance. At the same time, their lack of clarity about the battle's location is itself a surprisingly helpful clue to finding it: the best explanation of the confusion is to accept that the site lacks an obvious point of definition. This could hardly be the case if the battle occurred on the flanks of the town of Crécy-en-Ponthieu at the traditional location.

That said, some of our sources do seem to associate the battle with the town. While a number of our sources give us a generic 'Crécy' that could be anything from the region to the Forest to the town – a flexibility that could be why we have the Ponthieu/Picardy confusion – there's no question that Edward himself, in his letter of 6 September 1346, sites the battle as occurring *'apud villam de Cressy'*, which traditionalists have translated as 'at the town of Crécy', and case closed![23] The problem is, the meaning of the Latin word *apud* isn't remotely as straightforward as they would like to admit. Here are its possible meanings, according to the most standard scholarly reference, Oxford's *Dictionary of Medieval Latin from British Sources*:

1. at, near. b. at the house of. c. among, in the country of.
2. to (a place). b. (lying) towards (a compass point).

Such a range of meanings could honestly range us all over Ponthieu. So, setting aside the preconceptions of the *vulgato*, which did Edward actually mean?

In a letter written even earlier, on 2 September 1346, Richard Wynkeley relates that the battle occurred as the English were moving '*versus Cressi*' [towards Crécy] when the French came upon them '*in campo*' [in a field].[24] The next day, Edward writes in French that it happened as they were marching '*devers Crescy ... en plain champ*' [towards Crécy ... in an open field].[25] On 4 September Michael Northburgh repeats the very same thing.[26] The directional quality of these sources strongly indicates that the battle happened *before* reaching the town of Crécy, rather than *after* passing through it, as is required of the traditional location. So in writing *apud*, Edward presumably meant 'near' or 'towards' Crécy, *not* 'at'.

As it happens, a battle *on the way* to Crécy is likewise reported in sources as varied as a French administrative request by Robert de Dreuex – the battle was '*devant Cressy en Pontieu*' [before Crécy in Ponthieu] – and a Welsh panegyric by the poet Iolo Goch, to say nothing of various chronicle accounts.[27] Other accounts, like Jean le Bel's influential chronicle, comment on the field's distance from Abbeville rather than from the town of Crécy-en-Ponthieu, which is quite strange if it was on the opposite side of the latter town.[28] The same is true of eyewitness Johann von Schönfeld's letter of 12 September 1346, which places the battle between Abbeville and Crécy-en-Ponthieu, something the traditional site very definitely is not.[29]

The traditional location requires that the English, having somehow beaten the French to the north side of the Forest, would need to:

- cross the River Maye,
- seize the town of Crécy-en-Pontheiu, and
- take up a position north-west of the town.

The French would cross the same river. According to the *vulgato*, they would take up their own position on the heights before beginning their S-turns into the enemy. In the alternative, rotated scenario, they would cross the river *in the act* of making their assaults.

But *not one* primary source mentions any of this. No one crosses the river, much less attacks through it. No one seizes the town. The sources point again and again to a site that was *en route* to the town of Crécy, beside the Forest of Crécy south of that town, between it and Abbeville.

We can achieve greater specificity of location through the incorporation of additional avenues of evidence – like topography, place-names, and battle tactics, each of which will be introduced as we go along – but let's first recover what additional evidence we can glean from these textual sources.

Perhaps foremost among these sources is the simplest, which may explain why it is so often overlooked: Retford's *Kitchen Journal*. We've already followed his daily diary of the king's encampment during the campaign. It has consistently placed the king within the closest town to his march. Other sources confirm the practice this implies: the king was staying in the nicest housing they could find, not a field tent. This stopped being the case on 24 August, after the battle of Blanchetaque, when Edward was encamped '*sub Foresta de Cressy*' [beneath the Forest of Crécy] rather than in a town. The next night he was '*in Foresta de Cressy*' [in the Forest of Crécy] – good reason to think he was outside the town of Noyelles-sur-Mer (closer to Sailly-Bray) than within it. The following day was 26 August and the battle of Crécy. That night, Retford says the king was encamped '*adhuc sub Foresta de Cressy*' [still beneath the Forest of Crécy] (Figure 11). On 27 August, the king is '*in campis sub Foresta de Cressy*' [in the fields beneath the Forest of Crécy]. Only on 28 August does the *Kitchen Journal* report a move from this location, as the king lodged that night near Maintenay at the 12th-century Cistercian Valloires Abbey.[30]

Downtown Crécy-en-Ponthieu is a walk of less than ten minutes from the windmill above the town where Edward supposedly directed his great victory. To have taken that position Edward's army would have had to seize that town and controlled it completely. And yet, the *vulgato* would have us believe, no one ever mentioned the English king doing so, and never in the days afterwards did he make that short stroll *downhill* to find a better place to stay than in his field tent.

The *Cleopatra Itinerary* agrees almost entirely with the *Kitchen Journal*, though clearly it has not been copied from it. Across this same sequence it reports that after Blanchetaque the army stayed '*juste la Foreste de Cressy*' [beside the Forest of Crécy], followed on 25 August by a stay '*un altre cost de la Forest*' [on the other side of the Forest]. The night of the battle on 26 August the camp was in '*les champs devaunt la ville de Cressy in Pountyf*' [the fields in front of the village of Crécy in Ponthieu], and the following night, on 27 August, was spent '*en mesme le champ juste la Forest*' [in the same field beside the Forest]. Like the *Kitchen Journal*, the *Cleopatra Itinerary* reports that on 28 August the king stayed at Valloires Abbey.[31]

The itineraries aren't alone in connecting the battle directly to the Forest of Crécy. The anonymous writer of the early *Chronicle of the Counts of Flanders*, for instance, places the fight '*juxta oppidum de Abbatis-villa in Pontivo, in nemore quod dicitur Cressi*' [near the town of Abbeville in Ponthieu, in the forest that is called Crécy].[32] And identification with the Forest of Crécy is also given by the poet behind the *Crécy Poem*, the composer of the *Grand Chronicles*, William of Dene, Matthias von Neuenburg, and the English poet Laurence Minot.[33] The Italian Giovanni Villani similarly relates that the engagement occurred at '*a uno luogo e borgo di costa a uno bosco chessi chiama Cresci*' [a village and place bordered by a wood called Crécy], on '*uno colletto tra Cresci e Albavilla in Ponti*' [a small hill between Crécy and Abbeville].[34] Likewise, the writer of the early *Chronicon Estense* reports '*locum inter Cripsim et Labavillam in quodam maximo nemore*' [a place between Crécy and Abbeville in which was a great wood].[35] Writing sometime before 1355, the Bohemian chronicler Francis of Prague never mentions Crécy by name at all, simply stating that the great battle happened in '*tuta loca inter valles et nemora*' [a place of safety between the valleys and the forests].[36] Thomas Gray, in 1362, locates the battle 'passing the Forest of Crécy', as do many others.[37] And Thomas Burton, in his *Chronicle of Meaux Abbey* (1396), specifies that the battle occurred '*inter villam et forestam de Cressy*' [between the village and the Forest of Crécy].[38]

That Edward would have an interest in the Forest of Crécy is without question. From 1 December 1330 to September 1334, the surrounding region of Ponthieu was officially administered by the English king and his officials after it was surrendered to him by Queen Isabella, and he himself had twice stayed at Crécy in his youth in 1329 and 1331 – almost assuredly to hunt in the Forest. These connections were enough to ensure that the status of Ponthieu was yet one more source of tension between the crowns of England and France during the run-up to the Hundred Years War, though whether his two youthful jaunts in the Forest were enough to give the king of England the kind of 'home field' advantage that many historians trumpet is, to my mind, quite doubtful.[39]

Regardless, there is no doubt that Edward had at least *some* vague knowledge of the area, and that he would have seen the Forest of Crécy in particular as a focal point once he crossed the Somme. It was and had been a royal hunting ground, it was surely known to many of his men, it served as both a natural barrier and a potential point of retreat, and it had a history of being in his personal control. Viewed across the documentary evidence, therefore, it seems evident that the Forest of Crécy is an essential element of the battle's location.

Two weeks after the battle, Philippe VI ordered that payments be made to a loyal sergeant-at-arms who served in the battle at the '*mont de Cressy*' [Mount of Crécy].[40] The same topographic reference is given by Guillaume Flote, who was there, and possibly by John Ergom, who was not.[41] The extraordinary poem of Colins de Beaumont describes the battle occurring on a slope between a mount and a valley.[42]

Where some saw fields, others saw a forest, and still others saw a hill.

And a very few witnesses appear to bring the whole of this together. In related accounts, the *Chronicle of Artois* and the

Chronicle of Saint-Omer describe the English position as being on the fields near a windmill, close to a mount, with woods behind it. They also record a local place-name as *Buscamps*, likely meaning 'Forest-field'.[43] The Citizen of Valenciennes likewise sets the struggle *'dalés le bosquet de Cressy, sur une petite montaigne'* [near the woods of Crécy, on a small mountain].[44]

The Anonymous Roman provides a detailed picture of the battlefield, which is described as taking place by a broad valley beside *'uno castiello lo quale se dice Monte de Carsia'* [a fortress known as Mount Crécy] between the towns of Crécy and Abbeville, where the English king placed all his men *'nelli campi piani, a pede alla costa de Carsia'* [in the flat fields at the foot of Crécy's ridge]. This would be excellent information to help build upon for a topographic search, though he also describes this being eight leagues (22 miles) from Paris, rather than the nearly 100-mile distance between them even as the crow flies.[45] This doesn't mean his information must all be discarded – there could be a reason for the numerical error, including a copyist's mistake – but it must very certainly raise our eyebrows!

The number of references to a 'mount' of Crécy might seem to support the traditional location of the battlefield, but a location beside the Forest of Crécy is equally if not more fitting: still today the road westwards from the valley of the tiny hamlet of Domvast to the higher ground of the Forest is called the *Chemin du Monte du Forest de Crécy* [Road to the Mount of the Forest of Crécy]. And while the traditional battlefield is neither between Crécy and Abbeville nor remotely fitting to be described as 'flat fields', both of these descriptors would perfectly fit this alternative area.

THE ALTERNATE FIELD

Place-names are of much interest in investigating the traditional battlefield. There the place-names associated with the conflict were the Croix de Bohéme (though it's at some distance from the traditional site), the Chemin de l'Armée (though this name is more closely associated with the road south of the battlefield across the

Maye), the Moulin Edouard III (though this name doesn't appear on the earliest maps), and the Marché à Carognes (though this name is of uncertain connection to the battle itself). Each of these potential markers is at least partially negated upon closer scrutiny, and *none* require or demand the presence of a great battle and the slaughter of thousands.

Following the aforementioned Chemin du Monte du Forest up to the edge of the great wood, however, leads to an area at the north-eastern edge of the Forest of Crécy that yields place-name evidence that's more difficult to explain away. Here, settled fast against the eastern side of the Forest – along the road to Hesdin not far from the town of Crécy – is an area of comfortable fields on the plateau-like mount, roughly framed today between the great wood and the much smaller *Bois du But* [Wood of the Butte]. Though slightly higher slopes rise deeper in the Forest, this open strip of land is the high point on the road between Crécy and Abbeville, the dividing point between the water basin of the Somme to the south and the Maye to the north.[46]

This topography fits every essential requirement given by our documentary sources, including some of our most important records like those in the itineraries and Edward's own letters. Since at least our earliest records in 1832, the Abbeville side of this area, running along the eastern edge of the Forest, has been called the *Plaine de la Rondel* [Plain of the Shield]. The Crécy side, at the north-eastern corner of the Forest, is known simply as the *Au Ravage* [To the Violence]. The open area encompassed by the Forest and the Bois du But where they meet is today 600 to 700 yards square, though the plain continues southward along the edge of the Forest, sloping downward for over half a mile to the little chapel of Notre Dame de Foi and, the slope steepening sharply down yet another half-mile, to the village of Canchy. As it happens, Notre Dame de Foi, now in use as a local family mausoleum, is rumoured to have connections to the battle: Musgrave, writing in 1861, was certain the English stopped at this chapel, while in 1891 M. Jourdain reports similar tales about the French visiting the chapel to pray before the battle.[47] Regardless of the viability of such rumours, the high point of the Rondel further up the road would have been a highly suitable location for the English to position their troops in the late days of August 1346.

We saw earlier that some historians want Edward to have marched through the whole of the Forest of Crécy to get to the town of Crécy-en-Ponthieu. I've suggested that it's far more likely that he came around the south side of the Forest to meet the Hesdin road through this area. This is exactly what local traditions describe. Musgrave reported from his tour in 1860 that:

> the road he took from Noyelles to the chapel [of Notre Dame de Foi] is still visible. It is almost as wide as the modern highways; completely grass-grown, and though continually intrenched upon by various landed proprietorships cannot be missed through any part of its length. It is still called 'Le Chemin vert d'Edouard'. In the 14th century it was used as a medium of land carriage between Havre and Flanders, when Noyelles, at that time 'a large town', (as Froissart describes it) was a midway station for merchandize and shipping. The present main road between Abbeville and Montreuil sur mer was not formed till nearly four centuries after the date of these events.[48]

Arriving on the Rondel by these very roads, the English scouts would have surely recognized the potential of the high ground. The spot looks good today, and it was probably even better in 1346, when the plain hemmed in between the Forest of Crécy and the Bois du But would have likely been tighter. As Cassini's map shows – and the 1634 map of Tassin pushes it over a century closer to the battle – the position is a great one: the walls of the woods to either side might serve as natural guards for an army, protecting its flanks in addition to providing cover for supplies, reinforcements, and, important for this fight, archers.

That just such a battle was fought upon the Rondel is also suggested in the place-names that have survived here. It's tempting to argue that the name *rondel* [shield] itself derives from a battle, though it might just as easily refer to the very shape of this wide flat hill.

Not so easily explained is the Ravage, much less some of the other intriguing toponyms in the area that we can find on the previously discussed Napoleonic cadastral maps (these names, along with the topography, are incorporated on Figure 20). On the northern side of the Bois du But, back atop the Rondel, is a great triangle of field bordered by the Ravage on the west and the bisecting roads of the Chemin du Monte du Forest and the *Chemin des Maillets* [Road of Hammers]; for at least two centuries, the limit of our records, this stretch of land has been called *La Herse* [The Harrow], a word that Jean Froissart famously uses to describe the English position and tactics at Crécy.[49] The road leading from the Ravage northwards – that is, the very road that Philippe would take in fleeing the battle towards his loyal castle at Labroye – is the aforementioned Chemin de l'Armée, so named from this area to at least the Croix de Bohème some two and a half miles north of the Rondel.

Much closer than all this, the fertile fields immediately east of the Herse, on a slight downward slope through a depression in the topography, carry the name *Jardin de Génève*. Traditionalists have decried the possibility that this means the 'Garden of the Genoese', claiming instead that it refers to juniper bushes. As with Edward's *apud*, they do so against the dictionaries: according to the standard reference *Dictionnaire du Moyen Français*, the 14th-century word for a Genoese man is *Genevois*, while the word for a juniper bush is *genévrier*. Also, there aren't any junipers in the area.

If the Jardin de Génève marks the approximate location of the death of so many Genoese crossbowmen beneath that initial onslaught of the English arrows – if it marks where the hooves of the French knights charged over the top of them – then it makes sense that the area even further down this gentle slope carries the name *Enfer* [Hell]. Only where the ground begins to level off once more to the north, nearer the town of Crécy-en-Ponthieu, do we get *Paradis* [Heaven]. There is also, as a look back at Cassini's detailed map confirms, at least one windmill in the area, centrally located on the Rondel amid these many other clues.

One objection to locating the battle of Crécy here – aside from allegiance to tradition – is that a look at any map today will show that it sits directly to the west above the hamlet of Domvast, not beside the town of Crécy-en-Ponthieu. To this objection several points must be raised. As we have seen in the sources, not all references to Crécy refer to the village of Crécy-en-Ponthieu. We must also remind ourselves that Domvast, a hamlet today, was no civil jurisdiction at the time of the battle. In 1346 this little bundle of buildings at the foot of the Mont de Crécy was distinguished not as a town or market but only as the site of the now-vanished priory of Saint-Vaast, from which the current hamlet took its name. Beside this priory (which gave its name to a small wood just to the north-east of the proposed battle-site on the Rondel) stood a medieval *château féodal*, which was replaced by a *chateau bourgeois* that burned in 1907; today's church of Sainte-Marie-Madeleine is reportedly built on the site of the priory chapel, and only an early modern dovecote now remains from the former site. Because of its location, this could well fit the Anonymous Roman's reference to the battle occurring near 'a fortification known as Mount Crécy' – assuming we need to fit this detail to anything, that is. Details like this are a perfect example of the difference between explanation and application. I wouldn't rely on the Anonymous Roman's claims to identify a site, but it would still be useful if his details could be applied to a possible site.

More importantly, this priory, sitting at the base of the valley roughly three-quarters of a mile east of the Rondel site, might very well be behind Knighton's naming of the battlefield as 'Westglise': rather than a garbled mistake for distant Watteglise, the chronicler was far more plausibly referring to fields then known locally as being *ouest de l'église* [west of the church], which indeed they are.

In other words, modern Domvast itself may not appear in our records, but the key features of the church that was actually physically there in 1346 very much do.

* * *

This is a more likely location of the battle of Crécy.

As Thomas Burton said in his *Chronicle of Meaux Abbey*, it was a position 'between the town and Forest of Crécy'.[50] It was on the

Herse beside the Mount, the crest of the plains of the Rondel, a strip of farmland at the north-east corner of the Forest of Crécy, overlooking the Jardin de Génève. It makes strategic sense of the actions of both armies. It fits all the evidence on the ground and in the documents, even peculiarities like Knighton's reference to the field of 'Westglise'. As we'll see, the tactics even line up quite perfectly.

And nobody need be a fool.

So why, if everything fits here, did Guillaume de l'Isle place the battle elsewhere in 1704?

We can only guess. He knew that the battle was somewhere near Crécy. Like so many other interpreters, he might have thought this had to be a reference to the town rather than the Forest. In addition, de l'Isle probably knew the popular story that Edward had watched it unfold from a windmill. Though such mills were all over the countryside, it just so happened that there was a large one – a rare stone one, in fact – on the hillside above Crécy-en-Ponthieu (Figure 23). That might have been enough. He put it on his map, and a legendary location was born.

It may also be that he had an eye to the great 17th-century French historian Mézeray, who had claimed that Edward had lodged in Crécy, and that, with 'un bois derriere pour epaulement' [a wood behind his back], 'là il choisit sur une petite coline un lieu commode pour ranger son armée' [there he chose on a small hill a convenient place to arrange his army]. As we now know from the records of the remarkable Kitchen Journal (matched by all other sources), the supposition that the English king stayed in Crécy is a false one, and in this regard Mézeray may have unwittingly led de l'Isle and many others to false conclusions.

As for the rest of Mézeray, however, the famed historian might have been more right than he knew. The English upon the Herse would in fact be sitting on a small and convenient hill, with the wood behind their backs, facing away from the route to Abbeville. In fact, if the French attacked largely from the north-east as is here supposed, then as the day closed on 26 August 1346 they would have died, as Jean Froissart claims, charging directly into the setting sun – one more thing that cannot fit with the traditional location. Even the local historical identifications of burials at locations in the area at the Chapel of Moriamini and the Chapel of 300 Bodies might begin snapping into place, as they would now fall on expected lines of flight from the battle.

Our recognition that the traditional location is almost certainly not the location of the battle – that a far more likely site is to be found three and a half miles away on a small hill beside the Forest of Crécy – is not just a point of interesting trivia. It's not a mere correction to a point on a map or a humble suggestion that a placard be moved. To the contrary, changing the location of the battle fundamentally changes our understanding of what transpired there in late August 1346.

It's time for a new story.

The Battle of Crécy, 26 August

On the morning of 26 August, Colins de Beaumont awoke to church bells tolling over the streets of Abbeville. The sun was probably just warming the sky. It was the canonical hour of Lauds, around 6am. Monks were heading to their dawn prayers.

Colins was heading to war.

Behind the bells, the city would be buzzing with the preparations of an army who had been sleeping anywhere they could fit. Some had spent the night in tents pitched as close to the city's walls as possible. Others had slept on Abbeville's filthy streets. Colins was the herald of Jean de Hainaut, lord of Beaumont, one of the highest-ranked men in the army. He'd probably managed to procure a simple bed tucked away in a dusty corner of whatever nice home Jean had taken over.

Wherever he was, Colins awoke and tidied himself as best he could. He grabbed something to eat. Then he probably turned an ear to the streets, listening for the order to move out.

MARCHING OUT

In describing the movements of armies, historians will often say that the army marched from point A to point B – as I've repeatedly done in this book – but rarely do we stop to think about what this meant in reality.

Colins was one of some 20,000 men who would fight against the English king this day. Not all of them were French. King John of Bohemia was there, along with his son, Charles, who would become king after him. They had a few hundred German and Czech fighters with them, cavalry all. A few thousand Genoese mercenaries – hired by Philippe to defend against English attacks at sea – were now marching as land-based crossbowmen. King Jaume III of Majorca was there, too: he'd been kicked out of his lands by his brother-in-law, King Pedro IV of Aragon, and he was trying to get Philippe's support to win back his birthright.

Not all these men could move at once, so we shouldn't imagine the army as a single entity moving between fixed points. For the most part, they couldn't all *be* at a fixed point. In its movements a medieval army was like an inchworm: as the men at the front stretched forward, the men in the back bunched up in preparation to follow. Then, as the men at the front bunched up wherever they were going, the men at the rear stretched forward as they hurried to catch up.

The front of the army was the vanguard. The men here were mounted, so that they could best respond to threats or opportunities. It was, in theory, the most dangerous place to be, since it was that part of the army most likely to encounter resistance or ambush. Most days, though, it was the most comfortable place to be, since the roads – depending on the weather – would be less dusty or muddy than they'd be after several thousand men had tramped along them. For both reasons, being in the vanguard meant being in a place of honour. Men wanted to be there.

Less honourable was the rearguard, which protected the supply train. The rattling wagons were slow-going on the best of days, and on the worst of days getting them through the landscape could be a nightmare.

Few sources give us the picture of the mundane moments of everything that was happening across this long stretch of men as it made its way through the countryside. What detail most accounts offer is typically confined to the exciting narrative bits like battles and sieges. Medieval people, much as we do, liked to skip the boring parts.

But there are exceptions.

In 1304, King Philippe IV of France marched out of Arras, headed to Flanders to pay back the Flemings for the disastrous French defeat at the battle of the Golden Spurs. Among the many lower officers in his army was a man from Orléans named Guillaume Guiart. Wounded a week before the campaign's climactic battle of Mons-en-Pévèle on 18 August, Guiart decided to become a poet: between 1306 and 1307 he composed *La Branche des royaus lingnages*, a massive verse history of the French kings from the birth of Philippe Augustus to 1306. It is 21,510 octosyllabic verses in length – not a work for the faint-hearted.

It *is*, however, a work in which Guiart describes the logistics of moving a massive army in 14th-century France. It's as close as we can get to knowing what life had been like for the men who were about to come together and fight at Crécy.

Guiart describes how the orders to march were passed throughout the city by town criers shouting the news. Reporting to those assigned companies through which they received their wages, the soldiers would 'pack the road tightly', the poet recalls, 'All of them following in an orderly manner / The marshals and their banner-bearers / Who go in the first position in front of the army.'[1] Company by company, it took the army all morning to funnel out of Arras: the men filled the roads as they marched, kept in order by the men-at-arms who moved alongside them on horseback, herding them like sheep. Guiart pays particular attention to the time spent in hitching wagons, harnessing horses, loading carts, and all the other logistical necessities of the army's supply train. Boring these parts might have been, but as a soldier he knew they were unquestionably essential to the army's survival.

Guiart doesn't get into the specific numbers, but even if a road could handle 20 men abreast – many roads couldn't – and we assumed that their marching lines were a mere five feet apart – which is awfully tight if they were carrying anything at all – then an army of 10,000 men would be over 2,500 feet long on the march. Philippe's army in 1346 was twice that. It would have stretched at least a mile long on the march. And that's the men alone. The line of wagons ran single file, adding an enormous amount of length.

Guiart describes the tremendous racket that the whole thing made as it stretched and bunched its way from one place towards another:

And you would hear the rattling of carts,
The neighing of horses and blaring of trumpets,
The boys, who could not keep quiet,
Shouting and singing with joy.
I would do well to praise this last thing,
For can there be troubles on the road
If the heart is raised in joy?
…
No man could be found who could count them
Nor even imagine such a number,
Not in length nor in width!
God! how the saddled charger,
That the boy leads on the right side,
Shakes so proudly!
And with escutcheons on the saddles,
Golden horse bits and seat pads,
And bells and harness straps
On all the chargers I'm talking about,
Which were leaving so joyously,
They made a melodious sound.
The clerics chant motets; the militia dance;
The aged ones beg; the carters quarrel;
Young women chat and joke;
Sergeants hiccup; heralds cry;
Wagons with big barrels rumble
Drums sound; horns trumpet loud;
Banners clatter and tremble;
Asses bray; horses neigh;
The arms of the armed make noise;
Scoundrels yell and boys argue.
All the surrounding country resounds
With the great din that they all make.[2]

There's a good chance that some armies – especially during the Middle Ages, when they were fixed to a ground-based perspective of the world – heard each other long before they saw each other.

Guiart also describes what happened when the army had to set an encampment in the field rather than the city. This is a good example of how the English had probably spent the night before the battle of Crécy:

> With shovels and buckets
> They deploy tents and pavilions,
> As if in strong houses and halls,
> Furnished with trunks and luggage.
> Those on foot who do not have revenues,
> Not a penny do they have for tents,
> So they search out the limbs of trees:
> There would you see little branches cut
> And the sergeants dragging these
> And bending them towards little saplings,
> To make lodges and lean-to shelters
> From the branches they have gathered up.[3]

The encampment he was in, Guiart says, spread out so far that the 'perimeter and enclosure' – likely the circled wagons of the supply train – enclosed 'more than a great league', around two and three-quarter miles. Inside that great ring were smoke-filled tents, men cheating each other at dice, and camp followers plying the soldiers with watered-down wine and cakes baked in makeshift ovens that they cut into the ditches along the sides of the road. And at the centre of it all were the tents of the king, ringed with guards to keep out the riff-raff and enemy spies.

* * *

Some of our early sources, like the *Chronicle of Artois*, say that Philippe was so anxious to get moving that he had tried to leave even before he had heard daily Mass[4] – that is, around the time Colins was probably waking up. If so, the vanguard formed up around the king in a hurry: Jean de Hainaut would have rushed to ride alongside him, along with the other kings and the commanders of the army.

Colins was surely with them. He was a member of Jean's retinue, but more importantly he was a herald: if they encountered any of the enemy – or a local lord come to join the French army – then his skills might be required.

Jean le Bel tells us that when the vanguard was about three leagues (eight and a quarter miles) out of the city, Philippe was met by scouts. Measuring this along the king's route following the road from Abbeville through Saint-Riquier – Jean Froissart specifically tells us that part of his army was lodged there[5] – this would mean the reports came around the time the king was just reaching the Chaussée Brunehaut. This was the Roman road that he hoped to use to move around the English and cut them off. Odds are that the scouts had been instructed to meet him at the junction, where the next course of action could be determined. They brought news that the English were only about four leagues (11 miles) away. More importantly, they weren't moving.

Philippe must have been thrilled. If the English continued to hold position, his plan would work: using the speed of the Roman road, he'd swing around them and prevent them from advancing up the Hesdin road. From the junction he sent a handful of men – including a Bohemian leader called the Monk of Basel[6] – on a ride cross-country to observe and report on Edward's deployment. Other riders spread the word of the enemy sighting down the long line of march.

The situation parallels something Guiart describes happening in 1304. After his march out of Arras had begun – the vanguard well out in front, the rest of the army still squeezing out onto the road – news came that the Flemings had seized a bridge ahead of the French and taken up positions to attack them there: as we've seen repeatedly, the controlling of roads, particularly where they create choke-points at wet-gap crossings, is an essential strategy in war.

> But one gave counsel to the king
> That, if he wished to do harm to them,
> They ought to search out another crossing;

At that place where their army is gathered up
He has no chance of defeating them,
The road is too difficult for them to attack.
For this reason the king decided, without delay,
To turn his army in a completely different direction.
The people who had already left Arras
Were stopped by a soldier,
Re-routed to the countryside of Fampoux.[7]

As scouts and messengers relayed information to and through a marching column whose length could be measured in miles, this kind of piecemeal re-routing was inevitable and expected.

It happened now, on the day of the battle of Crécy. It was the first in a sequence of disasters for the French.

The quickest route for the vanguard, at the junction with the Chaussée Brunehaut, was to ride up the Roman road through Noyelles-en-Chaussée. Not far beyond that town, though, a smaller route branched off that could get them to the Hesdin road even faster. It angled down the valley of the Maye on the Cassini map. It's the D56 today.

This was the king's route, but it wasn't everyone's route. Philippe had left Abbeville early. His own vanguard had been forced to play catch-up. And they were on horseback, while most of the army was on foot. As a result, enough of his forces were trailing far enough behind that they would be re-routed – just as commonplace as Guiart describes it – to follow a different road to reach the enemy: just under three and three-quarter miles back, a road branched off from Saint-Riquier, passing through Domvast towards the town of Crécy-en-Ponthieu. It's the D12 today, and in 1346 it met the Hesdin road near the corner of the Forest of Crécy, at Marcheville. Philippe's scouts had told them that this was where the English were waiting: on the Hesdin road just south of *that* intersection, next to the woods.

So the French army split. They would meet at the English. All the better to surround and destroy the enemy, some must have thought.

Philippe and the front of the line continued on until they reached the Hesdin road themselves. Though the track of that older road has since moved, it's still easy to find the junction on the D56: where the two roads met – where Philippe and his fellow kings and commanders next paused – is where the Cross of Bohemia stands today (Figure 21).

Here, they were met by the Monk and the other riders that the king had sent ahead to reconnoitre the enemy position. The French king's war-council – his fellow kings of Bohemia, Rome, and Majorca, along with counts, dukes, and others, including Jean de Hainaut – gathered together near the crossroads. They listened as the riders described how the English were only a single league (two and three-quarter miles) up the road from where they stood.[8]

EDWARD'S POSITION

What was before them, according to the men who had surveyed the English lines, was a fixed defensive position. It's illustrated as Figure 20. Edward had placed his army at the high ground where the Hesdin road passed alongside the Forest of Crécy. It's called today the Mont de Crécy – and presumably was called the same back then – but from the French approach it would be mostly gentle slopes overlaid with fertile fields. Where the road ran across the high ground, it split the mass of the Forest proper from a smaller wood clustered around a small hillock beside the valley of Domvast: what is today the Bois de But. Edward had centred his army in the space between these woods. In his chronicle written around 1350, Matthias von Neuenburg informs us that Edward, knowing he was pursued, 'crossed the forest in one day, establishing himself, as if hidden, for battle in the morning beside the forest'.[9]

And so he was.

The trees themselves were a natural impediment to attack on two flanks, but to protect himself still further, he closed off the spaces between the two woods with his wagons, which were likely turned over onto their sides – 'axle-poles raised high', as the Anonymous

Roman describes them – so that they formed a makeshift wooden wall. This kind of field fortification is called a *wagenburg*, and many historians have been hesitant to accept that Edward had placed himself inside one. So far as I can tell, they're worried that having one makes the English king seem weak.[10]

According to William of Dene's account, at least, he very much was: Edward was 'greatly exhausted', with 'all his army weary from the journey because they had eaten little for the two days prior'.[11] Dene calls it 'fasting', probably reflecting an early attempt to spin their lack of supplies into a spiritual cleansing. No matter the label, it was physically weakening. The time since Blanchetaque could still be counted in hours, and before that there had been a relentless march from Paris. The English were simply worn down.

So a wagenburg was absolutely the smart move as the French approached. It brought Edward an extra measure of support. It's no wonder our sources describe such a formation again and again – whether modern historians care to notice or not.[12]

Edward hadn't known exactly which road would bring Philippe at first, but as the day had passed his men were scouting the French approach just as surely as the French were scouting the English position. He would have surmised that he was facing two lines of approach: one directly up the road from Saint-Riquier through Domvast (this is the road moving from the bottom right towards the upper left on Figure 14), and the other down the Hesdin road (shown in green). Though we can assume that the woods were generally more extensive in 1346, it should be noted that the eastern corner of the Forest of Crécy was an exception. The Hesdin road here has been replaced by paved roads that meet further out in the plain, and the Forest has subsequently recovered part of the old road's route. The English left, therefore, was likely inside the line of the trees today, intended to cut off the road itself.

Facing the fields between these two approaches, Edward opened a gap in the front of his wagenburg. Giovanni Villani calls it an 'entrance gap'.[13] Jean le Bel describes the same thing: Edward ordered his men to build 'a large wagenburg in front of the forest of all his army's wagons and carts, through which there was only a single opening, and he put all his horses inside.'[14] Edward surrounded himself with wagons, Matthias von Neuenburg says, 'so that the French knights could not attack them in any other place than the foremost wing of the army' – this likely means the front of the position – and his archers protected this area.[15] The author of the *Chronicle of Normandy* adds that Edward was using other existing landscape features: 'the English were well shielded by their wagons and by strong hedges,' he writes.[16] The basic layout even reached Jakob Twinger, writing his *Chronicle of Strasburg* in the last decade of the century, who knew that the English had been near a forest and were 'surrounded with wagons and carts, so that the soldiers could only ride into it at one end'.[17] Adding further detail, Geoffrey le Baker says the English horses 'were kept back with the supplies', at the rear of the wagenburg.[18]

The Anonymous Roman says the formation resembled a horseshoe, and that on its 'weakest flank' Edward ordered his men to 'dig a deep ditch'.[19] This claim has been dismissed by many scholars, since Jean le Bel says that where the positions were made 'there had been neither ditch nor pit'.[20] But the tense of le Bel's observation – and the fact that he was making it at all – is a bit odd: it seems to imply that there *were* diggings of some sort on the field at the time of the battle, but they had not been there previously. It's a statement, in other words, that on scrutiny appears to be correcting the record against people who claimed that diggings had been in place before the English arrival. We'd be hard pressed, after all, to suggest that the English undertook no fieldwork at all: not only would neglecting such a basic act of battle preparation be disconnected from Edward's personality, but the fact that the English undertook at least *some* diggings is confirmed in the eyewitness account of Geoffrey le Baker. He observes that the first division of the English dug holes in front of them – 'the depth and width of a foot' – to help protect against cavalry charges.[21]

What the Anonymous Roman describes is clearly something different from small holes, though, and it warrants some discussion.

A walk on the fields today reveals a natural fold in the landscape, arcing from the north side of the Bois du But towards the Hesdin road. Edward, if he was taking position here, would certainly have used this natural seam to give his men a height over his enemy. Against French approaching up the Hesdin road, this advantage would be admittedly slight. But against those coming up the road from Domvast it presented a sharper, higher slope. This would be helpful to him, since the presence of the Bois du But here, while working to protect Edward's flank, also greatly veiled his ability to see down this road: it was the weakest point of the English defence (Figure 24).

Today, along a roughly 300-foot stretch of the natural fold, the foot of the slope has been dug out. It's a deep ditch – perhaps 30 feet wide and 16 feet deep – facing the weakest flank of the English position, just as the Anonymous Roman suggests. So perhaps the first division's little ankle holes weren't the only diggings, and Jean le Bel was correcting whispers that the ditchwork here was too substantial to have been made by the English and had already been there: to the contrary, he's saying, the English really had dug it.

It should be noted, though, that whatever the English dug here – *if* they dug here – it is assuredly *not* the same ditch we see today. Could 10,000 desperate men have dug such a large trench feature in the hours they had? Probably so. But whatever was there in 1346, I suspect that what we see four centuries later has been much altered by both soil erosion and further digging. Lime pits are particularly prominent in the region, and an existing depression in the landscape would be a logical place to engage in such work.

Even if we discard the ditch completely, the sharp rise in the landscape here is an essential feature on the terrain. Its heights are the fields locally called the Herse, and together with the northern edge of the Bois du But they overlook a depression in the fields beside today's ditch. This natural bowl is the Jardin de Génève on our maps.

In 1346, Edward would have had his wagons lining the high ground here: across the front edge of the Herse and then curving westwards to the Forest. It was a wide frontage to defend: today, about half a mile from one side of the wagenburg to another.

It's hard for us to imagine such a sight. Its very size makes such a scene seem impossible.

But remember: Edward had landed in Normandy with roughly 14,000 men. By the time of Crécy he'd lost some to battle, desertion, or illness. Estimating a 10 per cent loss to this point in the campaign – we can only guess – he had roughly 2,500 men-at-arms, 8,700 archers, and 2,700 various infantry. The Citizen of Valenciennes says that the king 'made only two divisions of archers, placed on his two sides in the manner of a chevron'.[22] They were also among the carts, as Villani and others describe.[23] Importantly, as Geoffrey le Baker points out, they were 'on the sides of the king's army like supporting wings' – meaning both in the carts and angling out ahead of them – so that 'they neither impeded their own men-at-arms nor attacked the enemy head-on, but instead struck like lightning into their flanks'.[24] The opening in the wagenburg, in other words, had no archers directly in front of it. They were all on the sides. And if we split them evenly, there were 4,350 of them to left and right. The armoury of the Tower of London had provided them all with at most 40 arrows each at the start of the campaign beyond what they had themselves. How many they had now, we don't know. They had expended many – the French had already faced massed volleys of arrows at Caen, at Poissy, at Oisement, and even at Blanchetaque – but fletchers had surely managed to manufacture more along the way using seized French supplies. Even so, the arrows weren't an unlimited resource. They couldn't, as Hollywood likes to imagine such things, endlessly darken the sky with the killing shafts.[25]

As for the rest of the English forces, they began the battle dismounted, and they were formed up into three divisions. Our sources lack the kind of granular detail to enable us to know their exact sizes, but an even split would give each roughly 1,700 men. The prince of Wales was placed in charge of the first division – along with Sir Godfrey de Harcourt and the earls of

Warwick, Stanford, and Kent, who Jean le Bel says were there to 'guard' the young man.[26] All of them would have had banners announcing their presence. This line arrayed across the opening in the wagenburg. The frontage of this division, and thereby the width of the opening itself, depends on how far apart the men stood from one another, and how many ranks deep they were. Re-enactors have shown that Vikings in formation took up two to three feet of lateral space per man, but this was in the making of a shield-wall, a formation that demanded overlapping shields and the tightest packing possible. The warfare of the 14th century was very different, with weapons typically demanding more room for manoeuvrability. Let's assume an average of five feet per man on the field. Lined side by side, they would stretch 8,500 feet, but in combat they would be lined up some number of ranks deep, likely offset so that each man stood looking through the gap of the two men in front of him.

But how many ranks deep?

At the battle of Agincourt in 1415, Henry V deployed his forces in a line only four ranks deep, but our sources suggest that this was an abnormally thin formation. No such statement is made of Edward's line at Crécy. Let's assume, then, that his first division, standing across the opening of the wagenburg, was eight ranks deep. With 1700 men, and an average of five feet per man, we're looking at an opening just over 1,000 feet wide. This is all admittedly guesswork, but it seems reasonable enough.

The second division was just inside the wagenburg. The earls of Northampton and Suffolk were there, along with the bishop of Durham. The *Chronicle of Saint-Omer* suggests that they were 'drawn from one end to the other and had a great hedge of their carts so that one could not see their rear'.[27] The third division was 'in the rearguard and protected the tents and baggage' – likely on the south side of the English position, at least to some degree watching the Hesdin road as it ran along the Forest towards Abbeville. There was always the chance that the French could send forces converging in that direction, too.

Some of our sources suggest that the king himself was in the second division, while others say the third. The discrepancy, I suspect, is due to the fact that he was with the third division instead of the second, where he would be expected to be. As le Bel says, his division 'ought to have been between' the other two.[28] His second division in terms of command, in other words, was in the third position from the front of the fight, making it the third division of battle.

It wasn't cowardice that had sent him into the rear. It was the need to maintain command and control. Several sources describe a windmill within the English position, from which Edward watched much of the battle. Doing so would be a tremendous advantage for a military commander, since it would allow a 'bird's eye' view of the action. Such a windmill was probably one of the reasons people were drawn to associate the battle with the traditional site above Crécy-en-Ponthieu: there was once a prominent stone windmill there (see Figure 23). One has to say, though, that the stone windmill was really in the wrong place: if the king was with the third division from the front, the windmill ought to be towards the back of the field. Yet the traditional site would put this windmill near or even *at* the English front. The alternative site on the Rondel also had a windmill, as Cassini's map shows, and it would have been within the English wagenburg. Even better, it was in the rear of the position, where the king's second-turned-third division ought to be. From the height of its top, Edward would have had excellent sight lines onto the field of battle beyond, through what Villani calls 'the narrow, tight fighting area as wide as the opening of the wagenburg'.[29]

Edward's scouts had done their work well. The same tactics they had used against the Scots at Dupplin Moor and Halidon Hill – the same ones he had tried to use against Philippe when they had nearly fought in 1339 – would work perfectly on this field in northern France. The archers, protected by the woods and the wagenburg, would funnel the enemy into the opening at the centre of the horseshoe. There, the Black Prince and the first division stood dismounted, their banners beckoning the French to come to blows.

WHO ORDERED THE ATTACK?

When the commanders who had surveyed the English position described it to the French commanders at the crossroads on the Hesdin road to the north, a debate began. Minute by minute the stretched inchworm of their extended march was drawing itself up towards the enemy position by two roads, but the shadows were already long – Jean le Bel says it was already the hour of Nones, around 3pm.[30] The experienced leaders all knew that gathering and organizing the full array of 20,000 men could take many hours longer. The men of the militias, a large part of his army, were still in the rear of the march, according to the *Chronicle of Normandy*.[31] The last of them were probably still miles away.

Philippe pressed the Monk of Basel for his honest opinion, because he'd seen the enemy position first-hand. Reluctantly, the Monk said that he thought it unwise to attack such a prepared position given the late hour. Better to wait until the morning. Jean de Hainaut agreed. Philippe, he said, should head up the Hesdin road – along the ridge that the *vulgato* would have the king insensibly charging down from – to reach comfortable lodgings at the castle in Labroye. Others urged the king to fight here and now, to put an end to the damnable English this very hour.

We know the result of the debate: the French attacked.

We know the result of the attack: the French lost.

How we understand that loss depends on what we understand about what happened in that meeting, and this depends on whose story we listen to. Because while all our sources are in one sense equal – even the least of them could be telling us vital and accurate information – they are by no means all in agreement. And we don't approach them all with a clean slate. Some of our sources have been proven reliable and dependable: again and again the stories they've told us have connected up with the other sources of information we have. They have been proven 'true' – insofar as we can get to that. That doesn't mean that we know they're telling it straight *this* time, of course, but it means we're generally willing to trust them until proven otherwise.

But then there are other sources that we're *really* wary of. It might be that they've been proven wrong time and time again. It might be that they're quite distant in time or space from what we're looking at, and we're worried about how much information has shifted along the relay points between them. It might be that while they're trustworthy about most things, we know that in this instance they've very much got an axe to grind. One way or another, we don't want to rely on them incautiously.

It would still be good, though, to account for them. Just as we have to remember that our reliable person could get it wrong once in a while, we also have to remember that our unreliable person could get it right once in a while.

To put this in concrete terms here: we have a vast array of sources for the battle of Crécy. Among my first steps has to been to analyse this pool of data – the origin, biases, and dependability of each source – in order to find the ones that are most likely to be reliable. In formulating an initial hypothesis for what happened, I began with these voices. It was a gamble, but from an objective position it was the best bet to start with. Having acquired my working theory using our strongest sources, I could then refine it in the hope that, in its application, this theory would work with even our weakest sources. In the end, the historian is in the position of being like your favourite detective, checking the stories that her witnesses give her, patiently and methodically, to find the truth that explains what everyone said – including the person who was lying. I've cited Jean le Bel a lot in this book so far because, as near as anyone can tell, he's pretty damn reliable. So is Gilles li Muisit.

Which makes this moment in our story a problem:

Jean le Bel's source was Jean de Hainaut, who was there. He apparently told le Bel that Philippe had agreed with the advice of the Monk of Basel to attack the next morning, but 'none of the lords wished to turn back, and some who were in the front did not wish to return, because that act seemed to them to be dishonorable'.[32] The impetuous, glory-hungry lords pushed forward despite the king's wishes.

Gilles li Muisit's source was also Hainaut. But he apparently told li Muisit the complete opposite story from the one he gave le Bel: this time, it was Philippe who 'called his troops to arms', and he did so against the opinions of his gathered lords.[33]

Both explanations can't be true. Was one of the stories, despite what the two writers tell us, not coming from Jean de Hainaut? Had Hainaut not remembered it clearly? Had he lied to one of them? Or both of them?

Taking a broader look at our sources doesn't seem to help much. A number of sources agree with li Muisit that Philippe was the problem. The Citizen of Valenciennes says that Philippe 'wished to fight since he saw his enemies'. His lords didn't, but this wasn't a democracy. 'Sire, do what you want,' Jean de Hainaut replied, 'we will follow you.'[34]

But agreeing with le Bel, the chronicler Francis of Prague insists that Philippe was absolutely willing to hold back, but then King John of Bohemia, 'with his son, the Roman emperor-elect, powerfully took control of the gathering battle-lines' and led them forward.[35] Beneš Krabice tells the same tale in his *Chronicle of the Church of Prague*, so clearly a story blaming the dead king had gone back home with news of his death.[36] Was this story the true one? Or maybe it was meant to cast John in a bad light? Or, on the flip side, to show how positively driven the man was, even unto the end? For that matter, perhaps the story being told in Prague had nothing to do with the dead king and everything to do with the local politics surrounding his son and heir.

The story that reached the Anonymous Roman adds nuance to this 'blame Bohemia' narrative: when the English formation was described to him, the experienced-but-blind king said it would be 'impossible to defeat the English without suffering great damage ourselves'. He advised caution. In response, Philippe loudly expressed his disappointment that such a living legend of a warrior would shy from battle. Insulted and enraged, Bohemia insisted that there would be a fight, and that he himself would lead the charge.[37]

As for that, though, there is disagreement across the sources about how many French divisions went into battle and how they were ordered. The anonymous *Prose Brut* says there were four French divisions.[38] Pseudo-Murimuth says the French had seven.[39] The *Eulogium Historiarum* says it was eight.[40] Geoffrey le Baker says there were nine divisions, but matches with the Anonymous Roman's story that the king of Bohemia demanded control of the attack by putting him in the first division.[41] The Anonymous Roman, describing the actual divisions, says there were nine, but that the Genoese were in the first division; Bohemia was in the ninth.[42] The Citizen of Valenciennes also has nine divisions and the Genoese in the first, but he puts Bohemia in the third.[43] Perhaps, as Matthias von Neuenburg says, Philippe wouldn't allow Bohemia and his German troops the honour of going in front. The glory would belong to his French.[44] It may be that all the inconsistency is because of the fact that the army was still streaming in along the roads. Three divisions could be formed up immediately. A fourth shortly thereafter. And so on. But even so, the stories literally don't add up.

That we don't know for certain who ordered the attack – much less the shape and sequence of it – is frustrating, but it's also a clue in its own right. At a most basic level, clearly no one was anxious to take responsibility for such a catastrophic decision. It's human nature. As the saying goes, the more things change, the more they stay the same.

More importantly, though, the fact that people couldn't even agree on the number of divisions points to an army that was in significant confusion and disarray. This was probably the biggest problem that the French faced. It's also the most important thing for any military leader to maintain and the reason Edward would have been up in the mill: command and control.

No matter who they say ordered the charge, our sources speak with one voice that, in the event, there was no order. The writer of the *Chronicle of the First Four Valois Kings* reports that the French were still trying to put themselves into ranks when their mounts began to be cut down beneath them: 'Through haste and disorder the French were defeated.'[45]

Disordered they might have been, but they also would have been astonishing to behold – both for their numbers and for their finery. Jean Froissart describes them riding 'towards [their] enemies, [their] banners unfurled. It was a great sight so see these lords nobly mounted and prepared for battle, fully fitted out, with flowing banners, contingent after contingent in endless succession riding through the fields.'[46] The nobles among them were so confident that they were already boasting and making claims about which of the great lords of England they would claim for ransom. From what le Baker tells us, some of the foremost commanders were doing the same: the king of Majorca, he says, had called dibs on the king of England.[47] As a result of this, Philippe ordered the raising of the Oriflamme standard. By tradition, the raising of this flag upon the battlefield signalled that no quarter would be given, no prisoners would be taken.

Kill them all.

THE GENOESE DISASTER

The fighting began as the sun got low in the sky, according to both Geoffrey le Baker and Jean le Bel.[48]

It was at that point that the Genoese crossbowmen – a couple of thousand mercenaries, all on foot – marched forward at the English lines. Our sources are entirely consistent about this. They are also entirely consistent that the French came to the battle in complete disarray.

On the traditional site, this combination doesn't make sense. If the lines were coming to the field in a disorganized fashion, then for the Genoese crossbowmen to be the first lines into the battle they would have needed to be the first ones to get there.

But the Genoese were on foot.

There is no way they would beat the entirety of the vanguard – cavalry all – to the field.

Only the author of the *Chronicle of the Low Countries*, written around 1395, seems to sense that this might be a problem. He suggests that the Genoese were acting as part of the king's bodyguard, which would at least give them a reason to be near the front.[49] But why would Philippe be guarded by mercenary crossbowmen? They weren't a quick-response force. For that matter, they weren't even a tremendously useful first-response force. Crossbows pack a tremendous punch and require little training to operate – certainly relative to the longbow – but they're remarkably slow to load. Worse, the loading of them is essentially a full-body endeavour. When you're loading a crossbow, you're a sitting duck for the enemy.

The Genoese crossbowmen were thus a great fit for a fixed defence where they could move in and out of exposed points of fire as they loosed and loaded their crossbows. A field offence would be nothing like this.

The Genoese obviously knew this weakness. For this reason they had armour and large shields, called *pavises*, behind which they could find protection while they loaded their weapons. On the day of the battle – the day they were needed – these pavises were on wagons at the rear of the army. Worse, says the *Chronicle of the Low Countries*, they didn't even have their armour.[50] These deficiencies will be important when it comes to what happened to these men, but let's not get ahead of ourselves. For now, let's keep an eye on what we're being asked to believe at the start.

The Genoese were hired by Philippe to wage war at sea. We have their contracts.[51] But when the war had come to his lands, Philippe had summoned them into his army. He had subsequently used them for fixed-point defence – they defended the bridges along the Seine, for instance. But now, when it came to the march to the great battle, we're supposed to accept that Philippe had decided to use them as his personal guard. Trying to keep up with him and the others on horseback, they would be jogging themselves to exhaustion. And if they ran into anyone, they wouldn't have the key piece of equipment that they needed to be effective fighters by any stretch of the imagination.

Nevertheless, nearing the end of the day, the king threw them into the battle first. And when they failed – inevitably, one might say – he and his lords purposely set about running them over.

None of this makes sense.

In calling them the king's guard, the *Chronicle of the Low Countries* was likely trying to make sense of something that's nonsense. Just as we are.

Thankfully, there's a relatively easy fix to all this.

The Genoese weren't at the front of the whole army with Philippe. They honestly wouldn't have much use up there, and they couldn't have kept up even if they did. Instead, they were much further back in the column. Quite sensibly, they were closer to their pavises, which were on the carts in back. When the back portion of the marching column was re-routed at Saint-Riquier, however, they became the front of *that* part of the army that was marching up the road past Domvast.

As they came out of the valley, rising up towards the Rondel, the Genoese would have seen the English close on their left side: past the Bois du But and atop the Herse, rising above what would become the Jardin de Génève. From the Genoese perspective, it would have looked like a line of wagons at the end of a slight rise. There were some archers on the wagons, but there were far more of the Genoese crossbowmen. The shortest of walks and they could go at them.

It may be that seeing the enemy – right *there* – they simply decided to go in. But I think instead that Philippe, trying to create a plan on the fly, saw them arriving on his left and threw them forward. The idea would be to have them loose a few rounds of crossbow bolts into the enemy, before sending a punishing charge of his mounted knights against the cowering English defence. They'd blow open the weak side of the English wagenburg.

Nothing like this happened, because no one on the French side could see the bowl that the Genoese were marching into (Figure 25).

And no one could see the wing of English archers who were extended out through the Bois du But, perfectly flanking the Genoese approach. The crossbowmen marched forward. When they were in range of the English lines, they stopped and raised their loaded weapons.

They launched a volley.

The English archers ducked behind the wagons, and the Genoese bolts pummelled the wood. A few found flesh, but not many (Figure 26).

Philippe has a poor reputation in military annals, much of it due to his terrible defeat at Crécy. The traditional location only serves to blacken his reputation further: to send his forces into such obvious slaughter, Philippe – and every advisor in his service – would have had to be a fool. Yet the dead at the battle included the flower of French knighthood, as English sources are so keen to remind us. These were not debutantes at war. It's far more likely that Philippe and his advisors had good reason to be confident of victory at this moment. In what was essentially a race to cross the Maye, Philippe had won. Edward was trapped and had nowhere to go.

But Philippe was about to make his first clear mistake. We can see it in hindsight, but it should be said that on the field that evening things were far less clear. All he knew in that moment was that the Genoese had shot and there had been no response. The English had been silenced. The time to strike was now.

And so his first line of cavalry started forward.

The crossbowmen were meanwhile trying to reload their weapons for another volley. It was no simple task. First, the crossbowman would lift his weapon so that he could connect the 'bowstring' to a metal hook hanging from his belt. Next, he'd lift one foot into a stirrup at the front of the crossbow. Then, by stepping down while keeping his body upright, he'd push the bow forward while pulling the bowstring back: when it locked into place, he could pull it off his foot and the hook, load it with a bolt, and then prepare to launch it at the enemy (Figure 22).

Under the best of circumstances, this process took time. But according to our sources, it had just rained.

This rain, many of them explain, made the crossbows unusable because it shrank their strings and made them too tight to fire – whereas the English archers had unstrung their longbows and tucked the strings under their hats to keep them dry.[52]

This is hogwash.

It's a story that resulted from the best effort of battle-ignorant writers trying to make sense of the tales they'd heard: there were key differences between the longbows and the crossbows at Crécy, and it had something to do with the rain that had fallen.

The problem is, bowstrings don't get tighter when they're wet. They get *looser*. And no one was taking their bows apart on a field of battle regardless.

What *is* true is that the loading of a medieval crossbow of the period required balance on one foot, and this was much harder to manage on muddy ground. The Anonymous Roman captures the problem exactly:

> the Genoese were unable to shoot, because they were unable to load their bows. There had been a shower of rain and the soil was damp, so when the Genoese tried to load their weapons by putting a foot in the stirrup, the foot slipped and they could not plant it on the ground.[53]

Adding insult to injury, the longbows of the English had greater range than the crossbows of the French.

So as the Genoese struggled to reload in the muddy bowl of the Jardin de Génève – in the open, without the protection of their pavises – the archers at the wagons stood and took aim. What's more, the archers hidden in the wing along the brushy woods to their side did the same: the author of the *Chronicle of Flanders* says that 'the English shot their arrows and were very well shielded by the wagons and the hedges and the wood'.[54] The *Chronicle of the First Four Valois Kings* agrees: 'the English archers lay first in ambush in the hedges'.[55]

The slaughter began.

The Genoese caught in the bowl of the Jardin de Génève fell in great numbers, shot from the Herse and the Bois du But. They couldn't reload. They couldn't defend themselves. They were, as an eyewitness poet wrote, 'entirely useless'.[56] As Gilles li Muisit says, 'the English shot with such speed and in such numbers, that they were not able to defend against them'.[57] Each crossbow shot,

Giovanni Villani concurs, 'would be answered by three arrows from their bows, which formed a storm cloud in the sky'.[58] Death rained down.

Unprotected and unable to return fire effectively, the Genoese routed in panic – straight into the first line of the cavalry who were already charging towards the 'softened' English flank.

As Jean le Bel describes it:

> All the professional soldiers and Genoese were defeated, and they were finished and wanted to flee; but the divisions of the great lords were [so] exalting one on top of the other for envy that they did not wait, not one of them, but they charged, all in chaos and entangled without any order, so that they closed in on the professional soldiers and Genoese between themselves and the English; because there was nothing those men could do, they fell under the horses' hooves.[59]

The Genoese were trampled. As arrows struck the horses, they added their own horrible screams to the sounds of death. In wild terror, men were thrown in the tumult. And still more arrows hurtled in.

Geoffrey le Baker says that the French across the field heard the sounds of the dying, but it wasn't understood: 'From among these foot soldiers being trampled by the massive horses there arose a great wail of lamentation, which those in the rear of the French army thought came from dying Englishmen. As a result, each Frenchman pushed forward against the man in front.'[60]

According to Giovanni Villani, the English suddenly set off several small cannons they had here and there among the wagons: 'so loud and threatening that it seemed God himself was thundering, with great killing of men and gutting of horses'.[61] More French, still thinking the screams were dying English, kept coming, even as the ground was littered with their own dead.

The gunpowder weapons at Crécy have been a source of much confusion for interpreters of the battle. Sometimes their presence is ignored. Sometimes their role is overstated. Most historians have associated these cannons on the Crécy campaign with 100 'small engines called ribalds' that were ordered from the Tower Armoury in 1345, but Thom Richardson has shown that these were 'wheeled carts, made of wood and fitted with ten spears each lashed on with rope'.[62] They had no connection at all to Edward's artillery.

Our sources themselves provide only a little information on what the king specifically used at Crécy. The *Grand Chronicles* tell us that there were three artillery pieces on the English side; Jean Froissart says there were only two.[63] Froissart specifically names them 'bombards', as does Villani and another contemporary Italian source, the *Pistoian History*.[64] One thing we can be sure of, though, is that they weren't the large-scale anti-fortification weapons that we tend to call 'bombards' today: the use of artillery was still new enough to European warfare that the vocabulary used to describe it remained unsettled. Instead, the artillery pieces at Crécy were small, likely hand-cannons (Figure 27). When Edward later received ten guns from the Royal Armoury for his siege of Calais, eight of them were probably of this same type. The two 'large' ones remaining were probably descended from a small, vase-shaped cannon depicted in an illustration from 1326 (also Figure 27). That early weapon mainly shot bolts, but unlike the Roman ballistas that had come before it, it also belched fire and smoke. Villani says that the ones used at Crécy 20 years later shot 'small iron balls', but the weapon's sensory effects were very much unchanged: they were fired specifically to 'frighten the French horses and cause them to bolt'.[65]

The Genoese who had managed to survive the horror to this point still tried to retreat, but when the next waves of French rolling into the fray 'saw them turn and abandon the battle, they deemed the retreat treason, and they attacked them and killed many'.[66] The *Chronicle of Flanders* doesn't ascribe this accusation to anyone in particular, but other sources, like the *Grand Chronicles*, lay it at the feet of Philippe himself.[67] Froissart even has the king giving a dramatic declaration: 'Kill them! Kill these bastards! They are worth nothing in battle!'[68]

Many writers have suggested that this murderous action occurred the moment that the Genoese tried to pull back from the English arrows. But *if* there was any such order – I remain unsure – it can only have been after the surviving Genoese had at last peeled their way out of the fray. Any notion that the king would throw away the lives of his cavalry – which is what he'd be doing by throwing them into the deadly scrum to run down the Genoese on the mere *suspicion* of treason – is plainly nonsense. Run down in a side-action? Maybe. But it also could be that our sources are conflating two separate events. The retreat of the Genoese on the battlefield had done enormous damage to the French side, and in the days afterwards rumours swirled that their actions had been deliberate and treacherous in nature. The Genoese became scapegoats. This would certainly be more reasonable than a murderous order from the king in the midst of the action on the battlefield. It would also match what Edward was hearing. In a letter written on 3 September he passed along rumours that Philippe, 'after the defeat, went to Amiens, where he had a great number of the Genoese killed, for he said that they had betrayed him in his time of need'.[69] If he had heard anything about the French king slaughtering his own men *during* the battle, he surely would have mentioned as much: it would fit his narrative that Philippe was an enemy of his own people.

At any rate, we can be sure of the Genoese retreat into their own advancing lines. We can be sure of the horrifying pile-up as the French – arriving on the field by two roads in anxious disarray – kept coming forward into an ever-worsening press that made for ever more inviting targets. 'The Genoese tried everything in order to withdraw from the crush,' Froissart writes, while 'those on horseback could not retreat because of the great and impenetrable line of men-at-arms and horses behind them.'[70] In the confusion, it must have seemed as if the French were in a hurry to die.

Edward had been watching it all unfold from high atop the windmill near the English third line. He watched the arrows of his men rise and fall. He heard the screaming ahead of the Genoese and the cheers of his archers. He saw the panic of those trying to flee, the swirling dust of cavalry lines in chaos at that right side of his line.

Forced to stand and fight, Edward had perfectly matched his tactics to the terrain. He had already baited the French into a tragic sequence of assaults on his hastily constructed but remarkably effective field fortification. He was outfoxing his French adversary by the simple measure of being organized and in control.

He had no way to know that he was about to come to the edge of defeat.

Not just in this battle, but in the entire war.

THE BLACK PRINCE CAPTURED

At some point, the French king was able to piece together the horrific failure of the attempt on the English right. He responded by throwing his men against the entirety of the English line. If he couldn't destroy his enemies with a targeted tactical strike, he'd overwhelm them with sheer force of numbers. 'The princes and barons with their cavalry and men-at-arms approached the English lines,' Gilles li Muisit says, and 'they began to fight and war at different places'.[71] This wasn't mercenaries or militias of common men. This was the litany of lords who'd come to the fight. 'The flower of the whole knighthood of France', as Richard Wynkeley described it a few days later.[72]

The English position was built in expectation of exactly this kind of attack. Edward and his commanders knew they were outnumbered at least by two to one. If they were going to have any chance to succeed against those odds, it would be by negating that advantage. The wagenburg and the archers – both those upon it and those in the wings extending out from it – were designed to receive a wide frontal assault and funnel it, collapsing and constraining the enemy until they were only as wide as it suited Edward for them to be. That width was the width of the opening in his wagenburg: the width of his first division. The prince of Wales was there, and one wonders at his thoughts as he stood there, the lines of the French careening towards him on horseback. He wasn't yet the vaunted Black Prince. He was a 16-year-old young man. He'd been trained to fight. He knew the ways of war. But knowing a thing and doing it were two very different things.

The English archers loosed at the enemy charging him. Their arrows buzzed in angry swarms from left and right, swiping into the French flanks, forcing them to compress inward. The lines trembled as horses stumbled and men were thrown to the ground where others stepped and stumbled over them. The English cannons thundered with smoke. More and more riders were going down. Bodies were piling up. The left wing of archers might well have advanced to close their range: 'the English archers came down from the ridge into the wheat,' the Anonymous Roman writes, 'constantly shooting arrows into the men-at-arms, drawing their bows and releasing – Da, da, da – and putting all in peril. On the right flank [of the French] they cut down the horses, thinning the enemy ranks, the wounded retreating and the horses dead.'[73] Jean le Bel describes the chaos:

> And the other side's archers shot so marvelously that the horses, feeling the barbed arrows, which did marvels, did not want to advance: some rode against others as if deranged, others bucked dreadfully, others turned their backs to their enemies, despite their masters, because of the arrows that they felt, and others let their masters fall, because they were unable to do anything else. And the English lords standing on foot advanced and fell upon the men who were not able to deal with their horses.[74]

There's reason to think the French never reached the English lines. Geoffrey le Baker had said that the first division, with the prince of Wales in command, had dug ankle-pits to stop a cavalry charge if it came close, but this 'did not happen'.[75] It didn't happen, it seems, because at this point, seeing their enemy going down in heaps before them, the first division of the English abandoned their position and advanced.

This cannot have been a part of Edward's battle plan, which was built around patience, a prepared position, and superior tactical control … all of which was lost the moment the first division moved out into field. The opening in the wagenburg was now unguarded. The archers, who'd been destroying the French, couldn't shoot into the mass for fear of hitting their own men. And melee combat – what the English were advancing into – was the very definition of chaos.

Advancing was just about the worst thing the first division could have done short of dropping their weapons and turning in flight.

And it was done under the prince's command.

Why they went forward, we can only guess. A reasonable assumption is that the sight of so many French lords going down was just too much of a temptation to decline. Whether it was greed or bloodlust or simply a case of being unable to hold their water, the result was the same: a broken formation and a broken English plan.

Seeing the banners of the prince of Wales and the other English lords moving out to engage on foot, the French lords who hadn't yet gone forward saw the chance of a lifetime. They drove into the press, all angling for a shot at the crown prince.

It's hard to imagine what it was like in the minutes that followed. Colins de Beaumont feared he had no words to describe what he saw of the 'lords in the fray': banners were 'trampled' as their ranks broke 'in the plain, / Shields and helmets cast upon / The ground, lords perishing'.[76]

The Chandos Herald, as we'd expect, speaks of the total glory of the prince of Wales in the face of all this violence:

> On that day there was a battle
> So horrible that, without fail,
> There never was a man so hardy
> That he would not have been astounded by it.
> He who saw the great power
> And the force of the king of France,
> A great marvel he would have to tell!
> Seized by hatred and wrath
> They came together into the encounter,
> And having been bred to master arms

They did so very chivalrously,
So that not since the Advent
Did a man behold a more fierce battle.
There was seen many a banner
Finely worked of gold and of silk.
And there so help me true God,
The English were all on foot,
As those who were ready
And most eager to fight.
There was the good Prince himself,
Who in the vanguard, as befits a man,
So valiantly acquitted himself
That it was a marvel to see;
Little did he allow the attack
Of any man, no matter how hardy or bold.[77]

This was the party line in England, and it would become one of the great stories of the battle. Production of the myth started early. Geoffrey le Baker, able to look back at the battle through the lens of what the Black Prince would become, is engrossed by his magnificence:

Fighting the English men-at-arms, the French were cut down by axes, spears, and swords, and in the middle of the French army many were by the weight of the crowd crushed to death without any wound. In this dire meeting of the lines the bold Edward of Woodstock, the firstborn of the king, who was then sixteen years of age, showed his admirable valor to the French as he led the first line, piercing destriers, unhorsing riders, shattering helmets, breaking spears, skillfully evading blows aimed against him, supporting his men, defending himself, lifting fallen friends to their feet, and exhibiting an example to all of performing well; nor did he rest from such labors until the enemy retreated behind the rampart of dead men... These ceaseless attacks kept the Prince and those standing with him so engaged that he was compelled to fight from his knees against the great bulk of the enemy all around him. Then someone ran or rode to his father the king and, seeking help, pointed out the danger to his firstborn son; he was sent back with twenty men-at-arms to help the prince, and he found him and his men leaning on spears and swords, recovering their breath and resting quietly on long mounds of corpses, expecting the enemy's return. Thus from the setting of the sun the grim face of Mars was shown again and again to the third quarter of the night. Three times across these hours the French sounded the battle-cry, fifteen times they attacked, but at last they fled defeated.[78]

Froissart added still more flavour to the tale, minimizing the danger while removing the suggestion that *any* reinforcements were sent. In so doing, he memorialized the popular myth of the Black Prince at Crécy. Here it is from his abridged chronicle:

That evening neither the king of England nor any of his battalion descended from their windmill mount, however fierce the fighting became. Instead, the Prince and his battalion as well as the second battalion, which was in reserve and which came to their rescue, did all the fighting on that Saturday. I was told that some knights, to whom the king had entrusted the Prince, came to him because they feared the Prince was in danger, as his battalion was wavering under the assault of an increasing number of soldiers and knights who were attacking. They said to the king and his knights: 'Sir, send your battalion forward and come to the rescue of your son! He is being overwhelmed!' The king replied: 'Is my son the Prince so heavily attacked or is he so badly wounded that he cannot help himself?' 'No, sir,' they said, 'but he is being kept very busy.' The king then said: 'Return to him and do not come back to me today asking for help for whatever reason as long as he is not in mortal danger. Let the young man earn his spurs! This battle belongs to him and I don't want anything to detract from that.'[79]

It's easy to understand why pro-English writers would want to tout such a tale. It's superiority all the way down.

Step outside the English bubble, though, and things start to look very different. The *Chronicle of Normandy* plainly states that the prince advanced 'so far that it was said that the count of Flanders captured the Prince of Wales, but he was rescued quickly'.[80] The *Chronicle of the Low Countries* likewise reports that the prince was 'captured by the count of Flanders'.[81] The Citizen of Valenciennes claims that the prince was 'put on his knees twice, and Sir Richard FitzSimon, who carried his banner, took the banner and put it under his feet and went himself to protect and rescue his master.'[82] For a medieval knight to kneel with his banner at his feet was to do nothing less than surrender. FitzSimon had laid the banner down beside the prince in order to protect him: this is the prince, he was saying, take him for ransom, not death.

That banner, Colins de Beaumont tells us, was actually seized by the count of Blois, who was dismounted in the press 'with a meager retinue of men':

> There was his sword bathed in blood;
> There I saw him bleeding and wounded,
> Going on, fighting on foot,
> Always ahead without turning back,
> Until he brought the standard
> Of the Prince of Wales all the way to the ground
> And held it in his arms
> As he died. Lord, what valor![83]

The Anonymous Roman tells a significantly more complicated story, in which a count supposedly named Valentino 'saw his chance of hooking a large fish' and took control of the prince of Wales. But as Valentino, on horseback, was dragging the young man off the field, Philippe's brother, the count of Alençon, saw him. Aghast that Valentino should take a prisoner so far above his station – Valentino's position as a lesser noble might well explain why he is otherwise unheard of – he struck him with a mace and killed him. In the confusion, the prince took horse and rode back to the safety of the English lines. The count of Flanders, meanwhile, had witnessed it all, and he upbraided his countryman: 'Count Alençon, this is not the loyalty or respect you owe to the crown. The war was won and you lost it.'[84] Alençon, furious to be called out, now killed the count of Flanders with his already bloodied mace. At that point, a low-ranked retainer of Flanders attacked the murderous count, running him through with his sword.

Many of the details here don't fit with other sources: the Anonymous Roman stands alone in suggesting that the prince escaped on his own; everyone else has him needing to be rescued. And no other source records the deaths of Alençon and Flanders by 'friendly fire'. For that matter, most say that it was Flanders who captured the prince, not the otherwise unknown 'Valentino'.[85] This tale is suspect, to say the least. But the threat that the story relays through the voice of the count of Flanders is absolutely right. Had the French succeeded in seizing the prince of Wales, they could have extracted from the English the terms to end the battle – and likely a king's ransom, to boot. For the few minutes that the prince was in their hands, it's not an exaggeration to say that the French had potentially won the Hundred Years War.

The English knew the danger. Hints of it are in the English sources, though it's always muted. The *Anonimalle Chronicle* says 'the prince fought strongly and vigorously and endured heavy and punishing blows' until he was 'wounded and almost taken or defeated', but he was saved by 'the bishop of Durham, the earl of Suffolk, and the earl of Huntingdon and their men'.[86] And of course it was this peril that had sent panicked runners to the king in his windmill.

Did the king really respond with a haughty dismissal, so confident that his lad would earn his spurs that he wouldn't even deign to leave his windmill – even though the war could hang in the balance?

Not according to many of our sources. The *Chronicle of Flanders* plainly states that Edward left his wagons and charged out at the very point that the prince 'was captured by the count of Flanders'.[87] Giovanni Villani relates even more detail: as the French pressed forward, the prince and the others out front were pushed 'back against the wagenburg. The English would have been defeated had not King Edward devised an able manoeuvre, as he came out through an opening he ordered made among the carts, allowing him to swing round the enemy and attack him from the rear, coming to his men's relief by hitting the enemy hard in the flank.'[88] This was a destructive blow, as it only caused more of the French to mass up together, 'so that they piled one horse on top of the other, thus resembling what happened with the Flemings at Kortrijk [in the battle of the Golden Spurs]. In particular, they were impeded by the dead Genoese of the first division lying on the ground.'

Villani's association of this action with the Genoese dead would indicate that the fighting had been pushed south-east along the field towards the English right. This would make sense: *men move like water*, and this was downhill.

Where was the opening that the king made in the wagenburg at this point? There are three immediate possibilities. The first would be that it was somewhere on the line overlooking the Jardin de Génève itself, perhaps around the point where it met the Bois du But, close to where the Rue du Mont de Forêt rises up onto the Herse today. The second would be on the backside of the English formation beside the windmill, where the king's third division was located. If this was the move, then Edward's panic is underscored by the steepness of the slope down which he would have ridden into the Domvast valley: reasonable for an experienced rider, but certainly not for the weak of heart. A plan to ride down this slope in order to take the Domvast road around the Bois du But and directly into the French backfield would be a desperate one. And, as it happens, this very slope is labelled *Plant de la Folie* [meaning either The Foolish Plan or the The Foolish Plantation] on our earliest maps. The third possibility is the one I favour: an opening was made on the English left, probably at the road itself, near the Forest. This was the avenue of most speed, which was important with his son's life in the balance. Wheeling into the French from this direction, Edward would be driving the French across the front of his lines, down towards the Jardin de Génève, where the French were rolled into the chaos of the Genoese dead – just as our sources describe.

Whatever the route, the impact of Edward and the third division was a tremendous blow. 'In the fray so loud was the shouting,' the Anonymous Roman says, 'so great was the noise and the splintering of lances that it seemed as if two mountains had hit each other'.[89]

The prince was extricated and made safe. The immediate danger passed.

JOHN OF BOHEMIA FALLS

As we've already seen, there's uncertainty about when King John of Bohemia entered the fray. Some say he was one of the first to ride into the fight. But I think he most likely entered now, as the entrance of King Edward had blown apart any momentary advantage that the French might have gained. As Francis of Prague explains it, he and his men had recognized that the outcome was decided:

> When the nobles of the kingdom of Bohemia saw the dangers to his life approaching, they advised the king that he should withdraw from the battle with them, to which he responded that he refused to commit such a slander against his renown, nor to blacken his honor for such a reason, but he ordered them to lead him where the great attack, the vigor of war, and the crash of arms was. To which one of the nobles of the realm of Bohemia answered: We shall lead you to that place from which most of us, and you, will not return.[90]

Bohemia was so poor of sight that he needed guides to get him to his desired end. If his men wouldn't take him, Jean le Bel claims, he ordered them beheaded. He was determined 'that he might strike an enemy with his sword'.[91]

Two of his knights agreed to take him into the melee. One of them was the Monk of Basel.[92] They set the king's horse between them, then clipped chains from their armour between themselves and his mount. 'If he cannot see', Colins de Beaumont quotes the king as saying of himself, 'others will guide him forward.'[93] The Anonymous Roman says that he ordered his son, Charles, not to follow him, and that those who stayed behind should honour him 'as their king and lord, also commanding that they remove him from the battle.'[94] Charles had already been named (though not yet crowned) as king of the Romans; his father's impending death would bring the possibility of an additional title in Bohemia. According to Colins, the blind man then restated his determination to die in battle, and his invitation to others to follow him:

> I know it well, for I saw him
> Crying to his people: 'Charge!
> Lead me into the thickest fray
> Or, otherwise, drop my reins
> And chase my horse forward.
> God keep me from turning back!
> I wish to die here, I can do no better
> Than in the presence of my true Lord.'[95]

Just as the king followed the two knights pulling him into combat, others followed him in turn. The chronicler Jean de Venette says the king 'hit with his sword as many of his own men as of others because he was without sight'.[96] Most sources, though, picture his end more heroically. A little-known medieval Czech poem, for instance, names many of the knights who decided to make their last ride into battle with the king. They were, all together:

> A good, large, valorous retinue
> Crying out his battle cries,
> Having in their hearts the thought
> That it is impossible to suffer death
> While accompanying their lord.

The enemies lamented
When the Vulture's wings gleamed
And under them the dear knight
Cried out his battle cry 'From Prague!'
…
They clashed against the enemies,
With their knightly deeds
Comporting themselves nobly,
With their daggers and swords memorably
Hewing and stabbing with all their strength,
Tearing out their horses' veins
As they pierced them with their spurs.[97]

No matter their individual feats, their fates were united: death, and more corpses for the piles. 'Finally, the king of Bohemia's army was vanquished,' the Anonymous Roman says, 'as one grinds a little grain with a big pestle in a mortar.'[98] Jean de Batery, a French poet writing a tribute to the lords who died in the battle, says Bohemia carried his banner 'Through the fields where he passed / So nobly and courteously; / May there have been no pain nor suffering / That he might have felt!'[99]

A nice thought, but a doubtful reality. In fact, we have a sense of how the king himself met his end – not from stories, but from the physical remains in John's tomb in Luxembourg, which were examined by Czech anthropologist Emanuel Vlček. He found a partial skeleton and mummified soft tissues (Figure 28). They tell us much about the violent reality of what the men faced at Crécy. The king's heel had been sliced off, probably during the effort to dismount him. Whether from that blow or another, Bohemia was brought to the ground for what might have been his last moments. His right elbow was slashed – likely disabling his sword hand – and then a bladed weapon was stabbed through his left shoulder blade into his back. If he was on his stomach, someone rolled him over, because we know that the killing stroke came with his face to the sky. They probably didn't bother to take his helmet off. Instead, they thrust a dagger through his visor, through his left eye and into his brain. It's doubtful that the man who did the deed understood the irony. He wasn't the blind king in that moment. He was just a rich enemy. Even amid the chaos of the field, those riches were a target: at least three bone-splitting cuts were made across the king's wrist – probably an effort to steal his sword or the rings from his hand.[100]

John wanted to die with his sword in his hand.

He did.

DARKNESS AND FLIGHT

In the melee, says the anonymous eyewitness who wrote the *Rhyming Chronicle*, the 'men hunted there all so bitterly':

No man wished to give way to the other;
Men split many a helmet,
So that the entire brain and blood
Out of the head must fall.
Of the bitter battle we cannot describe,
For it was so horrible and so ghastly.
Eight helmets sprang from four.
Many bodies were struck down,
So that the intestines spilled out;
Men hewed off arms and legs
In the terrible chaos of battle.
Soldiers trampled many under foot,
Who nevermore rose again nor stood.
They came to a heap on both sides.
No one could avoid the other;
Men fought bitterly forward and back.
The sword went up and down.
Each slew there another lord;
The horses leapt all asunder ...
Those killed and those wounded,
Their blood leapt like rivers:
It was horrible to see.[101]

And so it went on and on, he says, as the fighting 'endured for a long time':

> Stabbing, smashing, blow on blow,
> No one gave another any release.
> Many hands, many legs,
> The slaughter of men all together;
> Many hooves, many bodies,
> Were there mangled unidentifiably,
> So that blood drained through the armor.
> ...
> So many noblemen were killed,
> That I can not name the number.
> One saw them falling in droves,
> And on both sides many were being slain,
> Like what on a forge has been done
> In the smithy and on the forge's anvil,
> There men fought in many place;
> Entirely everyone smashing, blow on blow;
> No one did but hit others;
> Each fought stuck in the ring.[102]

Our sources generally agree that Philippe fought well in the battle. He had multiple horses cut down beneath him and was perhaps wounded, but he fought on in desperate hope of salvaging a victory. So many others did, too.

But the sky was darkening fast. As the light dwindled, so did any hope of success. Jean de Hainaut, who had supposedly advised that Philippe not engage with his enemy so late in the day, now seized the reins of the king's horse. He insisted that the king leave. Jean Froissart gives him a great speech:

> Oh, dear lord and noble king, please control yourself. If some parts of your army have been lost as the result of madness and pride, that does not mean you should expose yourself or the Crown of France to such a great and dangerous risk. You are

still powerful enough to gather as many men as you have lost, if not many more. Never will your kingdom be so completely defeated that this would not be possible. So withdraw now to Labroye, which is close by. Tomorrow you will have more news and, God willing, also a clearer idea of which course of action would be best.[103]

The king, reluctantly, agreed. The two men, joined by such knights and retainers as had survived, fled by the same road that had brought them. As they rode, the sounds of battle diminished and then disappeared completely. After that, there was only the echo of their horses' hooves, pounding the Hesdin road in the dark.

On the field they left behind, the killing continued.

No general retreat was sounded to accompany the king's departure. Probably the French were in such confusion that they lacked the command structure to manage it – a truly damning possibility. The communications were so bad that militia were still coming to the battlefield long after the outcome was decided. Most left, but, according to the *Chronicle of Flanders*, the militia of Orléans stayed long past the retreat, continuing the fight: 'almost all of them were killed'.[104]

As darkness fell, all that the French abandoned on the field could do was try to survive. They fled in any direction they thought safe.

This moment was how most medieval battles ended: one side or the other eventually broke and ran. Though it marked the end of the fighting, it rarely ended the killing. It was often the case that most of those who died in battle were run down and struck from behind: first by opportunistic infantry and second by rampaging cavalry.

This didn't happen at Crécy. While many were no doubt killed the moment they turned their backs, a great many others slipped away. Singly or in small bands, they ran into the darkness – in silence, lest their voices bring the enemy upon them. 'They did not know where to go,' Jean le Bel says, 'because the night was so endlessly black, so they knew neither town nor village, and they had not eaten all day. Thus they were by groups, three here, four there, as men isolated, and they did not know whether their masters or parents or brothers were killed or had escaped.'[105]

Back on the bloodied battlefield, Edward refused to let his men chase the defeated enemy. He had won the day, but for all he knew his enemy had only pulled back to recover for another blow. Night had fallen, and he couldn't afford to have any of his men getting lost in the dark.

He was right to remain ready to fight.

The first day of the battle of Crécy was done.

The second day was about to begin.

The Second Day, 27 August

The morning found King Philippe in Labroye. It would have been past midnight when he'd arrived in exhaustion and despair.

Several of our sources report that he had been wounded in the face by an arrow during the battle, though the same is also said of the king of Majorca. The fighting was heavy enough that both men might have been struck, though the silence of French sources regarding a facial wound to Philippe makes me inclined to think that it was Majorca who was hit, and that field reports of *a* king being struck were attached to the wrong one.

Either way, it's doubtful that Philippe came through the fighting unscarred in body or in mind. Jean de Hainaut had told the king they might regroup in Labroye, but as each sleepless hour passed it must have become clearer and clearer there was nothing left to regroup. Everything was in disarray. He had no idea who had died, or even where the survivors might be. Few of his forces had followed him north-east up the Hesdin road. He was getting reports that they had streamed south-east down the Chaussée Brunehaut.

This shouldn't have been surprising. That was the road many of them had taken to get to the battle, so its familiar path was the most likely retreat. It was also – because men move like water – a good and fast road towards a destination of safety: the great walled city of Amiens.

The king rode in that direction at first light and reached Amiens that evening after taking his lunch in Doullens.[1] He was clearly giving the English position a wide berth. A cautious and smart approach in the moment – he probably knew less about the English situation than he did about his own side – but one that tragically only furthered the confusion of the French left behind on the battlefield, in Abbeville, or in Saint-Riquier.

As a result, even more men would die.

LIONS SLAUGHTERING LAMBS

That the battle of Crécy was a two-day affair is not widely known. But our sources are remarkably consistent that it was.

Before dawn, a thick fog blanketed the English tents huddled beside the battlefield. After fighting past nightfall, Edward and his men had stayed in their armour with a heavy watch around the perimeter of their wagenburg. They knew they'd done well on the first day of fighting, but all had been chaos in the growing black. The few who managed to close their eyes fell asleep to the moans of dying men in a thick, eerie darkness that had seemingly erased the world. The language of the cries told friend from foe.

Only when the first rays of the sun were burning away the fog did the king allow a company of tired men to ride out, 'to see if they might find any French regrouping'.[2] For all they knew, Philippe was coming back with more men. According to the *Chronicle of the Este Family*, Edward was particularly worried about the appearance of the second French army, which had been marching north from Gascony.[3]

The first riders found no such organization. There were only the militia who'd been scattered in retreat as darkness fell – all of them as uncertain as the English about what happened. War is confusing under the best of circumstances. At Crécy, the fog of the air only added to the fog of war, and the result was tragic slaughter. As Jean le Bel describes it, Edward's riders found the French:

sleeping in the woods, the ditches, and the hedges, and asking each other about the conflict and what might result, because they did not know what had occurred, nor where the king or the lords were. When they saw the English coming against them, they approached them because they thought that they were their own men, and the English were among them like lions among sheep, and they killed them at will. Another company of English ventured out, and they found another company of men before the battlefield wanting to hear news of their lords: some asked about their masters, some their parents, and some their companions. These English killed all they could find.[4]

The first organized French force wouldn't have appeared until the fog began to lift. The Este family chronicler says this was led by the duke of Lorraine, who marched towards the field with his men:

hoping to regain the field after a heavy fight, by which they would delay the men of the king of England, and hoping to find them tired and so on, but the contrary of that happened, because the king was prepared and ready with all his men, fearing the coming of the son of the king of France.[5]

Giovanni Villani says that this was preceded by an assault led by Charles, the son of the king of Bohemia, who rallied his men 'on a small salient near a wood' – Lorraine came upon the field 'ignorant who had been defeated the night before' and joined Charles' forces on the ridge.[6] This was likely the same position from which the assaults had been made the evening before.

If the duke was ignorant of the situation, it would be another clue to the route of Philippe's march to the battlefield. Men tend to flee as directly away from battle as they can, following familiar roads. But it seems no one had returned to Abbeville – if they had done so, Lorraine would surely have known what had happened the previous night. That the defeated French fled elsewhere must mean they thought the English were a threat in that direction. This makes no sense at all if we accept the traditional location of the battle. From there, the road to Abbeville was open, easy, and direct, leaving us to wonder why everyone was retreating to more distant Amiens (or, more puzzlingly, Labroye, which was behind the enemy!). But if we accept the site suggested in this book, the English stood literally *between* the French attacks and Abbeville, leaving no question why the defeated didn't return to that city and why Lorraine could march out from it in ignorance.

When his forces combined with Charles', this attack became the 'large and strong' contingent of French that Michael Northburgh says was fought off by the earls of Northampton, Norfolk, and Warwick that morning, in which at least 2,000 of the enemy were killed.[7] Geoffrey le Baker says the French were four divisions, and that the English, 'though weary from the previous day's labors, resisted them bravely, and after a bitter and great fight' defeated them.[8] The duke and most of his men were killed.

Giovanni Villani says Charles now fled to the abbey of '*Riscampo*'.[9] The standing interpretation has been that this refers to the abbey of Ourscamps, which is on the River Oise near Noyon, but I'm not so certain. That abbey is roughly 70 miles south-east of Crécy, which would be an awfully long way to go in so short a time – and a really strange journey to have made when he would have had to pass through Amiens to get there. Villani probably confused the fact that Charles reached what the *Chronicle of the Este Family* calls 'a certain abbey close by'[10] with the name that several local sources give to the battle-site itself: *Buscamps*, meaning 'forest-field'.[11] (That name, incidentally, again pushes us away from the town of Crécy-en-Ponthieu and towards the Forest of Crécy.)

Charles had already been named king of the Germans and now, with his father's death, he was the presumed king of Bohemia. He was done fighting for the French king. Whatever abbey he'd retreated to, it seemed he was only waiting for news that it was safe to retrieve his father's body from wherever it had fallen.

In total, Edward claims that some 4,000 more of the enemy were slain in the early hours of this second day.[12] The *Grand Chronicles* of France state that the English killed more on the second day of fighting than they had on the first.[13] The English, according to the chronicle of Pseudo-Adam Murimuth:

slaughtered the captives, despoiled the slaughtered, divided the spoils, and they cast lots among themselves over who would take what, since there was no resistance. For the French were like straying sheep, the shepherd away and the flock dispersed; not making a sound, they are led to the slaughter. The English were made rich men from poor men, some dancing, and some weeping and praising God for such a triumph, such a victory.[14]

THE BLIND KING AND THE BLACK PRINCE

At some point that morning they found the king of Bohemia.

The *Chronicle of Artois* claims that he was still alive, and that Edward had him carried into his own tent to be tended to by his personal surgeons. The king died when he was laid upon the bed and his wounds examined.[15] This is unlikely. Given the nature of the wounds he had suffered the previous night, his survival ought to have been counted in minutes rather than in the hours needed to reach the dawn. But could the story still be true? The body can fight hard to survive, even when survival is hopeless. If he *was* still breathing, he cannot possibly have been conscious. Certainly his sudden death after having been moved – an act that would have reopened wounds – would hardly be surprising.

Bohemia's body, like his ride into the battle, became a wellspring of myths. Among them was the story that it was the Black Prince himself who found him on the field: this is the moment imagined in Julian Russell Story's painting (see Figure 30). The possibly Shakespearean play *Edward III* has something like this, too: after Edward denies further support to his son – 'Tut, let him fight; we gave him arms today, / And he is labouring for a knighthood, man!'[16] – the prince enters in triumph, walking alongside a stretcher bearing the banner-enwrapped body of Bohemia.

Popular legends suggest that the young prince was so moved by the death of the blind king that he adopted the king's badge as his own: three white feathers within a crown, overwritten with the German *Ich dien*, meaning 'I serve'. It's a romantic notion, but it isn't true. John of Bohemia had no such heraldry – his coat of arms is consistently vulture's wings – and he had no such motto. Equally unlikely is the notion that the motto, which is nearly identical to Welsh *Eich dyn* (meaning 'Your man') when pronounced, is meant to honour the Welsh archers who did so much to bring victory in the battle. It would certainly be an unnecessary complexity to create a German homophone for an intended Welsh audience. Instead, the crest seems to derive from the family of the prince's mother, Philippa of Hainaut.

Another myth is the popular image of the young prince as the hero of the battle – though unlike the whole business of the crest and motto, we can say that his glorification started early. The Chandos Herald, for instance, was unsurprisingly keen to centre the victory on his lord:

> I know well that on that day
> The noble and valorous Prince
> Had charge of the vanguard,
> As it should be remembered,
> For you him and his courage
> The field was gained and conquered.[17]

Jean Froissart, too, sang the prince's praises. Though he says nothing of it in the first version of his chronicle, his second version includes a story of the king embracing his son in the kind of dramatic moment that makes his chronicle such a magnificent work of literature: 'Fair son,' Edward tells the young man, 'today the battle was yours. I don't claim to have had any part in it. God should be given praise when he has bestowed such a grace on you just after becoming a knight.'[18] Ever in pursuit of a good story, Froissart changes the speech considerably in the next version: 'Fair son, may God let you continue like this. You are my son and you have honorably fulfilled your duty today. You are now worthy of holding lands.'[19]

The truth was that the prince *hadn't* done the right thing. He wasn't the hero that these and later stories made him out to be. Whatever excuses he might have trotted out – bravery and boldness and all that – there was simply no reason for him to have left his position at the front of the wagenburg. Moving forward into the chaos of melee combat at the very moment that the English archers were safely making pincushions of the enemy had nearly cost his father everything. There can be no question that however many English died that day, a great many of the deaths could be laid at the feet of the 16-year-old heir to the throne.

In the tumult of battle – and in the fearful uncertainty that had followed – it's likely that there had been no chance for the king to confront his heir for the costly error. It probably only happened when the army's safety was secured, late in the morning of the second day.

Edward apparently chastised the prince publicly. That's one explanation for the story told by the Citizen of Valenciennes: 'King Edward of England asked the Prince of Wales, his son, if it was pleasing to him to enter and be in the battle, and if it was a good game. And the Prince silenced himself and was ashamed.'[20]

BURYING THE DEAD

The English salvaged and stole everything they could from the dead. Rings were cut from contorted fingers. Weapons were pulled from frozen grips. Armor was cut loose and ripped off bodies. Purses were ransacked. When it was done, the English had more arms and armour than they could use, and more than they could easily carry away to sell. As a result, the Citizen of Valenciennes reports, 'the king put all the remaining armor, used and new, good and bad, in a large place amid the field, and burned them all, so that no one could ever use them again'.[21]

Using a travelling altar that he had brought on the campaign, the bishop of Durham led the men in a Mass of thanks for the victory, then 'solemnly celebrated the Office of the Dead', Geoffrey le Baker says.[22] Following this, according to Giovanni Villani, the king ordered 'the ground consecrated so as to bury the dead, friend and foe alike, while the wounded he had separated from the dead and treated'.[23]

Other sources report that Edward only buried the fallen English. As Heinrich Taube von Selbach puts it, 'he remained after the engaging of the battle in the same place for two days, not wishing that any of those who were slain be buried'.[24] If this was so, it can only have been a spite imparted on those who weren't nobles, because there's little question that the bodies of men of status could be worth money and if so would be treated more humanely. Edward just needed to know who they were.

And so we return to the scene from the start of this book: Colins de Beaumont, Jean de Hainaut's herald, walking through a field of the still-unburied dead to a tent filled with the torn and bloodied symbols of the titled men.

Colins came on Monday morning, one of a handful of French heralds sent by Philippe, Jean Froissart says, to arrange for a three-day truce and search 'for their masters and their kinsmen in order to bury them'.[25] Shortly after the truce was declared, the *Kitchen Journal* records that Edward travelled eight miles to stay at Valloires Abbey – no doubt far better lodgings than 'in the field beneath the Forest of Crécy' where he'd been for two nights running.[26] He took with him the body of Bohemia, which Geoffrey le Baker says was accorded the honours befitting a king: 'they had it washed with warm water, wrapped in clean linen, and placed atop a horse-drawn bier'.[27] The bodies of other major lords were also taken to the abbey for burial.

It's likely that most of his army stayed behind for at least this final night. Carrying out the foul but necessary work of dealing with the dead took time, even if many were left to rot.

How many dead?

The Anonymous Roman says 60,000 French died, with the English claiming 1,500 pairs of gold spurs – this signifying the number of knights killed – along with 1,300 standards, signifying the number of titled men.[28] That total number of dead is a clear exaggeration – we think there were only about 26,000 total men in the French army at Crécy – but we can say that the number of knights killed is consistent with early reports. As we know, Edward claimed that 'in a small area where the first onslaught occurred more than 1,500 knights and squires died, even aside from the others who died afterwards on all parts of the battlefield' – plus the thousands who died in the second day of fighting.[29] In a letter written the next day, Michael Northburgh was more specific about the 'good men-at-arms' who died on the first day: there were 1,542, to which could be added 'militia and footmen'. This more exact number was presumably tied to the collection of spurs. Johann von Schönfeld, also an eyewitness, repeats the count of 1,500 'among the barons, knights, and nobles', with a total of 16,000 dead altogether.[30] Giovanni Villani, writing within a couple of years of the battle, summarized the stories he had at hand:

> In this bloody and unfortunate battle for the king of France, practically all those present who have written about it agree that about 20,000 cavalry and infantry were killed, and horses of innumerable quantity, of which more than 1,600 between counts, barons, knights bannered, and knights bachelor, without including the more than 4,000 mounted esquires, and as many captured; and nearly all those who escaped suffered arrow wounds.[31]

Far more conservatively, the *Chronicle of Flanders* says 1,200 knights and 2,800 other men were killed, for a total of 4,000 'and no more'.[32] Gilles li Muisit is close to this, reporting that the French lost some 700 'men-at-arms and cavalry' plus 4,000 infantry. This particular set of numbers makes one wonder if spurs were removed from 771 men, and that these 1,542 *individual* spurs were then miscommunicated – intentionally or not – as 1,542 *pairs*. Either way, the battle of Crécy saw a truly staggering loss of life. By the time we account for the multiple attacks on scattered militia on the second day and those who died of wounds later, at least 5,000 men died on the French side *at a minimum*.

What was the English cost to kill so many of their enemy?

A few days after the bloodshed, Richard Wynkeley says that on the English side 'two knights and one squire' were killed – none nobility – along with 'some Welshmen'.[33] Just ten days later,

Johann von Schönfeld was telling an even more impressive story, that Edward 'lost not even a single knight'.[34] Geoffrey le Baker would later write that fewer than 40 died on the English side – slightly more reasonable, but still improbable.[35]

Part of the problem of counting the dead is the question of who actually counts. Class distinction within medieval society was so marked that a report about losses might only be concerned with losses within a certain part of society. In a sermon given later that year, English clergyman Thomas Bradwardine insists that 'from our men not one lord, knight, or squire in that combat was killed, gravely wounded, or taken prisoner, that I know of, and among the other men very few'.[36] The 'other men', for many if not most of our sources, simply aren't even worth counting – much less remembering. Geoffrey le Baker, after reporting the French deaths among the 'knights and men of higher status', says it plainly: 'no one cared to count the others killed there'.[37]

There was also an understandable effort on the English side to minimize or even eliminate their losses – while maximizing those of the enemy. Gilles li Muisit seems to have recognized this problem:

> Of the English troops who fell, who, what kind, and how many, I did not discover what I can say to be the truth, therefore I will not say anything concerning this; however, according to rumor, many of them were killed there. It is not possible to believe that such a number of good and noble men and infantry fell [on the French side] without a very large number of their adversary also killed or wounded.[38]

Returning to the subject a little later in his narrative, he reports that 'among those of the king of England fell many princes and nobles, which I could not name, and a very large number of other English soldiers and archers. Many in this battle have said many things, but I give no credence to these things, and therefore I have not put them into my narrative.'[39] Jean le Bel is one of the few sources to suggest that very many English died: he says 300 of their knights were lost.[40] To this we would surely need to add some number of 'common' men, but even if we speculated a total English loss of 500 men – a number no source claims, but one that could be possible given the desperate melee in front of the wagenburg – this would still be 10 per cent (or less) of what their enemy had suffered, a truly remarkable discrepancy since they had been outnumbered in the fight by at least two to one.

In human terms, Crécy was a horrific tragedy. But in military terms, from the English perspective, it was a victory beyond all expectation. It was, as historians like to call such things, a decisive battle.

So what did it decide?

Epilogue

All the Days to Come

The military outcome of a battle is often relatively unimportant. Who wins, who loses – beyond the individual human costs, victory or defeat becomes collectively vital only in terms of how it changes political or social outcomes. The battle of Hastings in 1066 was a decisive battle not because William won, but because Harold and his brothers *died* when they did. It was unquestionably good for the Normans that they had the general victory on the field – the confidence of victory and having fewer deaths on your side is always a good thing as a military leader – but what made Hastings more than just another battle in an age full of them is the fact that in one day the Normans swept aside the opposing political leadership. The English had no means to organize further effective resistance to the invasion, and enormous social upheaval followed.

Political losses don't always have to be deadly. History is filled with political leaders who survived conflicts only to be killed – sometimes literally – in the courts of public opinion. This might have been less evident within the authoritative social structure of a pre-modern monarchy, but it was still present. There's a reason Edward was so keen to spin each and every event in the Crécy Campaign to put himself in the best light. It was good for his ego, but it was also necessary politics: without support at home he would be unable to keep his armies in the field.

The longer Edward's effort took, the greater the need for political spin became. Judged against his aim of seizing the crown of France and ending the war, the Crécy Campaign was a failure. There's no question he'd beaten Philippe in a battle that was about as one-sided as they come, but no one afterwards seriously thought Edward had won the throne of France. Nor did he march on Paris to try to press such a claim.

For that matter, Edward didn't even take the opportunity provided by the shattered and scattered local defence to capture Abbeville or in any other way secure his supposedly 'ancestral' lands of Ponthieu. This is the final nail in the coffin of the idea that Edward had wanted to fight at Crécy all along as part of a plan to stake his claim to these lands in particular.

No. He only fought here because Philippe caught up to him here. Everything beyond that fact was and is putting the best spin on an act of necessity.

As soon as he got the chance, after all, Edward left.

He had gone to Valloires Abbey on Monday 28 August, as soon as he had the safety of the truce. On Tuesday, he crossed to the north side of the River Maye, moving his lodgings from Valloires Abbey to the priory at Maintenay, where he buried the king of Bohemia. After the English departed, Charles would disinter his father and take him to Luxembourg for final entombment.[1]

The English army was now fully regrouped. With the three-day truce concluded, they once more began scouring the countryside. They marched north at a good pace, burning and pillaging as they had after Caen. Edward's next night, according to the *Kitchen Journal*, was spent at Saint-Josse, then Neufchâtel-Hardelot for two nights, followed by two nights somewhere near Wimille or Wissant.[2] On 4 September he stood before the walls of Calais. His long-awaited reinforcements and resupplies from England met him along the shoreline, and Edward dug in for a siege of the great port city.

Crippled by losses north and south – first the failure to break Aiguillon and then the devastating loss at Crécy – the king of France was unable to muster the strength and resolve needed to dislodge his enemy. Not now, and not in all the months to come. By the time the city opened its gates – its richest citizens surrendering in a dramatic scene captured in Auguste Rodin's remarkable 1889 sculpture, *The Burghers of Calais* (Figure 31) – the siege had lasted one day shy of 11 months. It was long enough that the English encampment to the west had become a virtual city of its own, called Neuville, meaning 'new town', holding its own market days each week.

Such was Edward's resolve to seize Calais over this long period that the story of the campaign quickly centred on it: many believe that taking the city was his plan all along, that he'd just taken an impossibly long and wandering route across northern France to get there. The final nail in the coffin of *that* notion is that after Blanchetaque the king didn't take the road to Calais, but instead made a run for the Flemish allies that he still thought were at Béthune.

The king of England obviously *did* decide to take Calais at some point, though. So when was it?

The plan probably firmed up over the first few days after the victory at Crécy, as the king acquired better intelligence. He now knew that his Anglo-Flemish army had failed to accomplish much and had been turned back to the Low Countries – they arrived in Ghent on 29 August. He knew that he himself had failed to dislodge Philippe from the throne. He didn't need a military victory at this point so much as a political one. He needed a tangible accomplishment that would rally the support of the nobles and encourage the continued investment of the foreign bankers on whom he'd come to rely. Crécy, for all that it was a glorious victory, wasn't remotely that.

But taking Calais would be.

The decision paid off. Calais became the most vital and prosperous English port on the Continent. Trade with the Low Countries and beyond boomed. The English Channel was more secure than ever. The English treasury was strengthened. The king of England may not have acquired a new crown after Crécy, but he added a jewel to his old one (Figure 32).

For the French, it was an equal loss. Having one of their great cities under foreign control was a biting thorn in their side. Some

40 years later, the French poet Eustache Deschamps was speaking for many of his countrymen when he wrote a poem whose refrain was '*Paiz n'arez ja s'ilz ne rendent Calays*' – 'There can be no peace if they don't release Calais.'[3] In taking the port, Edward ensured decades of death to come.

The Hundred Years War, which for a brief moment might have ended with the prince's capture at Crécy, would last until 1453. The French wouldn't regain Calais until 1558 – 211 years after its capture by Edward.

None of it would have happened without his victory on the fields of northern France. If his son had been captured, or if his own standard had fallen during those two days of fighting in 1346, history would have been very different indeed. There would be no later glories of the Black Prince. No Agincourt. No Joan of Arc.

It's strange to call a victory as overwhelming as Crécy a battle for survival … but when it comes to the English dream of holding lands in France, that's precisely what it was: a chance to continue the fight, to continue the war.

Appendix: The Location of Crécy

Our sources provide a variety of descriptions for the location of the battle of Crécy. The information provided by our 14th-century sources, cued to the order of their appearance within the *Crécy Casebook*, is listed below. Original language is provided in parentheses for transparency.

	Author	Short Title	Location
1	William Retford	*Kitchen Journal*	beneath (*sub*) the Forest of Crécy
2	–	*Cleopatra Itinerary*	into the fields before (*devaunt*) the town of Crécy in Ponthieu | on the same field beside the Forest
3	Colins de Beaumont	*On the Crécy Dead*	from the mount to the valley
4	Richard Wynkeley	*Letter*	towards (*versus*) Crécy ... in a field
5	Edward III	*Letter*	towards (*devers*) Crécy ... on the other side of the Forest
6	Michael Northburgh	*Letter*	in the Forest of Crécy | towards (*devers*) Crécy
7	Edward III	*Letter*	towards (*apud*) the town of Crécy
8	Philippe VI	*Payment to Loyal Men*	at the Mount of Crécy
9	Robert de Dreux	*Horses Lost at Crécy*	before (*devant*) Crécy in Ponthieu

	Author	*Short Title*	*Location*
10	Johann von Schönfeld	*Letter*	between (*iuxta*) a certain diocese of St. George [i.e. Abbeville] and a town called Crécy | near (*iuxta*) a certain village, which is called Crécy
11	Thomas Bradwardine	*Victory Sermon*	near (*apud*) Crécy
12	Jean de Batery	*Poem of the Eight Coats-of-arms*	in the battle of Crécy
13	–	*John of Bohemia Lament*	at (*tot*) Crécy
14	–	*Chronicle of the Este Family*	a certain place between (*inter*) Crécy and Abbeville in which there was a great forest
15	–	*Annals of Zwettl*	–
16	–	*Lanercost Chronicle*	towards (*usque*) Crécy in Ponthieu
17	–	*Chronicle of Guyenne*	in the hedge-enclosed land (*plassa*) of Crécy
18	–	*Crécy Poem*	in Crécy | beneath (*sub*) the Forest of Crécy
19	Guillaume Flote	*Horses Lost at Crécy*	of the Mount of Crécy
20	–	*Chronicle of the Counts of Flanders*	near (*iuxta*) the town of Abbeville in Ponthieu, in the Forest that is called Crécy
21	–	*Chronicle of Artois*	at (*a*) Crécy | next to a mill, its rear to a forest | the field was named Forest-field (*Buscamps*) by the people of the land where the battle was
22	–	*Chronicle of Saint-Omer*	at (*a*) Crécy | next to a mill and at their back was a woods | the field where the battle was is named Forest-field (*Bulescamps*) by the people of the land

	Author	Short Title	Location
23	–	Capture of Tifford	of Crécy
24	–	Rhyming Chronicle	–
25	Giovanni Villani	New Chronicle	at a village and place bordered by a Forest called Crécy | outside the village of Crécy, on a small hill between Crécy and Abbeville in Ponthieu
26	John of Hocsem	Chronicle	not far from the city of Amiens
27	–	Pistoian History	between (intra) Crécy and Abbeville
28	Jean de Winterthur	Chronicle	–
29	Gilles li Muisit	Major Chronicle	near (apud) Crécy
30	–	Grand Chronicles	near (empres) to a Forest that is called Crécy
31	William of Dene	History of Rochester	towards (versus) the Forest of Crécy
32	Matthias von Neuenburg	Chronicle	beside (iuxta) the Forest | towards (ad) a certain diocese
33	Anonymous of Leoben	Chronicle	between (iuxta) the town called Crécy and a diocese of St. George [i.e. Abbeville]
34	John of Tynemouth	Golden History	–
35	Pseudo-Adam Murimuth	Chronicle	near (apud) Crécy
36	Philippe of Orléans	Ransom Payment	at (a) Crécy
37	–	Chronicle of Siena	towards (verso) the village of Crécy
38	Jan van Boendale	Brabantese Stories	in the land of Ponthieu
39	Laurence Minot	Edward III in France	between (bitwixen) Crécy and Abbeville

	Author	*Short Title*	*Location*
40	–	*Polychronicon Continuation*	near (*apud*) Crécy in Picardy
41	Iolo Goch	*Panegyric to Edward III*	journey towards Crécy
42	Francis of Prague	*Chronicle*	a place of safety between (*inter*) the valleys and the forests
43	Marco Battagli	*Chronicle*	in a battlefield
44	Michael de Leone	*Housebook*	in Picardy between (*inter*) Crécy and Abbeville, about six leagues from Saint-Josse
45	Geoffrey le Baker	*Chronicle*	the field of Crécy
46	Anonymous of Rome	*Chronicle*	at the Mount of Crécy | valley between a castle known as Mount Crécy and a town called Abbeville ... in the flat fields at the foot of Crécy's ridge
47	Iolo Goch	*Panegyric to Rhys ap Gruffudd*	at (*yng*) Crécy
48	Richard Lescot	*Chronicle Continuation*	beside (*iuxta*) the Forest of Crécy
49	Guglielmo Cortusio	*History of Padua and Lombardy*	between (*inter*) Crécy and Abbeville
50	Jean le Bel	*Chronicle*	near (*prez*) Crécy in Ponthieu
51	Heinrich von Diessenhofen	*Chronicle*	between (*inter*) Crécy and Abbeville
52	Thomas Gray	*Scalacronica*	passing the Forest of Crécy
53	Thomas Bisset	*Gesta Annalia II*	near (*apud*) Crécy
54	Neplach of Opatovice	*Chronicle*	in France
55	Heinrich Taube von Selbach	*Chronicle*	in Picardy within the realm of the king of France near (*iuxta*) the city of Amiens

	Author	Short Title	Location
56	John Ergom	Commentary to John of Bridlington's Prophecy	Montjoy ... the name of the place on which the battle began
57	–	Brief Chronicle	near (apud) Crécy
58	–	Canterbury Chronicle	towards (versus) Crécy | near (apud) Crécy | on the field of Crécy
59	–	Eulogium historiarum	above (desuper) Crécy
60	Citizen of Valenciennes	Accounts	between (entre) Labroye and Crécy | near the woods of Crécy, on a small mountain
61	–	Chronicle of Saint-Trond	near (apud) Crécy
62	John of Reading	Chronicle	on the field near (iuxta) Crécy
63	Jean de Venette	Chronicle	near (iuxta) Crécy in Ponthieu ... securely beside a wood
64	–	Chronicle of Normandy	at (a) Crécy near (pres) the Forest
65	Beneš Krabice of Weitmil	Chronicle of the Church of Prague	in a most secure place between the waters and the woods
66	–	World-chronicle of Koln	in the territory of Ponthieu
67	–	Prose Brut (Common Version to 1377)	in a field close to Crécy
68	–	Chronicle of Flanders [version A]	near (pres) Crécy
69	Niccolò of Ferrara	World History	towards a very dense wood
70	Chandos Herald	Life of the Black Prince	near (pres) Crécy
71	–	Death of King John	–
72	Henry Knighton	Chronicle	towards (ad) the bridge of Crécy | on the field of Westglyse near Crécy

	Author	*Short Title*	*Location*
73	–	*Anonimalle Chronicle*	towards (*devers*) Crécy ... on the other side of the forest
74	Tilemann Elhen of Wolfhagen	*Chronicle of Limburg*	in France
75	Jean Froissart	*Chronicle [Amiens version]*	near (*pries*) Crécy
76	Jean Froissart	*Chronicle [Paris version]*	near (*pres*) Crécy
77	Jakob Twinger	*Chronicle of Strasburg*	a wood
78	–	*Chronicle of the First Four Valois Kings*	towards (*a*) the valley of Crécy
79	Thomas Burton	*Chronicle of Meaux Abbey*	between (*inter*) the town and the forest of Crécy
80	–	*Chronicle of the Low Countries*	at (*a*) Crécy, near (*pres*) the woods
81	Jean Froissart	*Chronicle [Chicago version]*	near (*pries*) Crécy

Suggested Reading and Acknowledgements

The Battle of Crécy: A Casebook, which I co-edited with Kelly DeVries (Liverpool University Press, 2015), was the first published appearance of many of the new accounts of the battle presented here. More importantly, that book provides readers with all the 14th-century primary sources we had at hand, both in translations and in original languages for those who can read them. I remain proud of the work, which won our first Distinguished Book Prize from the Society for Military History. I think I speak for Kelly in saying that we are both grateful to Robert Woosnam-Savage of the Royal Armouries for joining us on our first collective visit to the Crécy battlefield, where the first seeds of the project were planted. In laughter and in insight, I can't imagine better companions in travel and in life.

What Newton said about standing on the shoulders of giants remains true in most things – though history isn't physics, and I'm definitely no Newton. So it goes without saying that none of this present work could have happened without the historians who have written whole libraries of words about this famous battle.

I want to highlight three of these prior works in particular. These are the ones I'd recommend to anyone wanting the *vulgato* account. In alphabetical order by author: *The Battle of Crécy 1346*, edited by Andrew Ayton and Sir Philip Preston (Boydell and Brewer, 2005); *War Cruel and Sharp*, by Clifford J. Rogers (Boydell Press, 2000); and *The Hundred Years War, Vol. 1: Trial by Battle*, by Jonathan Sumption (University of Pennsylvania, 1990). Each study is uniquely strong, but taken together they are a triumphant encapsulation of scholarship built atop the received tradition. I may disagree with them – partially, mostly, or even wholly – but I cannot doubt that they are good books from dedicated researchers. Our disagreements can and should be carried out with respect and professionalism.

To that end, I'm absolutely grateful to the colleagues who have helpfully questioned various parts of this work over the years. Particular gratitude must go to John France and the gathered scholars of the medieval military history symposium that was held in his honour in Swansea, Wales, in 2014. It was there that I first publicly revealed an alternate Crécy, and the fact that it was welcomed with earnest discussion from John and other military historians – among them, a young Trevor Russell Smith, who has done much to keep me on my critical toes over the years – was a godsend.

In the writing and editing of this book, I owe thanks to Myke Cole. He has been not only enthusiastic in his support, but also generous in the application of his scholarly red pen. He is additionally a friend who continues to inspire with his dedication to selfless service and personal growth.

My agent, Paul Stevens, was one half of the team that made the dream of this book a practical reality. My thanks to him and to the other half: Marcus Cowper at Osprey Publishing. Kudos, too, to all the magnificent staff at Osprey who have shepherded the book to print.

I'm happy to acknowledge the support of The Citadel, the Military College of South Carolina, for providing me with time off to complete this book. Though Covid-19 played hell with my plans (and far worse for far too many of us), I always knew I had the full support of my school. Thank you, General Walters, Provost Selden, Dean Jones, and Scott Lucas.

My gratitude, as well, to my classrooms of cadets and veterans who were presented with various aspects of this book with the firm order that they prove me wrong. I continue to learn so much from each and every one of them. It's truly a privilege to teach young men and women who are dedicated to betterment of themselves and the world around them.

I have been fortunate to have a support network of friends and family who put up with me droning on about long-dead kings and long-forgotten landscapes. Their patience and their love has been everything.

I come full circle in dedicating this book to one of those friends: my once and future co-author, Kelly DeVries. For years Kelly has stood at the forefront of the field of medieval military history. Few can rival his expertise, and his wide-ranging and extraordinary scholarship means that his fingerprints are all over this book ... even the parts he might not agree with. But beyond his impact on the profession, I owe him personal thanks for how he welcomed me into a field where so many might have seen me as a stranger – and how in the process he became one of my most dear personal friends and mentors.

Thank you, Kelly.

Endnotes

PREFACE

1 Trans. Michael Livingston, in *Medieval Warfare*, ed. Kelly DeVries and Livingston (Toronto University Press, 2019), p. 5.
2 Winston Churchill, *History of the English-speaking Peoples: The Birth of Britain* (Dodd, Mead & Co., 1956), p. 348.

INTRODUCTION: THE CRÉCY DEAD, 28 AUGUST 1346

1 Edward III, *Letter to Thomas Lucy*, trans. Michael Livingston, in *The Battle of Crécy: A Casebook*, ed. Michael Livingston and Kelly DeVries (Liverpool University Press, 2015); hereafter known as *Crécy Casebook*, p. 59.
2 Gilles li Muisit, *Major Chronicle*, trans. Kelly DeVries, in *Crécy Casebook*, p. 129.
3 Johann von Schönfeld, *Letter to Passau*, trans. Michael Livingston, in *Crécy Casebook*, p. 67.
4 *Chronicle of the Este Family*, trans. Michael Livingston, in *Crécy Casebook*, pp. 86–87.
5 *Annals of Zwettl*, trans. Michael Livingston, in *Crécy Casebook*, pp. 86–87.
6 Jean Froissart, *Chronicles [Amiens Version]*, trans. Godfried Croenen, in *Crécy Casebook*, pp. 274–75; *Chronicles [Abridged Version]*, trans. Godfried Croenen, in *Crécy Casebook*, pp. 294–95.
7 Jean Froissart, *Chronicles [B/C Version]*, trans. Godfried Croenen, in *Crécy Casebook*, p. 337.
8 Thomas Burton, *Chronicle of Meaux Abbey*, trans. Michael Livingston, in *Crécy Casebook*, p. 303.
9 Edward III, *Letter to Thomas Lucy*, trans. Michael Livingston, in *Crécy Casebook*, p. 59.

10 Colins de Beaumont, *On the Crécy Dead*, trans. Elizaveta Strakhov, in *Crécy Casebook*, p. 27.

11 Ibid., p. 29.

12 Ibid., p. 39.

13 Ibid., p. 41.

14 Ibid., p. 45.

15 On Tolkien's re-creation of the Somme, see Michael Livingston, 'The Shell-shocked Hobbit: The First World War and Tolkien's Trauma of the Ring', *Mythlore* 25 (2006), pp. 9–22.

16 Colins de Beaumont, *On the Crécy Dead*, trans. Elizaveta Strakhov, in *Crécy Casebook*, p. 47.

17 Ibid., p. 49.

18 Ibid., p. 49.

19 Ibid., p. 51.

PART I: BEFORE THE CAMPAIGN, TO 1346

1 For the original language, see https://epistolae.ctl.columbia.edu/letter/139.html; translation my own.

CHAPTER I: ROOTS OF WAR, 1066–1308

1 Kelly DeVries, '"1066 and All That": English and French Strategic Rivalry During the Middle Ages', in *Great Strategic Rivalries: From the Classical World to the Cold War*, ed. James Lacey (Oxford University Press, 2016). I'm very much indebted to this excellent overview of the relationship between England and France in this period.

2 For a terrific look at them from the English perspective, see John Hosler's *Henry II: A Medieval Soldier at War, 1147–1189* (Brill, 2007).

3 For the original Latin of the letter, and other letters by Eleanor, see https://epistolae.ctl.columbia.edu/letter/141.html; translation my own.

CHAPTER 2: ISABELLA AND THE TWO EDWARDS, 1308–30

1 *Chronicon de Lanercost*, ed. J. Stevenson (The Maitland Club, 1839), pp. 242–44; *The Prose Brut*, ed. F.W.D. Brie (K. Paul, Trench, Trübner & Co, 1906–08), 1.218.

2 *Vita Edwardi secundi*, ed. N. Denholm-Young (1957), pp. 55–56.

3 Jonathan Sumption, *The Hundred Years War, Vol. 1: Trial by Battle* (University of Pennsylvania Press, 1990), p. 91.

4 Jean le Bel, *The True Chronicles of Jean le Bel, 1290–1360*, trans. Nigel Bryant (Boydell Press, 2011), p. 31.

5 Adam Murimuth, *Continuatio Chronicarum*, ed. Edward Maude Thompson, Rolls Series 93 (Eyre and Spottiswoode, 1889), p. 51.

6 For an edition of the poem, see T.M. Smallwood, 'The Lament of Edward II', *The Modern Language Review* 68 (1973), pp. 521–29; the translation here is my own.

7 I'm indebted here to the discussion of the poem by Claire Valente, 'The "Lament of Edward II": Religious Lyric, Political Propaganda', *Speculum* 77.2 (2002), pp. 422–39.

CHAPTER 3: WINE, WOOL, AND THE
MARCH TO WAR, 1202–1337

1 Hugh Johnson, *Vintage: The Story of Wine* (Simon and Schuster, 1989), p. 145.

2 Asa Briggs, *Haut-Brion: An Illustrious Lineage* (Faber and Faber, 1994), p. 107.

3 For an excellent study of Bouvines, see John France, 'The Battle of Bouvines, 27 July 1314', in *The Medieval Way of War: Studies in Medieval Military History in Honor of Bernard S. Bachrach*, ed. Gregory I. Halfond (Routledge, 2015), pp. 251–72.

4 Sumption, *Hundred Years War, Vol 1: Trial by Battle*, pp. 109–11.

5 Translation my own. The original text is printed in Thomas Wright's *Political Poems and Songs from the Accession of Edward III to that of Richard III* (Rolls, 1859).

6 The English had earlier planned to utilize something like these tactics – what many historians would call the 'English system' – during the Weardale Campaign in 1327, but because the Scots refused to give battle we can't know exactly what it would have looked like at that time. See Michael Prestwich, *Armies and Warfare in the Middle Ages: The English Experience* (Yale University Press, 1996), p. 318.

CHAPTER 4: THE HUNDRED YEARS WAR BEGINS, 1337–46

1 On the dating of this letter I am much persuaded by Sumption's argument that it probably arrived between 6 and 21 May; see *Hundred Years War: Trial by Battle*, p. 606 note 92.

2 For the letter, see Maurice Jusselin, 'Comment la France se préparait à la guerre de cent ans', *Bibliothèque de l'École des Chartes* 73 (1912), pp. 233–34.

3 *Calendar of Patent Rolls of Edward III, 1338–40*, p. 286. Such was the destruction that as late as 4 December 1342 the area was being given tax relief to help it recover.

4 Ibid., p. 180.

5 Thomas Rymer, ed., *Foedera* (The Hague, 1704–35), 2.1080. There is good reason, in fact, to think that the king had already defaulted on at least some of his loans.

6 *Chronographia regum Francorum*, ed. Henri Moranvillé, Société de l'Histoire de France (Renouard, 1891–97), vol. 2, pp. 80–81.

7 Jean le Bel, *Chronicles*, trans. Bryant, p. 81.

8 '1339 Campaign Diary', in *Oeuvres de Jean Froissart*, ed. Kervyn de Lettenhove (Brunelleschi, 1870), vol. 18, p. 90.

9 In *The Wars of Edward III: Sources and Interpretations*, ed. Clifford J. Rogers (Boydell Press, 1999), p. 72.

10 Jean le Bel, *Chronicles*, trans. Bryant, p. 81.

11 For Sluys and Tournai, see the examinations by Kelly DeVries: 'God, Admirals, Archery, and Flemings: Perceptions of Victory and Defeat at the Battle of Sluys, 1340', *American Neptune* 55 (1995), pp. 223–42, and 'Contemporary Views of Edward III's Failure at the Siege of Tournai, 1340', *Nottingham Medieval Studies* 39 (1995), pp. 70–105.

12 On this, and the Italian interest in Crécy more generally, see the excellent discussion by Niccolò Capponi, 'The Italian Perspective on Crécy', in *Crécy Casebook*, pp. 477–83.

13 Edwin S. Hunt and James Murray, *A History of Business in Medieval Europe, 1200–1550* (Cambridge University Press, 1990), pp. 116–17.

CHAPTER 5: THE CAMPAIGN BEGINS, 12–23 JULY

1 Quoted in Rogers, *Wars of Edward III*, p. 123.

2 Quoted by Sumption, *Hundred Years War, Vol 1: Trial by Battle*, p. 285.

3 Jean le Bel, *Chronicles*, trans. Bryant, p. 169.

4 Thom Richardson, *The Tower Armoury in the Fourteenth Century* (Royal Armouries, 2016), pp. 115–16. Contrary to the popular belief in quivers full of arrows, the evidence shows that the English archers typically carried their allotment of arrows in two sheaves at the waist tied together with hemp twine using a running knot. See John Waller

and Jonathan Waller, 'The Personal Carriage of Arrows from Hastings to the *Mary Rose*', *Arms and Armour* 7 (2010), pp. 155–77.

5 William Retford, *Kitchen Journal*, trans. Michael Livingston, in *Crécy Casebook*, p. 21.

6 Jean le Bel, *Chronicles*, trans. Bryant, p. 171.

7 In Robert Avesbury, *De Gestis Mirabilibus Regis Edwardi Tertii*, ed. E.M. Thompson (Rolls Series, 1889), pp. 358–59.

8 Jean le Bel, *Chronicles*, trans. Bryant, p. 172.

9 Ibid., p. 172.

CHAPTER 6: THE SACKING OF CAEN, 23–30 JULY

1 Jean le Bel, *Chronicles*, trans. Bryant, p. 172. For a discussion of the calculations involved, see Clifford J. Rogers, *War Cruel and Sharp* (Boydell Press, 2000), p. 252.

2 *The Acts of War of Edward III (1346)*, in *The Life and Campaigns of the Black Prince*, ed. and trans. Richard Barber (Boydell Press, 1986), p. 31.

3 Jean le Bel, *Chronicles*, trans. Bryant, p. 172.

4 Rogers, *Wars of Edward III*, p. 124.

5 Jean le Bel, *Chronicles*, trans. Bryant, p. 173.

6 Some later writers would insist that if they hadn't run out of shots, the crossbowmen might have prevented the destruction that was about to unfold. See *Cont. Manuel, 1339–46*, folio 163, cited in Rogers, *War Cruel and Sharp*, p. 247.

7 Edward III, *Letter to Thomas Lucy*, in *Crécy Casebook*, p. 55.

8 Ibid., p. 55.

9 Jean le Bel, *Chronicles*, trans. Bryant, p. 173.

10 On the extraordinary extent of the plunder, see Henri Prentout, *La prise de Caen par Édouard III, 1346* (Henri Delesques, 1904).

11 Rogers, *Wars of Edward III*, p. 126.

12 J.F.C. Fuller, *The Decisive Battles of the Western World*, ed. John Terraine (Granada, 1970), p. 311.

13 Charles Oman, *A History of the Art of War: The Middle Ages from the Fourth to the Fourteenth Century* (Methuen, 1898), p. 600.

14 Andrew Ayton, 'The Crécy Campaign', in *The Battle of Crécy, 1346*, ed. Andrew Ayton and Philip Preston (Boydell Press, 2005), p. 103.

15 Froissart 4.412–13, quoted by Rogers (*War Cruel and Sharp*, pp. 247–48), who suggests that because this information is nowhere else attested it might be the more reliable. I respectfully disagree.

16 Anonymous, but from the actions he describes the author was almost assuredly a member of the Black Prince's staff.

17 *Acts of War*, trans. Barber, pp. 28–29.

18 Ibid., trans. Barber, p. 30.

19 For a similar argument, see Sumption, *Hundred Years War, Vol. 1: Trial by Battle*, pp. 532–34.

20 Yuval Noah Harari, 'Inter-frontal Cooperation in the Fourteenth Century and Edward III's 1346 Campaign', *War in History* 6 (1999), pp. 389–90.

21 *Acts of War*, trans. Barber, p. 34.

22 Jean le Bel, *Chronicles*, trans. Bryant, p. 173.

23 I've previously argued that his change of plan at Caen might have been due to his surprise at how easily it had fallen, and his related concern that it could be taken from him just as easily (see 'Losses Uncountable: The Context of Crécy', in *Crécy Casebook*, p. 8). These thoughts may indeed have entered into his mind, but I now think they were outweighed by the larger economic and political contexts of the war.

24 For the best attempt to argue that a *chevauchée* to Calais was the plan from the very beginning of the campaign, see Rogers, *War Cruel and Sharp*, pp. 247–50.

25 Though it has provoked little comment from historians, in his letter of instructions home Edward also says that he is sending other letters, which have not survived, to his allies in the Low Countries. These are likely to have included his instructions for their corresponding actions.

CHAPTER 7: THE LONG ROAD TO PARIS, 30 JULY–16 AUGUST

1 We know that the earl of Huntingdon, for instance, headed home at this point, 'because of a very severe and dangerous illness', according to Edward's own letter from Caen (Rogers, *Wars of Edward III*, p. 126). He survived the illness.

2 Jean le Bel, *Chronicles*, trans. Bryant, p. 174.

3 Edward III, *Letter to Thomas Lucy*, trans. Michael Livingston, in *Crécy Casebook*, p. 57.

4 *Acts of War*, trans. Barber, pp. 36–37.

5 Ibid., trans. Barber, p. 37.

6 Jean le Bel, *Chronicles*, trans. Bryant, p. 175.

7 Gilles li Muisit, *Chronique et annales*, ed. H. Lemaître, Société de l'Histoire de France (Renouard, 1906), p. 158.

CHAPTER 8: THE BATTLE OF BLANCHETAQUE, 16–25 AUGUST

1 This is the traditional time and place for the letter's composition, though Rogers has made an interesting attempt to argue that it was written on 15 August (*War Cruel and Sharp*, pp. 260–61, note 125).

2 This is evident enough from the content of the letter, but more importantly we find it in the *Acta Bellicosa*, indicating that it was circulated through the English camp.

3 *Acts of War*, trans. Barber, p. 38.

4 Ibid., trans. Barber, p. 39.

5 Jean Froissart, *Chroniques de J. Froissart*, ed. Siméon Luce, 15 vols, Société de l'Histoire de France (Renouard, 1869–1975), vol. 3, pp. 151–52.

6 Jean le Bel, *Chronicles*, trans. Bryant, p. 177.

7 They were being prepared, though: the ships finally appeared at Boulogne on 4 September before connecting with the king the following day.

8 Wynkeley, *Letter to the Blackfriars*, trans. Michael Livingston, in *Crécy Casebook*, p. 53.

9 Bertrand Schnerb, 'French Army', in *Battle of Crécy*, ed. Ayton and Preston, p. 269.

10 See, in particular, Andrew Ayton, 'English Army at Crécy', in *Battle of Crécy*, ed. Ayton and Preston, p. 190.

11 Chandos Herald, *Life of the Black Prince*, in *The Life and Campaigns of the Black Prince*, ed. and trans. Richard Barber (Boydell Press, 1986), p. 88.

12 Rogers, for instance, suspects they both knew; see *War Cruel and Sharp*, p. 262. See also Ayton, 'Crécy Campaign', in *Battle of Crécy*, ed. Ayton and Preston, p. 87.

13 Jean le Bel, *Chronicles*, trans. Bryant, p. 178.

14 Northburgh, *Letter*, trans. Michael Livingston, in *Crécy Casebook*, p. 61.

15 Rogers, *War Cruel and Sharp*, p. 263, note 138.

16 Villani, *New Chronicle*, trans. Niccolò Capponi, in *Crécy Casebook*, p. 115.

17 Jean le Bel, *Chronicles*, trans. Bryant, p. 178.

18 Northburgh, *Letter*, trans. Michael Livingston, in *Crécy Casebook*, p. 61.

19 Wynkeley, *Letter to the Blackfriars*, trans. Michael Livingston, in *Crécy Casebook*, p. 53.

20 Jean le Bel, *Chronicles*, trans. Bryant, p. 178.

21 Chandos Herald, *Life of the Black Prince*, trans. Michael Livingston, in *Crécy Casebook*, p. 235.

22 Wynkeley, *Letter to the Blackfriars*, trans. Michael Livingston, in *Crécy Casebook*, p. 53.

23 *Accounts of a Citizen of Valenciennes*, trans. Kelly DeVries, in *Crécy Casebook*, p. 205.

24 Jean le Bel, *Chronicles*, trans. Bryant, p. 178.

25 Hugh was 18 years old when his father and grandfather were gruesomely executed by Isabella and Mortimer in 1326. He worked his way into the good graces of Edward III, however, and was made Baron le Despenser in 1338.

26 William Retford, *Kitchen Journal*, trans. Michael Livingston, in *Crécy Casebook*, p. 21.

27 Ibid., p. 21.

28 *Cleopatra Itinerary*, trans. Michael Livingston, in *Crécy Casebook*, p. 25.

29 Edward III, *Letter to Thomas Lucy*, trans. Michael Livingston, in *Crécy Casebook*, p. 57.

30 Chandos Herald, *Life of the Black Prince*, trans. Michael Livingston, in *Crécy Casebook*, p. 239.

31 Edward III, *Letter to Thomas Lucy*, trans. Michael Livingston, in *Crécy Casebook*, p. 59.

32 Colins de Beaumont, *On the Crécy Dead*, trans. Elizaveta Strakhov, in *Crécy Casebook*, p. 49.

PART 3: RECONSTRUCTING CRÉCY, 26 AUGUST 1346

1 *Rhyming Chronicle*, trans. Kelly DeVries, in *Crécy Casebook*, p. 111.

CHAPTER 10: THE ARMIES APPROACH, 26 AUGUST

1 Carte générale de la France, No. 4, feuille 12.

2 It is certainly the case that our earliest maps of the region that show any topography at all – like Nicolas Tassin's Gouvernement de Rue (1634) or William Blaeu's Nova Picardiae Tabula (1660) – consistently show the dominance of the wide expanse of the Forest of Crécy.

3 William Retford, *Kitchen Journal*, trans. Michael Livingston, in *Crécy Casebook*, p. 21.

4 Northburgh, *Letter*, trans. Michael Livingston, in *Crécy Casebook*, p. 61.

5 *Cleopatra Itinerary*, trans. Michael Livingston, in *Crécy Casebook*, p. 25.

6 Geoffrey le Baker, *Chronicle*, trans. Michael Livingston, in *Crécy Casebook*, p. 161.

7 Wynkeley, *Letter to the Blackfriars*, trans. Michael Livingston, in *Crécy Casebook*, p. 53, and Edward III, *Letter to Thomas Lucy*, trans. Michael Livingston, in *Crécy Casebook*, p. 57, respectively.

8 *Accounts of a Citizen of Valenciennes*, trans. Kelly DeVries, in *Crécy Casebook*, p. 205.

9 Jean Froissart, *Chronicles [Amiens Version]*, trans. Godfried Croenen, in *Crécy Casebook*, p. 261.

10 *Accounts of a Citizen of Valenciennes*, trans. Kelly DeVries, in *Crécy Casebook*, pp. 204–05, 207. A 'league' is, unfortunately, not an internationally standardized system of measurement in the period. I have made my conversions according to the Carolingian principle that a league was three Roman miles, each of which amounts to 1,000 paces – an approximate conversion rate of two and three-quarter miles per league today.

11 *Grand Chronicles*, trans. Kelly DeVries, in *Crécy Casebook*, p. 131.

12 Though not knowing the etymology, Wailly suggested an English encampment in this same area for tactical reasons alone. While he ultimately concluded that the exact location was unknown, he pondered whether the camp might be connected to an earthen fortification in the swamp just over a mile north of Noyelles-sur-Mer. I believe he was referring to Mont-Thomas, though I've not been able to confirm this. See Henri de Wailly, *Crécy, 1346: Anatomy of a Battle* (Blandford Press, 1987), pp. 45–46.

13 Giovanni Villani, *New Chronicle*, trans. Niccolò Capponi, in *Crécy Casebook*, pp. 115, 117.

14 Henry Knighton says the king was headed for this bridge when he encountered the French; *Chronicle*, trans. Michael Livingston, in *Crécy Casebook*, p. 247.

CHAPTER 11: FINDING CRÉCY

1 The student's name was J. Wesley Snyder III, and he was actually looking for the earliest map to mark the location of the battle of Agincourt, which this appears to be. See his 'The First Maps of Agincourt', *Medieval Warfare Magazine* 9.1 (2019), 25.

2 Seymour de Constant, 'Bataille de Cressy', *France Littéraire* 3 (1832), p. 565.

3 Bibliothèque municipale d'Abbeville, Collection Delignières de Saint Amand et de Bommy, vol. 8, fol. 26r.

4 Preston, 'The Traditional Battlefield of Crécy', in *Battle of Crécy*, ed. Ayton and Preston, p. 116, citing Jean-Paul Legrand, 'La Forêt de Crécy', *Bulletin Société Linnéenne Nord-Picardie* 8 (1990), pp. 13–20. The fact that Picard's map labels it simply as a stone cross is notable in this regard. A 19th-century watercolour depicting the Croix de Bohéme before its restoration, and including some of the early accounts of it, can be found at Bibliothèque municipale d'Abbeville, Collection Delignières de Saint Amand et de Bommy, vol. 3, fol. 123r.

5 Archives départementales de la Somme, ref. 3P1323/3.

6 For the Croix du roi la Boheme, see Archives départementales de la Somme, ref. 3P1346/5 (dated 1824); for the Chemin de l'Armée as it leads through Marcheville, see Archives départementales de la Somme, ref. 3P1414/1 (dated 1823).

7 It should be noted, however, that a lack of local place-names does not necessarily discount any location, especially during such a time of heightened French nationalism. The location of the 1415 battle of Agincourt is relatively certain to have occurred within the immediate vicinity of Azincourt, France, yet the relevant 1825 Napoleonic cadastral maps do not label anything associated with the engagement; see Archives départementales de la Pas-de-Calais, ref. 3P069/2.

8 Wailly, *Crécy*, p. 74.

9 [William Chambers and Robert Chambers], 'Wanderings Round St Valery', *Chambers's Journal* 751 (18 May 1878), p. 306.

10 Preston, 'Traditional Battlefield', p. 116.

11 George M. Musgrave, *By-roads and Battle-fields in Picardy: With Incidents and Gathering by the Way Between Ambleteuse and Ham; Including Agincourt and Crécy* (Bell and Daldy, 1861), p. 139.

12 De Constant, *Bataille de Cressy*, p. 74.

13 Philip Preston, who first brought substantial attention to it, says it runs 'between 2.5 and 5.5 metres above the valley floor': 'Traditional Battlefield', pp. 109–37.

14 Preston, 'Traditional Battlefield', p. 123. François Traullé had noted the problem of this feature in 1798, but his concerns did not enter into later studies of Crécy until Preston's thorough work; see 'Mémoire sur

la bataille de Créci, où les Français furent repoussés par les Anglais en 1346', *Magasin Encyclopedique* 4.2 (1798), pp. 483–504.

15 Michael Prestwich, 'The Battle of Crécy', in *Battle of Crécy*, ed. Ayton and Preston, pp. 139–57.

16 Preston, 'Traditional Battlefield', pp. 119–21. On the results at Towton, see Veronica Fiorato, Anthea Boylston, and Christopher Knüsel, *Blood Red Roses: The Archaeology of a Mass Grave from the Battle of Towton, AD 1461* (Oxbow Books, 2000).

17 Henry Knighton, *Chronicle*, trans. Michael Livingston, in *Crécy Casebook*, pp. 246–49.

18 Ibid., p. 249.

19 Preston, 'Traditional Battlefield', pp. 136–37. It was his acceptance of a Westglise–Watteglise connection, along with an awareness of the topographical problems of the traditional site, that led Traullé to suggest that the battle happened entirely beside Watteglise (see 'Mémoire sur la bataille de Créci').

20 Jan van Boendale, *Brabantese Stories*, trans. Kelly DeVries, in *Crécy Casebook*, pp. 146–47; and *World-chronicle of Köln*, trans. Michael Livingston, in *Crécy Casebook*, pp. 224–25, respectively.

21 *Polychronicon Continuation*, trans. Michael Livingston, in *Crécy Casebook*, pp. 148–51.

22 Thomas Bisset, *Gesta Annalia II*, trans. Michael Livingston, in *Crécy Casebook*, pp. 192–93; and Heinrich Taube von Selbach, *Chronicle*, trans. Michael Livingston, in *Crécy Casebook*, pp. 194–95, respectively.

23 Edward III, *Request for Supplies*, trans. Michael Livingston, in *Crécy Casebook*, pp. 62–63.

24 Wynkeley, *Letter to the Blackfriars*, trans. Michael Livingston, in *Crécy Casebook*, pp. 52–53.

25 Edward III, *Letter to Thomas Lucy*, trans. Michael Livingston, in *Crécy Casebook*, pp. 56–57.

26 Northburgh, *Letter*, trans. Michael Livingston, in *Crécy Casebook*, pp. 60–61.

27 Robert de Dreuex, *Horses Lost at Crécy*, trans. Kelly DeVries and Michael Livingston, in *Crécy Casebook*, pp. 64–65; and Iolo Goch, *Panegyric to Edward III*, trans. John K. Bollard, in *Crécy Casebook*, pp. 152–53, respectively. For chronicles, see, e.g. the *Chronicle of Lanercost* (*Crécy Casebook*, Item 16), Geoffrey le Baker (Item 45),

Pseudo-Adam Murimuth (Item 35), the *Chronicle of Canterbury* (Item 58), the *Eulogium historiarum* (Item 59), John of Reading (Item 62), and the *Prose Brut* (Item 67).

28 Jean le Bel, *Chronicle*, trans. Kelly DeVries, in *Crécy Casebook*, pp. 182–83. See also the *Pistoian History* (*Crécy Casebook*, Item 27) and the work of Guglielmo Cortusi (Item 49).

29 Johann von Schönfeld, *Letter to Passau*, trans. Michael Livingston, in *Crécy Casebook*, pp. 64-65. See also the *Chronicle of Leoben* (*Crécy Casebook*, Item 33).

30 William Retford, *Kitchen Journal*, trans. Michael Livingston, in *Crécy Casebook*, pp. 20–23.

31 *Cleopatra Itinerary*, trans. Michael Livingston, in *Crécy Casebook*, pp. 24–27.

32 *Chronicle of the Counts of Flanders*, trans. Michael Livingston, in *Crécy Casebook*, pp. 92–93.

33 *Crécy Poem*, trans. Michael Livingston, in *Crécy Casebook*, pp. 90–91; *Grand Chronicles*, trans. Kelly DeVries, in *Crécy Casebook*, pp. 130–31; William of Dene, *History of Rochester*, trans. Michael Livingston, in *Crécy Casebook*, pp. 134–35; Matthias von Neuenburg, *Chronicle*, trans. Michael Livingston, in *Crécy Casebook*, pp. 136–37; and Laurence Minot, *Edward III in France*, trans. Michael Livingston, in *Crécy Casebook*, p., 148, respectively.

34 Giovanni Villani, *New Chronicle*, trans. Niccolò Capponi, in *Crécy Casebook*, pp. 114–17.

35 *Chronicle of the Este Family*, trans. Michael Livingston, in *Crécy Casebook*, pp. 84–85.

36 Francis of Prague, *Chronicle*, trans. Michael Livingston, in *Crécy Casebook*, pp. 154–55. The Bohemian chronicler Beneš Krabice of Weitmil, in his *Chronicle of the Church of Prague*, utilizes Francis' work, but he adjusts many details, including the placing of the location relative to waters instead of valleys: '*in locis firmissimis inter aquas et siluas*' [in a safe place between waters and woods] (*Chronicle of the Church of Prague*, trans. Michael Livingston, in *Crécy Casebook*, pp. 222–23). Interestingly, the *Chronicle of the First Four Valois Kings* sites the battle '*à la valee de Cressi*' [towards the valley of Crécy] (trans. Kelly DeVries, in *Crécy Casebook*, pp. 298–99).

37 This according to Leland's abstract of it, which is all that survives; see Thomas Gray, *Scalacronica*, trans. Michael Livingston, in *Crécy Casebook*, pp. 192–93. For others, see Richard Lescot (*Crécy Casebook*, Item 48), the *Chronicle of Normandy* (Item 64), the *Chronicle of Flanders* (Item 68), and the *Chronicle of the Low Countries* (Item 80).

38 Thomas Burton, *Chronicle of Meaux Abbey*, trans. Michael Livingston, in *Crécy Casebook*, pp. 300–01.

39 For the most hard-fought argument in this direction, see Ayton, who has meticulously combed the sources to try to find evidence of any connections ('Crécy Campaign').

40 Philippe VI, *Payment to Loyal Men*, trans. Kelly DeVries, in *Crécy Casebook*, pp. 62–63.

41 Guillaume Flote, *Horses Lost at Crécy*, trans. Kelly DeVries and Michael Livingston, in *Crécy Casebook*, pp. 92–93; and John Ergom, *Commentary to Bridlington's Prophecy*, trans. Michael Livingston, in *Crécy Casebook*, pp. 196–97.

42 Colins de Beaumont, *On the Crécy Dead*, trans. Elizaveta Strakhov, in *Crécy Casebook*, pp. 48–49.

43 *Chronicle of Artois*, trans. Kelly DeVries, in *Crécy Casebook*, pp. 96–99; *Chronicle of Saint-Omer*, trans. Kelly DeVries, in *Crécy Casebook*, pp. 102–03 and 106–07, respectively.

44 *Accounts of a Citizen of Valenciennes*, trans. Kelly DeVries, in *Crécy Casebook*, pp. 208–09.

45 Anonymous of Rome, *Chronicle*, trans. Niccolò Capponi, in *Crécy Casebook*, pp. 168–69.

46 For these same reasons this is the dividing line between the oversight of Crécy and of Abbeville, a kind of political, ecclesiastical, and social no-man's land that might be expected to be described in vague and contradictory terms depending on the inclination of the author.

47 Musgrave, *By-roads and Battlefields*, p. 142; M. Jourdain, *Les Sanctuaires de la Sainte Vierge dans le Diocèse d'Amiens* (Typographie Piteux Frères, 1891), p. 463.

48 Musgrave, *By-roads and Battlefields*, pp. 142–43.

49 For a discussion of this, see Kelly DeVries and Michael Livingston, 'Froissart's *Herce* and Crécy', in *Crécy Casebook*, pp. 469–75.

50 Thomas Burton, *Chronicle of Meaux Abbey*, trans. Michael Livingston, in *Crécy Casebook*, p. 301.

CHAPTER 12: THE BATTLE OF CRÉCY, 26 AUGUST

1 The translation here comes from Michael Livingston, 'An Army on the March and in Camp: Guillaume Guiart's *Branche des royaus lingnages*', *Journal of Medieval Military History* 17 (2019), pp. 259–72, at p. 263.

2 Jean Froissart, *Chronicles [Amiens Version]*, trans. Godfried Croenen, in *Crécy Casebook*, pp. 263, 265, 267.

3 Ibid., p. 267.

4 *Chronicle of Artois*, trans. Kelly DeVries, in *Crécy Casebook*, p. 95.

5 Jean Froissart, *Chronicles [B/C Version]*, trans. Godfried Croenen, in *Crécy Casebook*, p. 319.

6 Some sources give his name as Heinrich, and the general perspective has been that he was a member of the Münch family from Basel, following the identification by Jules Viard, 'Henri le Moine de Bâle à la Bataille de Crécy', *Bibliothèque de l'École des chartes* 74 (1913), pp. 74–128. DeVries rightly questions this tradition; see 'The Tactics of Crécy', in *Crécy Casebook*, p. 451, note 17.

7 Livingston, 'An Army on the March and in Camp', p. 265.

8 Jean le Bel, *Chronicle*, trans. Kelly DeVries, in *Crécy Casebook*, p. 183. All told, Jean le Bel says, the king had gone about seven leagues (19 miles) from Abbeville. This and the rest of le Bel's mileage lines up along Philippe's route as just described – all leading to an English position on the Rondel, about 18 miles from that city.

9 Matthias von Neuenburg, *Chronicle*, trans. Michael Livingston, in *Crécy Casebook*, p. 137.

10 The most notable exception is Kelly DeVries, who provides an excellent, wagenburg-centred reconstruction of the battle, on the site presented here, in 'The Tactics of Crécy', in *Crécy Casebook*, pp. 447–67. While I have disagreed with his reconstruction in places – and thereby disagreed with *myself*, since I have previously been in complete agreement with his work! – my debt to his work, his friendship, and his feedback could not be overstated.

11 William of Dene, *History of Rochester*, trans. Michael Livingston, in *Crécy Casebook*, p. 135.

12 As DeVries notes, 13 different 14th-century authors describe the wagenburg, and only one of them appears to be getting his information from a previous account; 'The Tactics of Crécy', in *Crécy Casebook*, p. 449.

13 Giovanni Villani, *New Chronicle*, trans. Niccolò Capponi, in *Crécy Casebook*, p. 117.

14 Jean le Bel, *Chronicle*, trans. Kelly DeVries, in *Crécy Casebook*, p. 187.

15 Matthias von Neuenburg, *Chronicle*, trans. Michael Livingston, in *Crécy Casebook*, p. 137.

16 *Chronicle of Normandy*, trans. Kelly DeVries, in *Crécy Casebook*, p. 219.

17 Jakob Twinger, *Chronicle of Strasburg*, trans. Kelly DeVries, in *Crécy Casebook*, p. 297. On other details, he was clearly less than well informed, as he thought that Edward placed 30,000 archers in front of this formation, which would have been the equivalent of around a third of the population of London!

18 Geoffrey le Baker, *Chronicle*, trans. Michael Livingston, in *Crécy Casebook*, p. 161.

19 Anonymous of Rome, *Chronicle*, trans. Niccolò Capponi, in *Crécy Casebook*, p. 169.

20 Jean le Bel, *Chronicle*, trans. Kelly DeVries, in *Crécy Casebook*, p. 187.

21 Geoffrey le Baker, *Chronicle*, trans. Michael Livingston, in *Crécy Casebook*, p. 163.

22 *Accounts of a Citizen of Valenciennes*, trans. Kelly DeVries, in *Crécy Casebook*, p. 207.

23 Giovanni Villani, *New Chronicle*, trans. Niccolò Capponi, in *Crécy Casebook*, p. 117.

24 Geoffrey le Baker, *Chronicle*, trans. Michael Livingston, in *Crécy Casebook*, p. 163.

25 For an excellent discussion of the impracticality of imagining 'storms' of arrows at Crécy, see the chapter on 'Topography and Archery' by Andrew Ayton and Philip Preston in *Battle of Crécy*, ed. Ayton and Preston, pp. 359–62.

26 Jean le Bel, *Chronicle*, trans. Kelly DeVries, in *Crécy Casebook*, p. 187.

27 *Chronicle of Saint-Omer*, trans. Kelly DeVries, in *Crécy Casebook*, p. 105.

28 Jean le Bel, *Chronicle*, trans. Kelly DeVries, in *Crécy Casebook*, p. 187.

29 Giovanni Villani, *New Chronicle*, trans. Niccolò Capponi, in *Crécy Casebook*, pp. 118–19.

30 Jean le Bel, *Chronicle*, trans. Kelly DeVries, in *Crécy Casebook*, p. 187.

31 *Chronicle of Normandy*, trans. Kelly DeVries, in *Crécy Casebook*, p. 219. Though of a later date than many of our sources, this chronicle is particularly useful for noting such things as this differentiation between ranks of soldiers in the army – because its author was a former soldier himself, though he didn't serve at Crécy.

32 Jean le Bel, *Chronicle*, trans. Kelly DeVries, in *Crécy Casebook*, p. 183.

33 Gilles li Muisit, *Major Chronicle*, trans. Kelly DeVries, in *Crécy Casebook*, p. 127.

34 *Accounts of a Citizen of Valenciennes*, trans. Kelly DeVries, in *Crécy Casebook*, p. 207; *Chronicle of Artois* also says as much, as do the *Chronicle of Saint-Omer*, the *Grand Chronicles*, and Richard Lescot (*Crécy Casebook*, pp. 97, 105, 131, and 181, respectively).

35 Francis of Prague, *Chronicle*, trans. Michael Livingston, in *Crécy Casebook*, p. 155.

36 Beneš Krabice, *Chronicle of the Church of Prague*, trans. Michael Livingston, in *Crécy Casebook*, p. 223.

37 Anonymous of Rome, *Chronicle*, trans. Niccolò Capponi, in *Crécy Casebook*, p. 171.

38 *Prose Brut [Common Version to 1377]*, trans. Michael Livingston, in *Crécy Casebook*, p. 225.

39 Pseudo-Adam Murimuth, *Chronicle [Nero Version]*, trans. Michael Livingston, in *Crécy Casebook*, p. 142.

40 *Eulogium Historiarum*, trans. Michael Livingston, in *Crécy Casebook*, p. 201.

41 Geoffrey le Baker, *Chronicle*, trans. Michael Livingston, in *Crécy Casebook*, p. 161.

42 Anonymous of Rome, *Chronicle*, trans. Niccolò Capponi, in *Crécy Casebook*, p. 171.

43 *Accounts of a Citizen of Valenciennes*, trans. Kelly DeVries, in *Crécy Casebook*, p. 207.

44 Matthias von Neuenburg, *Chronicle*, trans. Michael Livingston, in *Crécy Casebook*, p. 137.

45 *Chronicle of the First Four Valois Kings*, trans. Kelly DeVries, in *Crécy Casebook*, p. 299.

46 Jean Froissart, *Chronicles [Amiens Version]*, trans. Godfried Croenen, in *Crécy Casebook*, p. 265.

47 Geoffrey le Baker, *Chronicle*, trans. Michael Livingston, in *Crécy Casebook*, p. 161.

48 Geoffrey le Baker, *Chronicle*, trans. Michael Livingston, in *Crécy Casebook*, p. 161, and Jean le Bel, *Chronicle*, trans. Kelly DeVries, in *Crécy Casebook*, p. 185, respectively.

49 *Chronicle of the Low Countries*, trans. Kelly DeVries, in *Crécy Casebook*, p. 305.

50 Ibid., p. 305. Jean Froissart later states the opposite (Jean Froissart, *Chronicles [B/C Version]*, trans. Godfried Croenen, in *Crécy Casebook*, p. 323), that they had marched all day encumbered by their armour. As DeVries points out, this is unlikely to have been true; see 'The Tactics of Crécy', in *Crécy Casebook*, p. 453.

51 For an excellent discussion of these contracts, see Kelly DeVries and Niccolò Capponi, 'The Genoese Crossbowmen at Crécy', in *Crécy Casebook*, pp. 441–46. This short but informative article is, as far as I'm aware, the first to question the unprecedented placement of the crossbowmen in the vanguard.

52 Notable examples of the tale are the chroniclers Jean de Venette and Jean Froissart (*Crécy Casebook*, pp. 215 and 287, respectively).

53 Anonymous of Rome, *Chronicle*, trans. Niccolò Capponi, in *Crécy Casebook*, p. 171.

54 *Chronicle of Flanders [Version A]*, trans. Kelly DeVries, in *Crécy Casebook*, p. 227.

55 *Chronicle of the First Four Valois Kings*, trans. Kelly DeVries, in *Crécy Casebook*, p. 299.

56 *Rhyming Chronicle*, trans. Kelly DeVries, in *Crécy Casebook*, p. 111.

57 Gilles li Muisit, *Major Chronicle*, trans. Kelly DeVries, in *Crécy Casebook*, p. 129.

58 Giovanni Villani, *New Chronicle*, trans. Niccolò Capponi, in *Crécy Casebook*, p. 117.

59 Jean le Bel, *Chronicle*, trans. Kelly DeVries, in *Crécy Casebook*, p. 185 (translation slightly revised); see also the *Chronicle of Normandy*, trans. Kelly DeVries, in *Crécy Casebook*, pp. 219, 221.

60 Geoffrey le Baker, *Chronicle*, trans. Michael Livingston, in *Crécy Casebook*, p. 163.

61 Giovanni Villani, *New Chronicle*, trans. Niccolò Capponi, in *Crécy Casebook*, p. 117. This was, as DeVries notes, the first battle-usage

of these weapons; see 'The Tactics of Crécy', in *Crécy Casebook*, p. 450.

62 Richardson, *Tower Armoury*, pp. 136–37.

63 *Grand Chronicles*, trans. Kelly DeVries, in *Crécy Casebook*, p. 131, and Jean Froissart, *Chronicles [Abridged Version]*, trans. Godfried Croenen, in *Crécy Casebook*, p. 287, respectively. The *Chronicle of Flanders [A]* likewise notes their presence, without numbering them (trans. Kelly DeVries, in *Crécy Casebook*, p. 227).

64 *Pistoian History*, trans. Niccolò Capponi, in *Crécy Casebook*, p. 123.

65 Giovanni Villani, *New Chronicle*, trans. Niccolò Capponi, in *Crécy Casebook*, p. 117.

66 *Chronicle of Flanders [A]*, trans. Kelly DeVries, in *Crécy Casebook*, p. 227. See also the Anonymous Roman, Richard Lescot, and Jean de Venette (*Crécy Casebook*, pp. 171, 181, and 215, respectively).

67 *Grand Chronicles*, trans. Kelly DeVries, in *Crécy Casebook*, p. 133; see also Gilles li Muisit and the *Chronicle of the Low Countries* (*Crécy Casebook*, pp. 129 and 305, respectively).

68 Jean Froissart, *Chronicles [Abridged Version]*, trans. Godfried Croenen, in *Crécy Casebook*, pp. 287, 289.

69 Edward III, *Letter to Thomas Lucy*, trans. Michael Livingston, in *Crécy Casebook*, p. 59.

70 Jean Froissart, *Chronicles [Abridged Version]*, trans. Godfried Croenen, in *Crécy Casebook*, p. 287.

71 Gilles li Muisit, *Major Chronicle*, trans. Kelly DeVries, in *Crécy Casebook*, p. 129.

72 Wynkeley, *Letter to the Blackfriars*, trans. Michael Livingston, in *Crécy Casebook*, p. 55. This phrasing would be echoed by a large number of later accounts of the battle.

73 Anonymous of Rome, *Chronicle*, trans. Niccolò Capponi, in *Crécy Casebook*, p. 173.

74 Jean le Bel, *Chronicle*, trans. Kelly DeVries, in *Crécy Casebook*, p. 185.

75 Geoffrey le Baker, *Chronicle*, trans. Michael Livingston, in *Crécy Casebook*, p. 163.

76 Colins de Beaumont, *On the Crécy Dead*, trans. Elizaveta Strakhov, in *Crécy Casebook*, pp. 37, 39.

77 Chandos Herald, *Life of the Black Prince*, trans. Michael Livingston, in *Crécy Casebook*, p. 237.

78 Geoffrey le Baker, *Chronicle*, trans. Michael Livingston, in *Crécy Casebook*, p. 163.

79 Jean Froissart, *Chronicles [Abridged Version]*, trans. Godfried Croenen, in *Crécy Casebook*, pp. 291, 293.

80 *Chronicle of Normandy*, trans. Kelly DeVries, in *Crécy Casebook*, p. 221.

81 *Chronicle of the Low Countries*, trans. Kelly DeVries, in *Crécy Casebook*, p. 305.

82 *Accounts of a Citizen of Valenciennes*, trans. Kelly DeVries, in *Crécy Casebook*, p. 209.

83 Colins de Beaumont, *On the Crécy Dead*, trans. Elizaveta Strakhov, in *Crécy Casebook*, p. 39.

84 Anonymous of Rome, *Chronicle*, trans. Niccolò Capponi, in *Crécy Casebook*, p. 173.

85 We could speculate that Valentino was a lesser nobleman in Flanders' retinue, which would explain both his absence from other records and the general impression from others that 'Flanders' took the prince. This is far more complicated, though, than the simple likelihood that the story of the prince's capture had grown muddled by the time it got to the Anonymous Roman.

86 *Anonimalle Chronicle*, trans. Kelly DeVries, in *Crécy Casebook*, p. 251.

87 *Chronicle of Flanders [A]*, trans. Kelly DeVries, in *Crécy Casebook*, p. 229.

88 Giovanni Villani, *New Chronicle*, trans. Niccolò Capponi, in *Crécy Casebook*, p. 119.

89 Anonymous of Rome, *Chronicle*, trans. Niccolò Capponi, in *Crécy Casebook*, pp. 171–72.

90 Francis of Prague, *Chronicle*, trans. Michael Livingston, in *Crécy Casebook*, p. 155.

91 Jean le Bel, *Chronicle*, trans. Kelly DeVries, in *Crécy Casebook*, p. 189.

92 The other, according to Marco Battagli, was the lord of Rosenberg (*Chronicle*, trans. Michael Livingston, in *Crécy Casebook*, p. 159).

93 Colins de Beaumont, *On the Crécy Dead*, trans. Elizaveta Strakhov, in *Crécy Casebook*, p. 33.

94 Anonymous of Rome, *Chronicle*, trans. Niccolò Capponi, in *Crécy Casebook*, p. 175.

95 Colins de Beaumont, *On the Crécy Dead*, trans. Elizaveta Strakhov, in *Crécy Casebook*, p. 37.

96 Jean de Venette, *Chronicle*, trans. Michael Livingston, in *Crécy Casebook*, p. 215.

97 *Death of King John*, trans. Jan Biederman and Václav Žurek, in *Crécy Casebook*, pp. 241, 243.

98 Anonymous of Rome, *Chronicle*, trans. Niccolò Capponi, in *Crécy Casebook*, p. 175.

99 Jean de Batery, *Poem of the Eight Coats-of-Arms*, trans. Elizaveta Strakhov, in *Crécy Casebook*, p. 73.

100 Jan Biederman and Václav Žurek, 'The Bohemian Participation in Crécy', in *Crécy Casebook*, p. 440. For Vlček's study, see his *Jak zemřeli: Vyznamné osobnosti českych dejin z pohledu antropologie a lékarství* (Academia, 1993), pp. 70–104.

101 *Rhyming Chronicle*, trans. Kelly DeVries, in *Crécy Casebook*, pp. 111, 113.

102 Ibid., p. 113.

103 Jean Froissart, *Chronicles [Amiens Version]*, trans. Godfried Croenen, in *Crécy Casebook*, p. 273.

104 *Chronicle of Flanders [A]*, trans. Kelly DeVries, in *Crécy Casebook*, p. 229.

105 Jean le Bel, *Chronicle*, trans. Kelly DeVries, in *Crécy Casebook*, p. 185.

CHAPTER 13: THE SECOND DAY, 27 AUGUST

1 Gilles li Muisit, *Major Chronicle*, trans. Kelly DeVries, in *Crécy Casebook*, p. 129. Similar routes are reported across the sources.

2 Jean le Bel, *Chronicle*, trans. Kelly DeVries, in *Crécy Casebook*, p. 187.

3 *Chronicle of the Este Family*, trans. Michael Livingston, in *Crécy Casebook*, p. 87.

4 Jean le Bel, *Chronicle*, trans. Kelly DeVries, in *Crécy Casebook*, p. 189; translation revised to correct an error in the published version.

5 *Chronicle of the Este Family*, trans. Michael Livingston, in *Crécy Casebook*, p. 87.

6 Giovanni Villani, *New Chronicle*, trans. Niccolò Capponi, in *Crécy Casebook*, pp. 119, 121.

7 Northburgh, *Letter*, trans. Michael Livingston, in *Crécy Casebook*, p. 61.

8 Geoffrey le Baker, *Chronicle*, trans. Michael Livingston, in *Crécy Casebook*, p. 163.

9 Giovanni Villani, *New Chronicle*, trans. Niccolò Capponi, in *Crécy Casebook*, p. 120.

10 *Chronicle of the Este Family*, trans. Michael Livingston, in *Crécy Casebook*, p. 87.

11 See the *Chronicle of Artois*, trans. Kelly DeVries, in *Crécy Casebook*, p. 99, and the *Chronicle of Saint-Omer*, trans. Kelly DeVries, in *Crécy Casebook*, p. 107, respectively.

12 Edward III, *Letter to Thomas Lucy*, trans. Michael Livingston, in *Crécy Casebook*, p. 59.

13 *Grand Chronicles*, trans. Kelly DeVries, in *Crécy Casebook*, p. 133.

14 Pseudo-Adam Murimuth, *Chronicle [Nero Version]*, trans. Michael Livingston, in *Crécy Casebook*, p. 143.

15 *Chronicle of Artois*, trans. Kelly DeVries, in *Crécy Casebook*, p. 99; the claim is repeated by the *Chronicle of Saint-Omer* (trans. Kelly DeVries, in *Crécy Casebook*, p. 107).

16 *Edward III*, Scene 8, lines 1589–90.

17 Chandos Herald, *Life of the Black Prince*, trans. Michael Livingston, in *Crécy Casebook*, p. 239.

18 Jean Froissart, *Chronicles [Abridged Version]*, trans. Godfried Croenen, in *Crécy Casebook*, p. 293.

19 Jean Froissart, *Chronicles [B/C Version]*, trans. Godfried Croenen, in *Crécy Casebook*, p. 335.

20 *Accounts of a Citizen of Valenciennes*, trans. Kelly DeVries, in *Crécy Casebook*, p. 211.

21 Ibid., p. 211. If this is true and not just an exaggerated remembrance of typical field recycling – which could involve the melting down of some pieces – then it would seem likely that the English army's smiths used charcoal from their forge wagons to start the burn by using the pile itself as a kind of self-contained field forge.

22 Geoffrey le Baker, *Chronicle*, trans. Michael Livingston, in *Crécy Casebook*, p. 165.

23 Giovanni Villani, *New Chronicle*, trans. Niccolò Capponi, in *Crécy Casebook*, p. 121.

24 Other sources might imply as much, since they make a point of saying that Edward buried *his* men but are silent on the treatment

of the French dead. See, for example, the *Pistoian History*, Geoffrey le Baker, and Heinrich von Diessenhofen (*Crécy Casebook*, pp. 125, 165 and 91, respectively).

25 Jean Froissart, *Chronicles [Abridged Version]*, trans. Godfried Croenen, in *Crécy Casebook*, p. 277.

26 William Retford, *Kitchen Journal*, trans. Michael Livingston, in *Crécy Casebook*, p. 23.

27 Geoffrey le Baker, *Chronicle*, trans. Michael Livingston, in *Crécy Casebook*, p. 165.

28 Anonymous of Rome, *Chronicle*, trans. Niccolò Capponi, in *Crécy Casebook*, p. 177.

29 Edward III, *Letter to Thomas Lucy*, trans. Michael Livingston, in *Crécy Casebook*, p. 59.

30 Johann von Schönfeld, *Letter to Passau*, trans. Michael Livingston, in *Crécy Casebook*, p. 65.

31 Giovanni Villani, *New Chronicle*, trans. Niccolò Capponi, in *Crécy Casebook*, p. 121.

32 *Chronicle of Flanders [A]*, trans. Kelly DeVries, in *Crécy Casebook*, p. 229.

33 Wynkeley, *Letter to the Blackfriars*, trans. Michael Livingston, in *Crécy Casebook*, p. 55.

34 Johann von Schönfeld, *Letter to Passau*, trans. Michael Livingston, in *Crécy Casebook*, p. 65.

35 Geoffrey le Baker, *Chronicle*, trans. Michael Livingston, in *Crécy Casebook*, p. 165. In the subsequent 'Abridged' version of his chronicle, Jean Froissart says the English lost three knights and around 20 archers (trans. Godfried Croenen, in *Crécy Casebook*, p. 275).

36 Thomas Bradwardine, *Victory Sermon*, trans. Michael Livingston, in *Crécy Casebook*, p. 69.

37 Geoffrey le Baker, *Chronicle*, trans. Michael Livingston, in *Crécy Casebook*, p. 165.

38 Gilles li Muisit, *Major Chronicle*, trans. Kelly DeVries, in *Crécy Casebook*, p. 129.

39 Ibid., pp. 129, 131.

40 Jean le Bel, *Chronicle*, trans. Kelly DeVries, in *Crécy Casebook*, p. 189.

EPILOGUE: ALL THE DAYS TO COME

1 Giovanni Villani, *New Chronicle*, trans. Niccolò Capponi, in *Crécy Casebook*, p. 121.

2 The first is named by the *Kitchen Journal* (trans. Michael Livingston, in *Crécy Casebook*, p. 23), while the second is claimed by the *Cleopatra Itinerary* (trans. Michael Livingston, in *Crécy Casebook*, p. 27). This probably reflects different parts of the army encamping in different locations.

3 Deschamps, *Oeuvres complètes*, ed. August Queux de Saint Hilaire and Gaston Raynaud (Firmin Didot, 1878–1903), item 344, lines 10, 20, 30, 40, 50, and 56; translation my own.

Index

References to maps are in **bold**.